WITCHES RUN AMOK

Disney
HOCUS
POCUS

THE ORAL HISTORY

SHANNON CARLIN

HYPERION AVENUE

LOS ANGELES • NEW YORK

First Edition, August 2024
10 9 8 7 6 5 4 3 2 1
FAC-004510-23201
Printed in the United States of America

This book is set in Agmena Pro
Designed by Stephanie Sumulong

Library of Congress Cataloging-in-Publication Control Number: 2023936935
ISBN 978-1-368-09466-5
Reinforced binding

www.HyperionAvenueBooks.com

Logo Applies to Text Stock Only

To Billy & Jeanne,
the best parents a girl could ask for

Author's Note

This book was assembled from a number of sources, primarily from nearly one hundred new interviews I conducted with members of the *Hocus Pocus* cast and crew, as well as Disney executives, fans, cultural critics, drag performers, and Salem locals. I also used archival material, such as interviews I did with members of the cast and crew in 2018 as part of a piece I wrote for *Bustle* tied to the film's twenty-fifth anniversary, including quotes that were never before published. Since not everyone was available to speak, I used other published interviews about the movie and the people who starred in and created it. Archival quotes include the year in which they were originally said or published, and brackets are used throughout the book for clarity. Some quotes have been edited for length and clarity. A list of sources is in the back.

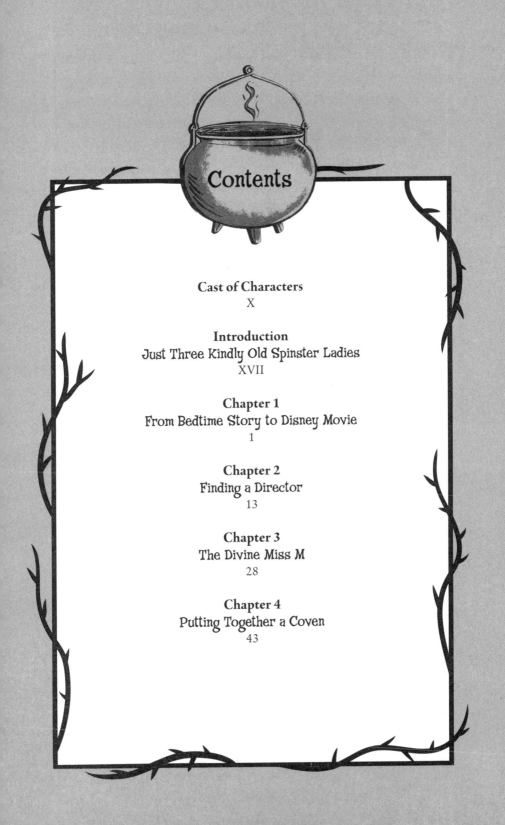

Contents

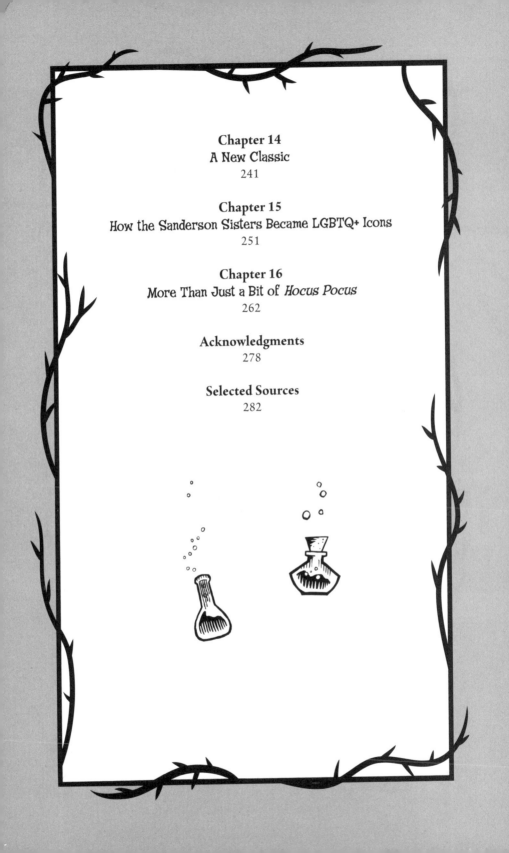

Cast of Characters

The Visionary

David Kirschner . . . . Creator/Writer/Producer

The Leader

Kenny Ortega . . . . Director/Choreographer

The Writers

Neil Cuthbert . . . . Co-screenwriter

Mick Garris . . . . Co-screenwriter/
Co-executive Producer

The Witches

Bette Midler . . . . "Winifred Sanderson"

Kathy Najimy . . . . "Mary Sanderson"

Sarah Jessica Parker . . . "Sarah Sanderson"

The Cast

Larry Bagby . . . . "Ernie 'Ice'"

Thora Birch . . . . "Dani Dennison"

Stephanie Faracy . . . . . . "Jenny"

Tobias Jelinek . . . . "Jay"

Doug Jones . . . . "Billy Butcherson"

Omri Katz . . . . "Max Dennison"

Karyn Malchus . . . . "Headless Billy Butcherson"

Joseph Malone . . . . "Skeleton Singer"

Jason Marsden . . . . Voice of "Binx the Cat"

Michael McGrady . . . . . "Eddie the Cop"

Sean Murray . . . . "Thackery Binx"

Vinessa Shaw . . . . "Allison Watts"

Amanda Shepherd . . . . . "Emily Binx"

Steve Voboril . . . . "Elijah"

Don Yesso . . . . "Mortal Bus Boy"

The Crew

Pamela Alch . . . . Script Supervisor

Chris Bailey . . . . Cat Animation Supervisor

Russell Bobbitt . . . . . . Prop Master

Colin Brady . . . . Animator: Binx the Cat

Rosemary Brandenburg . . Set Decorator

John Debney . . . . Composer

Tony Gardner . . . . Animatronic Cat Effects Artist/
Makeup Effects Designer/
Special Makeup Effects Artist

Steven Haft . . . . Producer

Kevin Haney . . . . Makeup Artist for
Bette Midler

Mary Hidalgo . . . . Casting Assistant

Peggy Holmes . . . . Choreographer

Steve LaPorte . . . . Makeup Artist

Rick Lazzarini . . . . Miniature Flying Witch
Puppets Creator

Larry Madrid . . . . Head Animal Trainer

Cheri Minns . . . . Makeup Artist for
Sarah Jessica Parker

Nancy Patton . . . . Art Director

Margaret Prentice . . . . . Special Makeup Effects Artist

William Sandell . . . . . . Production Designer

Marc Shaiman . . . . Composer/Lyricist/
Musical Arranger

Carolyn Soper . . . . Visual Effects Producer

Mary Vogt . . . . Costume Designer
Brock Walsh . . . . Lyrics and Incantations
Ralph Winter . . . . Executive Producer
Chet Zar . . . . Special Makeup Effects Artist

Additional Players

Michele Atwood
CEO, *The Main Street Mouse*; Co-founder, House of Mouse Expo

Mat Auryn
Author, *Psychic Witch: A Metaphysical Guide to
Meditation, Magick & Manifestation* and *Mastering
Magick: A Course in Spellcasting for the Psychic Witch*

Kimmy Blankenburg
@KimmyBlanksHocusPocusLife; *Hocus Pocus* Devotee

Bonnie Bruckheimer
Co-producer

Tina Burner
Creator/Star, *Witch Perfect*

Peaches Christ
Creator/Producer/Star, *Hocum Pokem*

Rachel Christ-Doane
Director of Education, Salem Witch Museum

Becky Coulter
Marketing Director, Alfred Coffee

William Cuthbert
@SpookyWil; Cohost, *The Black Flame Society* Podcast

Leonardo DiCaprio
Actor

Lt. Governor Kim Driscoll
Mayor of Salem, 2006–2023

Allison Dubrosky
@HocusPocusCollector; Cohost, *The Black Flame Society* Podcast

Belissa Escobedo
"Izzy," *Hocus Pocus 2*

Kate Fox
Executive Director, Destination Salem, 2007–2023

Amanda Yates Garcia
Author, *Initiated: Memoir of a Witch*

Drew Gaver
"Bev," Drag Performer

Heather Greene
Journalist/Editor/Author, *Lights, Camera, Witchcraft: A Critical History of Witches in American Film & Television*

Kahmora Hall
"Drag Queen Sarah," *Hocus Pocus 2*; *RuPaul's Drag Race*, Season 13

Nicole Halliwell
National Drag Entertainer

Jordan G. Hardin
Director of Food & Beverage, Alfred Coffee

Blake Harris
Screenwriter, *Hocus Pocus 2*

Daniel Henares
Filmmaker

Taylor Paige Henderson
"Young Winifred," *Hocus Pocus 2*

David Hoberman
President, Walt Disney and Touchstone Pictures, 1988–1994

A. W. Jantha
Author, *Hocus Pocus and the All-New Sequel*

Jeffrey Katzenberg
Chairman, Walt Disney Studios, 1984–1994

Alexis Kirschner
Daughter of David Kirschner

Liz Kirschner
Wife of David Kirschner

Dr. Catherine Lester
Lecturer, Film and Television

Gail Lyon
Creative Executive, Walt Disney Studios, 1991–1994

Janet Maslin
Film Critic, *The New York Times*, 1977–1999

Ernest Mathijs
Professor of Film Studies, University of British Columbia

Jennica McCleary
Performer/Producer/Bette Midler Tribute Artist

Nneka McGuire
Writer

Xavier Mendik
Professor of Cult Cinema Studies, Birmingham City University;
Director, Cine-Excess International Film Festival

Ginger Minj
"Drag Queen Winifred," *Hocus Pocus 2*; *RuPaul's Drag Race*

Nell Minow
The Movie Mom™; Contributing Editor, *RogerEbert.com*

Debra OConnell
President, News Group and Networks, Disney Entertainment

SaraRose Orlandini
Founder, SugarMynt Gallery

Tanya Pai
Director of Newsroom Standards and Ethics, *Vox*

Dr. Carmen Phillips
Editor-in-Chief, *Autostraddle*

Mark I. Pinsky
Author, *The Gospel According to Disney: Faith, Trust, and Pixie Dust*

Matt Piwowarczyk
Cohost, *All Things Cozy* Podcast

Paula Richter
Curator, Peabody Essex Museum

Jodie-Amy Rivera
Internet Personality

Vicente Saintignon
Actor/"Clair Voyance," Drag Queen

Brian Sims
Author/Performer, BORAH! Brewington Snaggletooth XIII;
Registered Respiratory Therapist, Brigham and Women's Hospital

Ilene Starger
Vice President of Casting, Walt Disney and
Touchstone Pictures, 1991–1994

Alex Steed
Cohost, *You Are Good* Podcast

Desson Thomson
Film Critic, *The Washington Post*, 1987–2008

Megan Townsend
Senior Director Entertainment Research & Analysis, GLAAD

Ron Underwood
Director

Aaron Wallace
Author, *Hocus Pocus in Focus: The Thinking
Fan's Guide to Disney's Halloween Classic*

Gillian Walters
Cohost, *All Things Cozy* Podcast

Mara Wilson
Actor/Writer

Susan Wloszczyna
Film Critic, *USA Today*, 1989–2001

Jessie Wolfson
Daughter of David Kirschner

James M. Wood
Vice President/General Manager, El Capitan Theatre

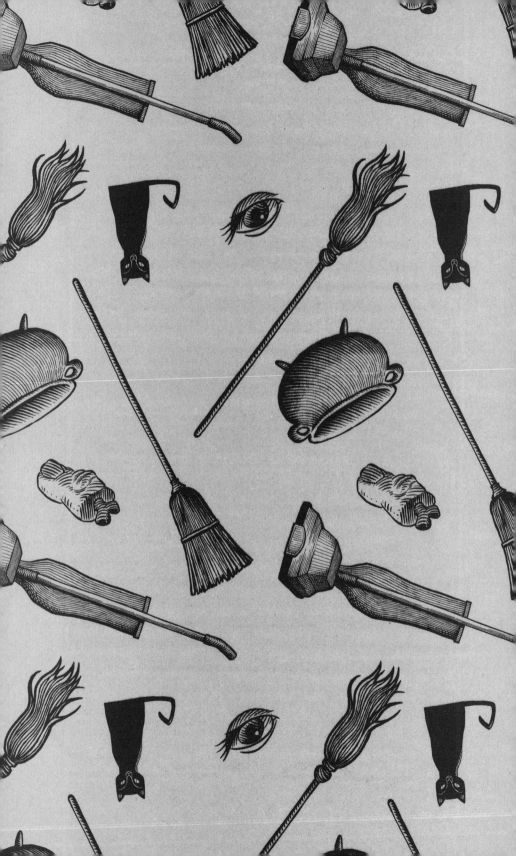

Introduction

JUST THREE KINDLY OLD SPINSTER LADIES

Those who have grown up watching *Hocus Pocus* on Freeform during the basic cable network's yearly "31 Nights of Halloween" event might not be all that familiar with the movie's humble beginnings. The PG-rated Disney family film is now considered by many to be the most popular Halloween movie of all time. (Though Michael Myers, the big bad of John Carpenter's 1978 classic *Halloween,* might take umbrage with that.) But *Hocus Pocus* was destined to be forgotten when it was released in July 1993—one month after Steven Spielberg brought dinosaurs back from extinction in *Jurassic Park*—to lower-than-expected ticket sales and middling reviews. The summer release date may seem unthinkable now to anyone with a calendar, but three decades ago, Halloween was just a day, not the seasonal event it has become. Summer was then the prime time to release a kids' movie, but unfortunately, based on the box office, neither children nor their parents were really interested in celebrating All Hallow's Eve in July.

Yet, the story of *Hocus Pocus*'s eventual success is one of happenstance and second chances—not unlike that of the Sanderson sisters, the seventeenth-century witches played by Bette Midler, Sarah Jessica Parker, and Kathy Najimy, who were accidentally resurrected by a tie-dye-loving high schooler and recent Salem, Massachusetts, transplant (and, lest we forget, virgin) who lit the Black Flame Candle in an attempt to impress his teen crush. Unlike those witchy women who were hell-bent on stealing the souls of little children in order to obtain eternal youth, the movie managed to overcome the challenges thrown its way. Due in no small part to a dedicated fan base that turned *Hocus Pocus* into a spooky season staple way before Disney understood exactly what they had.

When I was growing up in the '90s, every October (and sometimes September, too) gave me a reason to press play on my VHS copy of *Hocus Pocus*. I don't remember the first time I saw the movie—my mom says we rented it from the local video store and watched it enough times over the course of the three-day rental period that she quickly realized she was going to have to buy a copy for the house. But I do remember how much I loved watching it over and over, year in and year out. (I was initially a Sarah Sanderson fan, until I saw Thora Birch in *Now and Then,* at which point I became more of a Dani Dennison girl.) In some ways, I can't remember life before *Hocus Pocus.* It's a movie that has just always been there and, if Disney has its way, it always will be. In 2022, *Hocus Pocus 2* had the biggest opening for a streaming movie ever recorded, according to Nielsen tracking information, opening up the very real possibility that we will get the HPCU, aka the *Hocus Pocus* Cinematic Universe.

Before working on this book I never bothered to consider whether *Hocus Pocus* was a quote-unquote "hit" because I never cared whether the go-to Halloween movie of my childhood that featured three witches, a talking cat, and a lovable sometimes-headless zombie topped the box office on its opening weekend (it didn't; it came in fourth place, behind *The Firm, In the Line of Fire,* and *Jurassic Park,* earning $8.1 million on a reported $28 million budget) or earned critical praise (it didn't; Roger Ebert called it *"a film desperately in need of self-discipline"* and, with his partner in reviews, Gene Siskel, named it one of the worst movies of the year alongside long-forgotten films *The Beverly Hillbillies* and the Burt Reynolds kid comedy *Cop and a Half*). To me, a child who absolutely loved *Beetlejuice* and *The Addams Family,* the bawdy humor and overall spookiness of *Hocus Pocus* was cinema at its finest. Back then, the film's more risqué jokes went right over my head. I was probably in my teens before I even thought to question how that bus driver managed to keep his license when he spent more time eyeing the passengers than he did the road. Yet the jokes I did get still make me laugh all these years later, perhaps even more so than they did back then. (Winifred whispering, *"He has a little woman"* to her sisters while visiting the house of their presumed "Master," a Devil played by Garry Marshall, in an uncredited role, is far and away my favorite throwaway line.)

Nostalgia is certainly an important factor in how *Hocus Pocus* found its audience decades after its release. Millennials, like me, who grew up watching it when they were little have begun showing it to the children in their own lives. Yet my generation's penchant for sentimentality doesn't fully explain why this decades-old family film has become such a fascination of Boomers and Zoomers, inspiring yearly pilgrimages to the filming locations in Salem that require extra police to keep any overzealous fans in check. This movie should have gone the way of other underwhelming '90s movies like *Free Willy,* which beat *Hocus Pocus* at the box office in its original run, but doesn't appear to have any chance of being reclaimed anytime soon. Yet, here it is, more popular than ever. In 2023, *Hocus Pocus* was rereleased in theaters for its thirtieth anniversary and cracked the top ten at the box office. Not bad for a three-decade-old movie!

So why has *Hocus Pocus* managed to not only survive, but thrive in the years since its release? After collecting the stories and memories of those most closely involved with the film, as well as diehard fans, pop culture experts, Salem locals, former Disney executives, real witches, and drag performers, it's hard to pinpoint why or even how the Halloween movie about an immortal talking cat fighting to reunite with his sister in the afterlife became the cultural phenomenon it is. That's the most intriguing part of the *Hocus Pocus* success story: There is no silver bullet. It was many things that helped it become the iconic film it is today: creator David Kirschner's sincerity, director Kenny Ortega's artistry, Bette Midler's commitment, a creative and tireless crew, a connection to Halloween, an unabashed campiness, and, yes, nostalgic fans looking for a reason to return to a time when movies and life seemed a little simpler. What became clear to me after writing this book (and hopefully to you after reading it), is that *Hocus Pocus* has put a spell on the world—one that seems unlikely to be broken anytime soon.

Chapter 1

From Bedtime Story to Disney Movie

In the early 1980s, David Kirschner, the producer behind the Child's Play *horror film franchise, led by a murderous doll named Chucky, dreamed up a fantastical tale for his two young daughters about a teenage boy who was turned into a cat by three witches. It's not exactly kiddie fare, but it is the inspiration for* Hocus Pocus.

David Kirschner (Creator/Writer/Producer):

It didn't even start as a bedtime story. We were sitting on the porch of our house and there was a black cat that lived next door. He was a friendly fellow. I think one of the girls said, "It's such a pretty cat." I said, "But did you know that it's actually a boy?"

Alexis Kirschner (Daughter of David Kirschner):

My dad, who always made up elaborate stories to keep us intrigued, told us, "The witches turned the boy into a cat because he was trying to save his sister." It's a scary thought, to be turned into a cat and stuck that way forever.

Jessie Wolfson (Daughter of David Kirschner):

To this day, I'm honestly a little weird with cats because of my dad.

David Kirschner:

When I was a boy, I rescued a black cat. I was probably seven or eight and I knew my parents would kill me. We had two dogs and I brought it to my bedroom and for a few days it was living in there. I didn't even think about the whole concept of poop, I just loved this cat, but I got caught because of the scents, and the cat was let go. I just always remembered that cat, so when I saw this cat next door, it just kind of pulled on heartstrings from when I was really little. Every night they wanted to hear this same story, and I would add to it. I was kind of the in-house entertainment. It was Liz, my wife and my partner, who said to me, "You should really do something with this."

Liz Kirschner (Wife of David Kirschner):

Literally when I first heard it, I just said, "Oh my God." It just struck a chord. Halloween has always been an important holiday in our lives. We've just celebrated it from the moment we first met. Hearing that story really inspired me to say, "You have to write that. You've got to share that with the world."

While in the early stages of writing this story, Kirschner was busy pitching another personal project. An American Tail, *the 1986 animated feature directed by Don Bluth, told the story of a young Russian-Jewish mouse named Fievel who, while emigrating from Russia to New York City in 1885, gets separated from his family. After Jeffrey Katzenberg (at that time the Walt Disney Studios Chairman) passed on the project, Kirschner caught a lucky break.*

David Kirschner:

I was fortunate enough that Kathleen Kennedy, who runs Lucasfilm these days and was Steven Spielberg's producing partner back then, saw an article on me in the *LA Times* when I was first starting out. She asked to meet me. I had no idea who Kathleen Kennedy was, but I certainly knew Spielberg. She came to my office and I presented *An American Tail* to her. I didn't seem to make her laugh and I didn't seem to make her cry at the parts that I thought I would. After I'm done with the pitch, she said, "Can I use your phone?" I thought, *Oh she's going to call a taxi.* She called Steven and said, "You need to see this kid's work, like, now." The next day, I presented *An American Tail* to Steven at his Fourth of July party. He said to me, "What's more exciting than what I see before me is what you still have up there." Out of the corner of my eye, over Steven's shoulder, I see Liz just crying so hard. I'm trying to enjoy this moment, but also so frightened Spielberg's going to turn around and see a woman just hysterical on his couch.

Liz Kirschner:

That was an amazing experience. *An American Tail* was Dave's first film and it's never been that easy again. That was unbelievable, but that's not how things normally happen.

David Kirschner:

After that I had Spielberg pixie dust all over me. I say that because, after passing on *An American Tail,* all of a sudden I got a phone call from Jeffrey Katzenberg's office in 1984. They wanted to see if I had anything else that I'd like to talk about. I remembered what Liz had said to me about this story that originally was called the *Halloween House* and so I said, "Well, I have a story that I've created." They said, "Can you come in tomorrow?" I said, "Oh, I can't for about the next ten days." It wasn't that I was busy, because I wasn't, I needed to begin to do artwork and put things together for the pitch.

Alexis Kirschner:

I remember just sitting next to my dad and him drawing the storyboard sequence for his meeting to present *Hocus Pocus.* He had also found a vacuum because one of the witches flies on a vacuum in the story he told. I just remember him being so excited about all the props that he was going to use for his meeting.

Liz Kirschner:

There were kids who lived in our neighborhood who were a little older than our daughters. We gave them paper bags and they decorated them with witches and black cats to look like little Halloween bags. It was their original art, which was wonderful. I remember going to the market and buying a gazillion pounds of candy corn. I think we were just caught up in the excitement that he was going to pitch this to Disney. Growing up, Disney was everything to us. It was thrilling to be a part of that.

David Kirschner:

I asked Disney if I could get into the conference room about thirty minutes early. When the executives walked into the room, the lights were turned down low and I had a mop, a broomstick, and an Electrolux vacuum cleaner with the engine hollowed out hanging from the ceiling on monofilament wires so they looked like they were flying. I had a cauldron filled with dry ice and Liz had sent me there with about fifteen pounds of candy corn, which I made into a serpentine design on the conference table where the executives would sit. When they came in, they smelled the candy corn; they smelled their childhood. They laughed and made some jokes; they were not particularly supportive. Jeffrey said, "Oh, show-and-tell time." This was the same guy that passed on *An American Tail*, but there was a little more respect there. It had nothing to do with me. It was the fact that Spielberg chose something that Jeffrey Katzenberg passed on. I presented all of the artwork I had done and I said, "Halloween is a billion-dollar business"—which, in 1984, it was. Now it's a ten-billion-dollar business—"and there are no movies out there for families." I'm not even sure Jeffrey Katzenberg heard the rest of my pitch after that. He really responded to that fact. I could just see his eyes light up.

Jeffrey Katzenberg (Chairman, Walt Disney Studios, 1984–1994):

I'm afraid that was too many years and too many pitches ago to recall.

David Kirschner:

Jeffrey said, "Okay, well, thank you. We'll let you know." I walked away wondering if they were just being polite and were going to pass on it. I loaded up my dolly and made a bunch of trips to the parking lot. As I loaded the last stuff in my car, Jeffrey's assistant came running out to the parking lot and said, "Jeffrey does not want you taking this anywhere else. He wants it." I said, "That's good, right?"

Jeffrey Katzenberg had bought David Kirschner's idea for a movie then called Halloween House, *inspired by his short story of the same name, published in* Muppet Magazine *in the early 1980s. Kirschner had never written a script before, but found a kindred spirit in Mick Garris, a story editor on the Steven Spielberg–executive produced TV series* Amazing Stories, *who would go on to become a legendary horror filmmaker. The two wrote the first script together in 1986, but it took nearly a decade, a false start with one director, and multiple script rewrites before Disney greenlit the project.*

Mick Garris (Co-screenwriter/Co-executive Producer):

I was thirty-three years old when I got a call from Steven Spielberg. He had read the spec script I had written, which, I found out years later, was the very first script for *Amazing Stories*. They asked me to do another one right away. Halfway through [writing] that, they asked me to be the story editor [on *Amazing Stories*]. I was literally on food stamps, and then I was working for Spielberg. That was my first job, and that's how David knew of my work. I loved David immediately, just his imagination. We both had that Amblin sensibility.

David Kirschner:

The truth was, I really didn't know many other people that wrote screenplays so I asked Mick if he would want to be part of this, and he said, "Yeah, sure." Mick Garris is considered, I mean, truly considered a master of horror. He has directed many Stephen King stories and is a great writer. Mick loved the story and kind of glommed onto the darkness, which is so normal for Mick.

Mick Garris:

I couldn't help but write something a little darker than what they made. The one big difference with my script—and it's a big difference to me, not to everybody else—but I wrote the movie about twelve-year-olds because when you're twelve, that's when Halloween is the most potent time in your life. When you're sixteen, you're stealing the candy from the twelve-year-olds. We knew going in that it was a Disney movie, but I have childhood memories of the blue smoke that comes out of the gun after they shoot poor Old Yeller, so Disney is not afraid of darkness.

David Kirschner:

Between the two of us, it was pretty dark, but there would be many, many other writers that would work on the script later, at least twelve, including Neil Cuthbert, who came in to punch up the jokes.

Neil Cuthbert (Co-screenwriter):

This was the spring of '91 and I was very much a working screenwriter at that time. Disney approached me with the project. They sent me the Mick Garris script, which I read, and really liked. I thought it was a great story. This project had been around for a while. There were three or four additional scripts between Mick and me. I remember they said, "Oh, we don't need to show them to you." When I do something like this, I want to read all of them because I'm not opposed to taking other people's good ideas, but there wasn't much there that was usable from our point of view. They were basically all discarded. They kept going back to Mick's script. Mick and I have the writing credit, even though we've never met, but it was his version underneath it all that made this movie happen. It was his version that Jeffrey Katzenberg and Disney kept saying, "It doesn't work yet, but we want it to work."

Gail Lyon (Creative Executive, Walt Disney Studios, 1991–1994):

I was what they called a creative executive on the project, which means you're responsible for helping to choose writers and then sort of babysitting, if you will, the creative decisions and the creative progression of the project. I had read some stuff of Neil's and [then Senior Vice President, Production] Michael Roberts and I asked our bosses to read it. They said, "Look, go after this guy." So we did. That's how it used to happen—and by the way, I think it's how it still happens. Michael and I worked with Neil really closely and we got very much into the DNA, for better or worse, of how the script progresses. Anytime you're dealing with things like magic or witchcraft, there's an unspoken set of rules that you need to sort of follow internally, even if they're never spoken about in the movie.

Neil Cuthbert:

A lot of things weren't defined in the first version, but the story was there: the witches running around Salem looking for the book, the zombie boy, the talking cat. All that stuff was in that original story. What the studio wanted was essentially a pretty major rewrite that would develop the comedy in the piece, develop the witches as personalities, and develop what they used to call "a fish out of water" comedy. It was really an expression I got so sick of hearing at the time.

Vinessa Shaw ("Allison Watts"):

The original script was scary. It was more like the *Wizard of Oz*. Being a *Wizard of Oz* fan, I remember reading it and being, "Oh, this is my opportunity to do my *Wizard of Oz*," you know? It was much more in that vein. It was more dramatic; magical but dramatic. I don't know who decided to make it more comedic, but it became so much better. That's when some of the camp that people love became part of the movie.

Ralph Winter (Executive Producer):

It feels pretty lofty that we might be compared to *The Wizard of Oz*. That might be a scarier movie than anything we had.

Mick Garris:

"Hansel and Gretel" was definitely an influence, not so much *Wizard of Oz* for me. I wasn't seeing the bright candy-apple colors that the movie is made in. That's very much Kenny Ortega's contribution; he gave it a personality.

Neil Cuthbert:

It really was more like a horror fantasy movie. It wasn't funny. I mean, it wasn't unfunny; it wasn't like a real horror movie. It wasn't full of gore, but it was played pretty straight. The book, the kids, and the talking cat, all of that was built into the first version, but the tone of it was very different.

In 1988, Ron Underwood, who would go on to make the 1990 horror-comedy Tremors, *was hired to direct the film then still known as* Halloween House.

Ron Underwood (Director):

This was the first feature film I was hired to direct, so it was a big deal. I was thinking when I was offered it, *Wow, there's never been a Halloween movie for kids.* I know it was Mick's script that I read; it was pretty early in the process. I had been doing educational short films, [and] when that market dried up, I did children's television. I did an adaptation [for television] of a Beverly Cleary book, *The Mouse and the Motorcycle*, which had a talking cat in it. There was a talking cat [in this film], so Disney came to me knowing I could do talking cats. I think that's literally why I got hired.

Mick Garris:

I saw *The Mouse and the Motorcycle* and thought it was charming and very impressive. I remember meeting Ron and thinking he had great ideas. Disney, like a lot of the other studios, like[s] young imaginative filmmakers. Not just because they're imaginative, but they're also less expensive and they're easier to control. I don't know why it ended up not going to Ron, other than maybe it's a big movie for a first-time director.

Ron Underwood:

I liked Mick Garris's script. I wanted it to be a kids' movie, but I also wanted it to have some bigger scares. I don't know if Disney really wanted to make it any scarier. I don't remember how the whole thing ended, whether *Tremors* just got momentum at that point and I dropped out [to direct that], or they said, "The heck with this guy!" I don't even remember. It's kind of weird, though; both *Tremors* and *Hocus Pocus* weren't hugely successful at the time, but both of them have had long lives. I love that about them.

Omri Katz ("Max Dennison"):

I remember some of the early illustrations of the movie: Bette Midler's character had sharp, nasty teeth. She kind of looked like Bram Stoker's *Dracula*, just super creepy. Those are the illustrations I saw just before I jumped on board, but I was just like, "Wow, this is cool!"

Tony Gardner (Animatronic Cat Effects Artist/Makeup Effects Designer/Special Makeup Effects Artist):

My original script breakdown included demonic versions of the witches, truly scary pointy-tooth creatures; the bullies aging into old men; Emily having the life sucked out of her and seeing her skin sink into bone and having her die on camera.

David Kirschner:

One of the darkest elements of our original story actually remained, which is sucking the lives out of children. They did keep that, but they softened it a great deal and surrounded it with a good deal of comedy.

Thora Birch ("Dani Dennison"):

I mean, sucking the lives out of little children is an insane concept, especially for a ten-year-old brain. Oddly enough, my dad was a huge Carlos Castaneda fan so we all had to read [the controversial Peruvian-born anthropologist and author's] books and they were talking about auras and life forces and all that; I was hooked on this story right away.

Kathy Najimy ("Mary Sanderson"), 1993:

It seems scarier on paper, but when you get me and Sarah and Bette in our characters and in our costumes, with the jokes everywhere and running around and bumping into each other, the sucking the lives out of kids becomes so secondary that it's not scary anymore.

Neil Cuthbert:

I grew up watching the great Hollywood sibling comics, like the Marx Brothers, the Three Stooges, [as well as the comic team of] Laurel and Hardy. I read the script and thought, *Wow, this is an incredible opportunity to create that for three women.* To make the sisters more like a comic ensemble where they love each other, but they also hate each other.

Mark I. Pinsky (Author, *The Gospel According to Disney: Faith, Trust, and Pixie Dust*):

I saw many of these Disney movies as a child myself and I became reacquainted with them when I had children. I was writing a bit about religion in my job at the *LA Times* at the time, and I noticed there seemed to be a systematic set of values that was presented [in Disney movies]. Good is always rewarded, evil is always punished, but above that, there's sort of a belief in belief. You need to believe in a greater power of some sort, but it was never very specific. It wasn't Christian or Jewish; Walt Disney made a commercial decision not to make it an identifiable theology. He chose magic in the benign sense. What struck me in regard to *Hocus Pocus* is that it was more ambiguous. The witches were funny and kind of evil, but not darkly evil. It was a real departure. It was kind of like, "There is evil in the world, but don't worry about it." In the end, good triumphs over even ambiguous evil.

Steven Haft (Producer):

David [Kirschner] is the Walt Disney of the next generation, a true Hollywood conceptual artist and creator. We now talk about a so-called "creator economy," but in the '90s, we were still fairly close to a studio system, there were many fewer humans who had the title "creator" because it was a very narrow funnel that you had to get through to get your creations financed and made. Of that much smaller cohort who got to call themselves creators, you look across Hollywood and see Walt Disney; Rod Serling, who created *Twilight Zone;* Gene Roddenberry, who created *Star Trek;* George Lucas, who created *Star Wars*; and David Kirschner. He belongs in that elite very short list of genius Hollywood creators.

Mick Garris:

David was the only one who was there from beginning to end. He is definitely the father of *Hocus Pocus*. It's his baby, and I'm proud to be a stepparent. Without David's imagination and loving spirit, this movie wouldn't exist.

Chapter 2

FINDING A DIRECTOR

A fter parting ways with Ron Underwood, the studio's search for a director led them to a familiar name: Kenny Ortega, a choreographer who had worked with Michael Jackson, Cher, and KISS before choreographing notable 1980s films such as Dirty Dancing, Xanadu, *and* Ferris Bueller's Day Off. *He made his feature directorial debut in 1992 with* Newsies, *a Disney musical based on the New York City newsboy strike of 1899 that starred a young Christian Bale. The movie wasn't a success—it made back less than a fifth of its $15 million budget at the box office—but the studio saw promise in Ortega's skills as a director.*

Jeffrey Katzenberg:

Kenny had done *Newsies* for us and, even though it was a disappointment at the box office, it was always one of the favorite films I've worked on. So, I was eager to have him work his magic on this movie.

David Hoberman (President, Walt Disney and Touchstone Pictures, 1988–1994):

Newsies was a big leap for Kenny, you know? We all really loved it and were surprised that it didn't perform at the box office.

David Kirschner:

Jeffrey recognized that Kenny was talented and, I give Jeffrey credit for this, he wanted to give him a second bite of the apple, so he handed him *Hocus Pocus.*

Steven Haft:

People think of Jeffrey as being a tough boss, which in some ways he was, but he had this very endearing nature and deep loyalties to people. That's how you end up with Kenny on the biggest-budget live-action film in Disney history. A budget of twenty-eight million dollars doesn't sound like a lot of money, even then, but Disney wasn't making expensive movies and this was the number-one-biggest-budget movie they had ever made and they gave it to a guy, who, on his last film, had taken it, I mean, I've heard numbers, I've never seen the numbers, but someone told me he delivered *Newsies* for many millions more than his budget. My job [as a producer on *Hocus Pocus*] was, "Don't spend my money." The studio was terrified.

Ralph Winter:

I think *Newsies* was tough on Kenny in terms of the way it was perceived. He wanted to do a good job [on *Hocus Pocus*]. He wanted to correct anything that he thought might have been a misstep on *Newsies*. He never referenced it, but I think it was in all our minds. He was a hard worker; he was involved and willing to do whatever it took to make it happen.

Kenny Ortega (Director/Choreographer):

When I first met with Jeffrey Katzenberg, he invited me to Disney with the invitation to do two features. At that time, everybody was saying, "The musical is dead." Jeffrey wanted to take a shot at it, which was thrilling to me. He had a script, *Newsies*, which he wanted to develop into a musical, and he basically said, "If you'll do this one, you can pick the next one." I was overjoyed to do *Newsies*; I loved the premise, I loved the children's crusade, I loved everything about it so it was a no-brainer. It was my first film, and I wish I would've had more time in prep, and just more time with all those musical production moments. But, overall, I'm grateful for having been invited to do it.

Bonnie Bruckheimer (Co-producer):

I do remember that he wasn't the first choice. I don't remember who else they were talking to. [Bette Midler and I] saw *Newsies* and we didn't see why a movie like this would be right for him. I'm not saying that we didn't want him, I mean, *Newsies* was entertaining, but it didn't seem like it was related to a movie like *Hocus Pocus*.

Aaron Wallace (Author, *Hocus Pocus in Focus: The Thinking Fan's Guide to Disney's Halloween Classic*):

It is widely reported that Steven Spielberg was involved with the production in its early days. That he came very close to directing it, that there was a whole pitch meeting, and that he came to the set once it was in production. I had the opportunity to meet and to work with Mick Garris and essentially his recollection was that there was this pitch meeting and Spielberg was very involved. David Kirschner remembers it differently.

Mick Garris:

We were planning on [*Hocus Pocus*] being something we would take to Steven. It was the most spectacular pitch I've ever been a part of, and that's entirely because of David. He brought in pumpkins, candy, and other harvest things. He laid it out on the conference room table at Amblin; it was just gorgeous and mind-boggling. It was just the two of us and Steven, maybe [Spielberg's] development executive was there, too, but we're telling this story and we can see Steven's face light up. Then David let it be known that Disney was involved, and it changed everything. To this day, I still don't know why we would be pitching the movie to Amblin if it was a Disney project. At that time in particular, Amblin and Disney were very competitive with one another; they were going after the same audience. Steven did not want to be working with that studio. Ironically [in 1994] Steven and Jeffrey Katzenberg, who was [Chairman of Walt Disney Studios] at the time, teamed up for [a new studio named] DreamWorks. They not only became friends, but partners.

David Kirschner:

Mick Garris tells a story that I have no memory of: We presented it to Steven, he loved it, but didn't want to make it with Disney. Mick and I have different memories of that chapter in the *Hocus Pocus* story. Believe me, I would much rather the reality be that, but about a year or so after *Hocus Pocus* came out, Liz and I were at the Amblin Christmas party and Kathy Kennedy came up to me and said hello. Then she got right to business, "You know, you really hurt Steven." I was thinking, *Little me? How could I ever hurt Steven? I would never hurt Steven!* She said, "The fact that he made your first film happen for you, and you didn't even give him the opportunity to see *Hocus Pocus*." I remember feeling hot tears in the back of my eyes and saying, "Kathy, I so completely messed this up. Disney just asked if I had something else, I said yes, and I am so sorry."

Liz Kirschner:

It was such a horribly uncomfortable moment that I think I slinked away. I didn't want to be part of that conversation, which is terrible. I probably should have been there to support Dave.

David Kirschner:

I did something terrible, and it wasn't to be an insensitive person, but I was insensitive in the sense that when Jeffrey said, "Do you have anything else?" And I said yes. I didn't even think, *Oh my god, Steven Spielberg has just given me the break of my life and here I have another project and maybe I should run it by him first.* If I had a time machine, I would go back and try to make it right.

Liz Kirschner:

Not that you want to upset Steven Spielberg, but there was a story that he wanted to hear of Dave's. He thought, *Why didn't Dave bring it to me?* I mean, there's a positive spin to that, right?

Aaron Wallace:

My background is as a lawyer, and in the context of eyewitness testimony, very often you can have three individuals who are in the same place at the same time, and even a week later, they all remember it differently, let alone thirty years later. My feeling is Mick and David are probably both right and there's some connecting fact that has gotten lost to time. But the nexus between Steven Spielberg and *Hocus Pocus* is so fascinating. This notion that the film is "Spielbergian," notwithstanding any actual connection he may or may not have had with the film. When you just look at the filmography of Steven Spielberg, rather clearly one of the most celebrated filmmakers of all time, the Godfather of the Blockbuster, you look at some of his themes: a quest for restoration of a broken family, a coming-of-age story very often in the context of an encounter with the supernatural, this sense of wide-eyed wonder. His reputation in the early days was as the big kid with the camera. I get that same sense watching *Hocus Pocus*. Kenny Ortega's approach to the lens has that same sense of awe, and it's an awe for Salem and an awe for the magic and the mystery of Halloween. You do get that same kind of filmmaking finesse alongside the type of story that Spielberg has told so many times. Perhaps it becomes no surprise to learn that Spielberg may have had an actual connection to the film.

William Sandell (Production Designer):

When I saw the script, Kenny wasn't signed on yet. The execs at Disney were sitting around and said, "You love Halloween. Here's a Halloween script." I said, "Well, who's gonna do it?" They said, "Well, we'd like Kenny to do it." I was the production designer on *Newsies*. They said, "He'll probably hire you because it looks like you guys have a good relationship. So go get him." I was out there like an agent. I heard Kenny say later, "Bill Sandell was following me around!" I came this close to losing the project.

Kenny Ortega:

Right off the bat, Bill Sandell is a brilliant production designer whom I have missed all these years with a full heart. I adore him. I had no intention of going to anyone else other than to him so that's a bit of an exaggeration, I think, on his part. . . . Jeffrey came to me and said, "Bette Midler is looking for a family-friendly film. She has a daughter.

She wants to do something that she can watch. We have this script called *Hocus Pocus* and, if you're interested, we'd love to present you to Bonnie [Bruckheimer] and Bette as the director." I was Toni Basil's assistant choreographer on the [1979] movie *The Rose*, in which Bette was nominated for an Oscar, so I had already worked with her and I was madly, madly, madly in love with her. My answer was yes before even reading the script. Really and truly it was "Yes, and thank you, and I'll be happy to read the script."

Russell Bobbitt (Prop Master):
Kenny Ortega and I were just dear friends after working together on *Newsies*. We just really hit it off and became besties. No one said besties then, but it's what we were. It was kind of a no-brainer to go from *Newsies* to *Hocus Pocus* because at that point, we were part of a team that we didn't want to break up. Kenny and I just connected in all ways, shapes, and forms. I have a dear place in my heart for him. He was the choreographer for almost any big name you can mention. He's worked with every diva there was. He was a diva expert. He truly schooled himself really quickly into translating his dance training to film and storytelling. For that reason alone, I think everybody was always in awe of him. Everyone felt like they belonged in that atmosphere and that was because of Kenny.

Neil Cuthbert:
Kenny Ortega was very nice to work with. He was a good guy, and, by the way, directors are not all good guys. Especially the new ones who don't always know what they're doing.

Thora Birch:
Kenny was this great ball of fire and energy who genuinely loves kids. He was always like, "Oh, Thora, so great!" And then he'd give me a big old hug. His capacity to compartmentalize and just focus on who he was dealing with in that moment, I really respected that. It just provided a

sense of warmth to the set that I think I probably needed because there were intimidating factors, you know?

Michael McGrady ("Eddie the Cop"):
I really liked Kenny a lot. I loved his style. I loved the way he worked on the set. He was cognizant, more or less, of who I was. I was not a name, I was nobody big. But I did *The Babe* with John Goodman, and I did *Diggstown* with James Woods and Lou Gossett Jr., and I was on a trajectory of working with big stars on big movies. When *Hocus Pocus* came along, my agents actually didn't want me to do it. They said, "It's a small role, it's only one scene." I had two young girls at the time who had never seen me in anything because I'm usually beating somebody up. My argument was, "I want to do a family-friendly movie so my kids can finally see what I do for a living." My agents were like, "Well, we think it's a really bad move, but it's your career." When I showed up on the set, I met Kenny and instantly just thought he was fantastic. He was very classy, really knew what he wanted. I actually saw *Newsies* and I was so impressed with how creative it was. I thought, *This could turn out to be a cool little film.*

Ilene Starger (Vice President of Casting, Walt Disney and Touchstone Pictures, 1991–1994):
Kenny Ortega is very smart, ebullient, hardworking, and gifted, and I enjoyed working with him. He was an actor and choreographer before segueing to directing, and his awareness of rhythm and movement are invaluable, as they add pacing and fluidity to his projects.

Vinessa Shaw:
The magic behind this movie is Kenny Ortega. He being so talented as a choreographer brings a sort of musicality to the movie without it being a musical.

Mary Vogt (Costume Designer):
As a choreographer, you're a teacher. He manages to be a teacher without being condescending. He's very sincere and disciplined. You can't be creative as a dancer unless you are disciplined.

Tobias Jelinek ("Jay"):
His musical sensibility is rather flawless and it's seamlessly woven into *Hocus Pocus*. There's a real dance-like quality to so many of the scenes.

Jason Marsden (Voice of "Binx the Cat"):
I only worked with Kenny for a couple of days. I remember this hippie-looking dude with long hair and shorts and I think a tank top, but my stepfather was a ballet choreographer so I grew up around that. I would notice in the scenes they would show to me, the dynamic between Sarah, Kathy, and Bette was very musical, very choreographed, and very fluid. I could see the choreographer's influence on that.

Peggy Holmes (Choreographer):
Kenny is just like oozing rhythm. That's just who he is. He approaches his projects with that rhythm inside of him.

Steven Haft:
One of the world's smallest lists is choreographers-turned-successful-directors. [*Singin' in the Rain* director] Stanley Donen, who I'm a great fan of, and Kenny Ortega are on that list. If you look across Kenny's body of work, he earns his due on this very esteemed list, but he's a handful.

Vinessa Shaw:
Kenny came on set with such energy and passion. It was infectious. There were so many times where he was just, "More, you guys!" because we're just these lethargic teenagers. He was like a much nicer Willy Wonka just entrancing us with every move.

Omri Katz:

He's extremely enthusiastic and brings that to the set. I think he was just so thrilled to be a part of this industry. Still today, when I talk to Kenny, he's so excited about everything he works on.

Rosemary Brandenburg (Set Decorator):

Kenny is so playful and so into movement and creative and just a superb person. I really enjoy him very much. He was just the smartest, neatest guy. It was just a real privilege to work with him.

Michael McGrady:

I just want to put on record: Out of all the directors I worked with, Kenny was one of my favorites of all time. He's a person who just loves people. He's an artist. He has that empathy for the artist and what they do and how vulnerable they have to be.

Amanda Shepherd ("Emily Binx"):

Just meeting him for the first time, I could just tell he was an incredible person. It was strange, I almost felt like I knew him. He was just so relatable and just so kindhearted. As a child, you pick up on those things. I had gone to auditions with so many different directors and producers, and nobody gave me that feeling of love and made me feel like I was supposed to be there.

Tobias Jelinek:

I had forgotten this, but we all had stationery with *Hocus Pocus* and our name on it. He would write little notes, "Miss you!" "Love you!" "Stay cool!" Little pep talks just to keep everyone feeling loved.

Ralph Winter:

The tone of the film is all Kenny. He's gregarious, very outgoing. He's very involved. He was great with the kids. He was trying to get them to have fun and get into the part. The same with the ladies, he was very good with them in terms of drawing out more performances, more choices, more ideas. I thought he was very giving.

Russell Bobbitt:

There were times where we would have to stop shooting and Kenny would do a ballet lesson or a tap lesson. We'd all sit around in a circle and Kenny would tap-dance for us. There were house parties on the weekends. We would hang out and he'd barbecue. We were a tight-knit family in the San Fernando Valley. I still feel like I could go knock on his door and we would just pick up where we left off.

William Sandell:

In showbiz, there are egos and then there are the nice guys. Kenny was a nice guy.

Mary Vogt:

I didn't notice a big difference in how he treated people. Whether you were an extra or Bette Midler, he treated everyone the same. I had never really seen that, and I have not really ever seen that again.

Steven Haft:

Kenny had three talented lead actresses to play with, so there was a rehearsing-in-real-time kind of atmosphere on set. There was also a tight budget. I've run a mile here and I've run a mile there on different films, but *Hocus Pocus* required me to run a marathon. It was the most robust undertaking I was ever confronted with.

David Kirschner:

It was a constant stream, a deluge of notes on this project. What's amazing to me is even as it was being shot, Kenny Ortega's patience with the studio was beyond my understanding. He was such a pro and always so calm. If he disagreed, he kind of talked it through with them. I learned a great deal from him, someone who was so young in their career at that point, about being a good listener. As opposed to just being ready to fight, which most people do in this business. He was such a consummate gentleman.

Kenny Ortega's supportive leadership style was why so many on his crew were willing to fight for his vision of the fantasy film.

William Sandell:

Production designers like myself are tasked with a pretty big responsibility. The studio's giving you a lot of money and they want to know how it's being spent. Are they going to get bang for their buck? At the end of the day, there ain't much art direction in art direction because I'm in front of a bunch of studio suits explaining where the money went, where the money's going to go, and why I need more money. I remember one very distinct morning, it was show-and-tell. Jeffrey Katzenberg was coming to the art department to see what we were doing. We had a big, beautiful tabletop model of the witch house and the waterwheel and the trees. Mary [Vogt] had all her beautiful fabrics that she was anticipating dressing the ladies in. Katzenberg walks in, [says], "I don't even know if I will make this movie." He's like, "Why is this house in the woods?" Later on, Mary and I were laughing because the script calls for a witch house in the woods. He was saying things like, "I'll put this whole thing in turnaround."

Rosemary Brandenburg:

That was one incident that I frankly will never forget. We had created a wonderful mock-up of the witches' house with a little working waterwheel and a little bit of water going through. It was just the most gorgeous model. The idea was to present to the studio execs what we're going to build and make sure everybody was on board. They were trying to save money and [Jeffrey Katzenberg] just went, "This is just too much. We don't need all this. We've got some really fine actresses here with some snappy dialogue. We could do this movie in front of black curtains. It would be just as funny." I mean, that was a very dispiriting moment, believe me.

Mary Vogt:
They kept saying, "The girls are fish out of water" and they could "do the whole thing against a black curtain with black leotards." Jeffrey was the one who was really [saying], "It doesn't matter what it looks like; it's more about the actors' performances." I had sketches and we were looking at them and he was like, "Oh, none of this is important and none of this matters." I was like, "Yeah, well, you got a real problem." I started to get annoyed. I had just done *Batman Returns*, so I was feeling pretty cocky. I thought, *Well who the hell are you?* because studio heads come and they go. I just thought, *Well, you're probably going to be gone next year anyway.*

Rosemary Brandenburg:
Yes, of course there were wonderful performances by some wonderful actresses with some snappy dialogue, but I don't think the film would have the staying power it had unless we had gotten the funds to make some really interesting sets. I give Bill [Sandell] 100 percent credit for that. He muscled through and did some diplomacy, made a gesture toward economizing and somehow managed to convince the studio that this was still a good idea.

William Sandell:
Jeffrey Katzenberg was very confrontational, I don't know what his issue was, but there must have been more to that story that I don't know. It was a rocky project from the beginning since Disney had been sitting on that script for years. But he must have liked what he saw that day because he greenlit the movie.

Mary Vogt:

The studio backed down because it became obvious that we weren't going to give up. I think that this was a good lesson: You don't have to push very hard, just don't give up. It's not even a fight. If you fight with them, they get energized. The last thing you want to do is energize people against you. I'm more into boring people into agreeing with me.

Ralph Winter:

I remember I'd get a call from Jeffrey, I don't know, five after seven in the morning, and then it's a three-minute conversation, "Ralph, how are we doing on *Hocus Pocus*? You got everything you need?" and "Yeah, I think everything's good." He goes, "Good. Just checking in. I'll call you next week." He would give feedback. He'd be blunt about things, but look, we had some laughs and it was hard work. We never had a problem. I respected what he did, and he respected what I did.

Mary Vogt:

Jeffrey was very talented, you couldn't take that away from him, but I think he was hurt by something. That's the only way to understand that meeting.

Steven Haft:

The thing that was going on was [Executive Vice President] Marty Katz, Disney's longtime head of physical production, the one that deals with budgets and things like that, was leaving right at the beginning of *Hocus Pocus*. Marty was Jeffrey's partner in keeping these studio pictures on tight budgets. He was being replaced by a guy named Bruce Hendricks. *Hocus Pocus* was the first picture being done in the Hendricks regime and Bruce was terrified because it was Jeffrey's biggest-budget film ever. Jeffrey only gave him the job as acting Head of Production when Marty left and the "acting" part of his title came down to, "If *Hocus Pocus* goes awry, you do not get this job." Poor Bruce was both terrified and trusting because he had been a deputy under Marty. He knew all the Kenny lore and he knew that he only had his job if we didn't fuck this up. He ended up having a career of twenty-five years running physical production at the studio under Jeffrey and Dick Cook [Chairman of the Walt Disney Studios, 2002–2009], but his whole job tenure came down to this film not going as *Newsies* had gone.

Chapter 3

THE DIVINE
MISS M

*T*he makers of Hocus Pocus *saw the witchy trio as a girl group, not unlike the Supremes or the Ronettes. The search for an actress to play Winifred Sanderson, the powerful and controlling eldest sister, was like choosing the perfect frontwoman. Whoever played Winnie had to sing, figuratively and literally, on screen. She had to be a good witch and a bad witch that fans would love, but also fear, at least a little bit—not an easy tightrope to walk. Bette Midler was a performer who could seemingly do it all. She got her start in the bathhouses of New York in the 1970s, under the stage persona "The Divine Miss M." In 1979, Midler made her big-screen debut in* The Rose, *a musical drama loosely based on the life of Janis Joplin that also earned Midler her first Academy Award nomination. From there she starred in a string of hits for Touchstone Pictures, the Walt Disney–owned production company known for its adult fare, including* Down and Out in Beverly Hills, Ruthless People, *and* Beaches. *In 1991, Midler had hit a bit of a skid in her career, starring in back-to-back films that were met with less-than-stellar reviews:* Scenes From a Mall, *a comedy starring Woody Allen that was named one of the worst movies of the year by Siskel & Ebert; and* For The Boys, *a musical dramedy that had her teaming up with James Caan to little acclaim. When* Hocus Pocus *came along, it seemed Midler was looking for a chance to do something different.*

David Kirschner:

Around 1991, I got a call from Jeffrey Katzenberg saying, "Bette Midler has committed to the movie and you've got a green light now." That came out of nowhere for me, by the way. I didn't even know Bette was being considered because it had been years of just waiting and waiting and another writer and then waiting and waiting. Honestly, I was beginning to think, *This is never going to happen.*

David Hoberman:

Sister Act was written for Bette, and when she passed, we went to Whoopi [Goldberg]. Once I committed to Whoopi, I'd forgotten whether she could sing or not. I remember calling her and saying, "By the way, can you sing?" And she said, "I can get by." After Bette passed on *Sister Act*, she was to my knowledge the first person we went to for *Hocus Pocus*. We had a deal with Bette. She was a big star at the time, and we thought that she would be a good draw and that we could build around her.

David Kirschner:

Bette's casting was Disney's idea. My idea was Cloris Leachman because of *Young Frankenstein*. I had brought it up to the studio when I first pitched it in 1984. There was the, "Hmm, okay." If they even gave it any more thought, they probably quickly realized, "She doesn't open movies." But she's just brilliant in my mind. Bette was known for her amazing albums, her tours, and then obviously all the movies that she did. She had a very loyal following. She was kind of a four-quadrant superstar, you know?

Mick Garris:

I saw Winifred as someone who was bigger than life, someone like Bette Midler, so I couldn't have been happier.

Jeffrey Katzenberg:

Bette was a rock star, figuratively and literally. From the time we came to the studio in 1984, she was the queen of Disney. Everything she did was a hit. So she was often our first choice for a part, and for this film she was truly a no-brainer.

Aaron Wallace:

I have a line in my book, "Bette Midler was an unlikely Mickey Mouse," and it's so true. She'd started performing in bathhouses in New York, not typically what we think of as a family-friendly venue. Some of her early music-making was very sort of adult, if not in content, in its public performance style. Her first film was an R-rated movie, *The Rose*, that deals with a lot of serious, heavy-duty adult stuff. The movies that she made were with Touchstone, which was Disney's sort of first foray into R-rated filmmaking. They didn't want to use the Disney name, so they created this other label, and it was really Bette Midler who launched Touchstone Pictures to great success with a string of raunchy, bawdy R-rated comedies. And then comes *Hocus Pocus*. I think the fact that that was her reputation up to that point is not insignificant to *Hocus Pocus*'s unique stature amongst Disney family films; it could be edgier than the usual Disney film in large part because of Bette Midler's persona. The casting was so unusual that she herself was sort of cracking jokes about how strange it was that she was headlining a Disney film.

Dr. Carmen Phillips (Editor-in-Chief, *Autostraddle*):

Hocus Pocus is a kid's movie, so Bette Midler did become a kid's icon. But so much of her career is for adults. I wanted to see all the things that she did, which is a weird negotiation you have to have with your parents where they're like, "You're a little small for all of this." I think the first time I saw her concert, none of the jokes made sense to me, but I loved that she wore a mermaid skirt. There aren't probably a lot of Black girls who grew up obsessed with Bette Midler, but I really did. I just thought she made time stop, I don't know how to describe it.

David Kirschner:

From what I understand, Jeffrey Katzenberg discussed this movie with Bette and sent her whatever version of the script they had at that point. There was enough there that she said yes to it, but she wanted some changes.

Neil Cuthbert:

I remember my script was the one that they showed to her finally. It was green-lit because Bette would do it. I mean, Bette was the queen. I did two or three drafts of the script. I wrote it over the summer, and I think around Thanksgiving they green-lit it. Then they did what they do so often with comedies. They said, "Thanks very much, we'll take it from here!" About eight months went by and I heard that it was going forward and Bette had been cast. Then I got a call at nine thirty p.m. on the East Coast on a Saturday night. "We need you back on the project right away." The next day I was on a plane to California, met Kenny Ortega, who was a really lovely guy, and who was in the middle of putting it all together. They stuck me in a little room right in the Disney offices so I could be close to everything and I started rewriting my brains out. The idea was to restore what had been lost from the script they'd green-lit, add a bunch of new stuff, and kind of just put it all together as quickly as possible. So I did. I was there in LA for three or four weeks putting the script back together. They couldn't show Bette the script because it was a monstrous cut and paste. In the old days, before computers were completely used, they would take sections from all the various scripts, print them out, and paste them together. It was literally Frankenstein's monster. That's just why they called me back. They get to the point where things are so screwed up, they don't know what to do. Out of desperation, they call in the original writer and say, "Put it back together," which is a nice payday because they're not fooling around at that point.

Ralph Winter:

Bette's casting gave it stature. A lot of times when you're evaluating what project you're going to work on, you wonder if it's really going to get made. When you know that a star like Bette's signed on, it's, "Okay, this is getting made." I don't think it's the same movie with anyone else from that moment.

William Sandell:

When I signed on, Bette wasn't attached, but once she was, I just said, "This is going to be a big movie!"

Mary Vogt:

It was a comedy and it was Bette. When you have an actress like that, it really creates the feeling for the whole project.

Bonnie Bruckheimer:

Because I was Bette's partner [at our production company All Girl Productions] at that point, I worked with her on everything that she did. She has a very busy life and we both had young children [at the time of *Hocus Pocus*]. She needed someone who could deal with the studio, so I don't know if it was Jeffrey or David Hoberman who finally said, "Well, you're around and we need you." I had nothing to do with the development of the movie, but once we started shooting, I was there on the set every day. Kenny had it very under control; it wasn't as if he needed anybody to help him, but I was the support role. I was a support for Bette under difficult circumstances. She trusted me. If they asked her to do something that I thought was too much for her, I would have a voice and say that, but that didn't happen very much.

Amanda Shepherd:

I knew of her from my mother because she introduced me to *Beaches* and *The Rose*. I was like, "Oh my God, this woman is a legend!" Even as a young kid, I knew that working with Bette Midler was a big deal.

Vinessa Shaw:

I had watched *Beaches* religiously with my friends and we'd bawl our eyes out. I was a huge fan of Bette Midler at the time.

Kathy Najimy, 2022:

I don't know if you know this, but growing up, I was a crazy, sycophant fan of Bette Midler's. I did crazy things like jumping off a mountain, onto a piano, onto the stage at her human rights concert [1977's *A Star Spangled Night for Rights*] at the Hollywood Bowl—then running backstage to find her dressing room and having guards carry me away. One time, at the Greek Theatre . . . I used to sing telegrams for a living, and I had a big white furry bunny suit. After her concert, I put the bunny suit on and went backstage and said, "I have a telegram for Bette Midler." I sang her this big song, and I handed her a telegram that said, "I love you, from Kathy." She said, "Kathy? Who's Kathy?"

Bette Midler ("Winifred Sanderson"), 1993:

It turned out that Kathy Najimy was an old fan of mine and that she had come looking for me once when I lived on Barrow Street in New York City, and she had left a letter and a picture for me or something like that. And she reminded me of all this, and of course I had to say, "Kathy, I was unaware at the time," but she took it well.

Omri Katz:

I wouldn't say back then that I was necessarily starstruck, but I was already such a fan of a lot of the movies Bette Midler had done, like *Down and Out in Beverly Hills*, *Beaches*, and *Ruthless People*, so I was pretty stoked to be working with her. But now I look back and I'm like, "Holy shit, I can't believe I got to work with her!"

Thora Birch:

I was so in awe of her, but also there was an element where the Dani in me was kind of like, "All right, you're cool, but I don't know." I have a rebel's heart, unfortunately, often to my detriment. I get that from my mom's side.

Mary Vogt:

Bette was great to work with and she was really funny. Oh, she was so funny. She was also kind of a little monster sometimes because, you know, she's a diva. People may think that's a bad word, but she's definitely a diva.

Neil Cuthbert:

I think Bette was very demanding. Ultimately, in a good way. I think they would've toned her down, but she knew to go big.

Winifred's over-the-top look in the film was a serious point of contention.

Mary Vogt:

We were preparing the film at the Disney lot in Burbank. It was really exciting because I live in Los Feliz, which is where Walt Disney and his brother first lived when they came to Los Angeles. They had their first studio in the area where my grocery store is now. Their actual little studio building that they started in was picked up and moved to the Disney lot. It was called the Shorts Building and that's where my office was on *Hocus Pocus*. It was a very modest building. There were original drawings of Mickey Mouse hanging up and they weren't the cells, but they had the actual backgrounds of *Snow White*, *Pinocchio*, and *Sleeping Beauty*. I just thought they were so gorgeous and the colors were so astonishing, so I kept thinking, *Color, you know, it's got to be color for* Hocus Pocus. When you think of Bette, you think of color. I mentioned it to Kenny, and he was like, "Well, the studio thinks that witches wear black." It's true in *Snow White*, the evil witch was in black, but the evil stepmother was in purple and green. Bette is more like an evil-stepmother type. Kenny had to talk to the studio because they had to be convinced. I said to him, "Well, maybe you should tell him to go to the animation building to see what they do at this studio." Like, maybe they don't really understand what they do here.

Kevin Haney (Makeup Artist for Bette Midler):

I know that they had gone through a lot of other people to create Winifred's look and the look of her sisters. Some people were doing storybook witches and that really wasn't what Bette wanted. Bette wanted something different and found the balance between evil comedy and sympathy.

William Sandell:

I got a call one day early in pre-production. It was one of these calls, "Bette Midler wants to see you down in her makeup trailer right away." Bette had a little makeup trailer off her office with [her producing partner] Bonnie Bruckheimer, so naturally I went down right away. There was this butting of heads with the studio. They wanted to see the Bette Midler that they were paying for. She was obviously the big draw. She wanted to play a witch, bless her heart, and she wanted to look like a witch. I have photos from that day. She was trying on eyebrows and teeth and would spin around in her makeup chair and try to terrorize me. She had me laughing so hard. I couldn't even speak.

Kenny Ortega:

Bette came into this project with such enthusiasm. She was really in charge and was really steering and guiding [the look of Winifred]. She had something in her mind. I remember when she first turned around and looked at me as Winifred, I was just overwhelmed with joy and excitement.

Neil Cuthbert:

I remember a couple of times I'd be working with Kenny and the phone would ring and he'd have to go running out because there'd be a Bette issue. Bette really is that character, I mean, she was in charge. I remember one time in particular that there was panic because she just found those teeth and everybody was like, "We got to get rid of those teeth, but Bette loves the teeth!"

Pamela Alch (Script Supervisor):
I was sitting with Kenny in his trailer when someone from Disney came down. "You've got to get her not to use those teeth. We want people to know it's Bette Midler!" There was a lot of back and forth for the first week [of filming]. They kept asking if we would reshoot the scenes. They really did not want her to wear the teeth, but she was absolutely adamant she was keeping them. She felt it was part of her character. Without them she was just Bette Midler. She wanted to be Winifred Sanderson.

Peggy Holmes:
I remember it was Bette who had the idea of having those teeth for Winifred. When she did that, it's my impression, that's when the character really came to life for her.

Kevin Haney:
Bette handed me a cast of her teeth that a dentist had taken. I started working on those immediately. The concept was kind of like a rat or a rodent. They weren't really buckteeth, they were just the right amount of bizarreness to change the way she looked. She was able to just work with them so well. I mean, even when we were doing tests at her house, she'd look in the mirror and she'd make one of her faces, and it was so wonderful. It was, "Oh yes, these will work."

Mary Vogt:
The costume had to work with the whole thing: the wig, the makeup, and the big teeth. Before she put it all on, I thought, *Well, this is either going to look great or it is gonna be a huge embarrassment for all of us.*

Kevin Haney:
When she came out in the Winifred costume and the wig, I was almost in tears. It was just, "Oh my God, this is so wonderful that we're doing

this." Katzenberg was not really happy about it. He's from the old school of, "We paid for Bette Midler, let's see Bette Midler," but Bette didn't want to do it without the teeth.

Jeffrey Katzenberg:

Bette's instincts about herself are unerring, from her character to her costume to her teeth. So, no, I had no concerns about her look. She is simply a brilliant performer and I had learned to completely trust her.

Gail Lyon:

It's funny because I do remember watching dailies at the studio as they were first coming in and thinking, "Wow, those teeth on Bette, that's a decision." It was a topic of conversation from honestly, day one of shooting. In some weird way, it's part of the lore now, but because it was such a specific campy decision, at the time, there was a lot of discussion about it.

Kenny Ortega:

Both [Bette Midler and I] were a little thrown when we first heard Disney thought that she had gone too far with the makeup, the hair, and the teeth. I think what ended up happening was we pulled back a little. We found a happy middle place with the teeth and everything else stayed, which I think enabled us to begin shooting the film with everyone, especially Bette, happy.

William Sandell:

The studio and Bette came to an agreement. They met in the middle where she was. I always thought that was funny, her fighting the witch battle. When she asked [what side I was on], I always said, "I'm backing you all the way, Bette. I think you should be a witch. That's what I signed up for, a movie about witches, so I'm with you."

Bonnie Bruckheimer:

Mary Vogt did the costumes, which were amazing, but it was Bette's idea to do the teeth. She's a comedian and she wanted to be really funny in this role, all-out funny, so she created the whole thing. She doesn't usually like to look unattractive in a movie. She was always beautiful in her movies, but she felt that this was necessary, and so she stuck with it the whole time.

Some of Bette Midler's biggest fans have made a profession out of mastering her witchy ways.

Nicole Halliwell (National Drag Entertainer):

I started as a Bette Midler fan before becoming a *Hocus Pocus* fan. I remember seeing a commercial for *Hocus Pocus* when I was eight or nine. I saw it was Bette and rented the VHS. I must have watched it at least twenty times in a week. I was so enthralled with this character. I started imitating her, trying to do her voice and her mannerisms.

Peaches Christ (Creator/Producer/Star, *Hocum Pokem*):

I was looking at Bette Midler's performance in that movie and just was so intimidated by her level of commitment. Her performance is extraordinary. I cannot imagine how exhausted she must have been at the end of every single day. Every part of her, every fiber of her being is in every cell of that performance, it's just wild.

Taylor Paige Henderson ("Young Winifred," *Hocus Pocus 2*):

I used to watch [*Hocus Pocus*] every year for fun on Halloween. When I finally got the role [in *Hocus Pocus 2*], it was more of a character study. I had never watched the movie in that way and I started seeing so many new things, new "Winnieisms." A "Winnieism" is something that Winifred does; the way she uses her hair, her teeth, her hands. That was one of the first things I noticed. I was like, "Oh, she's up here with her hands, always saying something." One thing Bette had talked to me about was Winnie's hair. She said, "Most of it will probably be packed in there, but she has these tiny little curls that are out of place." She said, "If you move your head and your hands enough, they'll move around and it's so cute," so I definitely used that a lot.

Jennica McCleary (Performer/Producer/Bette Midler Tribute Artist):
From the age of sixteen, I started being asked, "Do you know who you look like?" The answer was always "Young Bette Midler." When I was younger, I looked significantly more like her, and I didn't really know what to do with that. Eventually, every time someone said, "Do you know who you look like?" I said, "Bette I do!" Fast-forward, I've been doing a tribute to her for fourteen years now. In 2015, I was the first person that Disney hired since Bette Midler to fill Winifred's shoes in the *Hocus Pocus Villain Spelltacular Show* [in Walt Disney World]. The key to nailing Winifred is the hands. It's all about the hands, the little twists. I find that her subtleties in face are very important as well, but being on the Magic Kingdom stage, it kind of comes back to the physicality. How else do you make that play all the way down Main Street? I am sure Broadway is great—I hope to someday find out—but flicking your fingers in the air, saying those six words ["I put a spell on you"], and listening to twenty thousand people lose their minds still gives me chills.

Mary Vogt:
There's a lot of Bette in Winnie. The role combines so many of the performance attributes that Bette Midler is best known for. It's a brassy, bold, and assertive character. It's comedic, it's musical, but there's also this thread of old Hollywood that runs throughout. Bette has always taken a cue from old Hollywood, but she talked about basing her performance as Winifred on Margaret Dumont [who starred in seven of the Marx Brothers' movies] and looking back to the days of vaudeville and to early Disney villains from the '40s, '50s, and '60s. I think Winnie

was a role that allowed her to fuse all these parts of her personality, or at least her stage persona, into one role.

Kevin Haney:
I loved working with Bette. Her energy is just so phenomenal. She's like an untapped resource. We should be looking into her as a power source instead of solar.

Those involved with the project felt that, as the film's marquee star, there was immense pressure on Bette Midler to turn Hocus Pocus *into a hit for Walt Disney Studios, which was looking to make its mark on the live-action family-film market after the success of 1989's* Honey, I Shrunk the Kids.

Ralph Winter:
Actors are putting themselves in someone else's hands. They don't know how the final thing's going to go. They're not editors; they're not shaping the movie in terms of what's going to be there. They have to trust that Jeffrey Katzenberg, Kenny Ortega, David Kirschner, and everyone will come through with the right stuff. It's always a bit risky for an actor to put themselves in someone else's creative hands.

Omri Katz:
Bette was already focusing on her next production, the TV adaptation of *Gypsy*. Literally, when Kenny called "Cut," she was right back to her trailer doing vocal training. I'd walk by and I'd hear, *"La, la, la, la, la, la, la, la, la."* She was extremely professional and very involved in her own craft. That was her lifeblood, her passion, and you could see that.

Amanda Shepherd:
To be honest, I didn't really see much of Bette off set. She's an icon, so it seemed like she was kind of separate from everybody else. She went on set, did her thing, and then she was gone, but watching her was

mesmerizing, just absolutely mesmerizing. She was really turning into a totally different person.

Peggy Holmes:

I'm a choreographer who loves to choreograph things that don't look choreographed. Coincidentally, Bette Midler loves that kind of work also. She does a lot of homework, but then when she's filming, she lets it all go so she could still be in the moment.

Mary Vogt:

I think what people like about Bette's performance is that it's authentic. I think if you look at any movie that's successful, it's because there's an authenticity to the character that the audience can feel. I think that people pick up on that. People don't like pretension and they don't like when people are acting. It's got to come off real. It's Bette. She's over-the-top, but she's not self-conscious. Not trying too hard because if someone else said the things she said, they would look like they were trying too hard. But for her, that's natural. She's not saccharine; she's kind of edgy. I think the audience really responds to that.

Tony Gardner:

Everybody brought their best effort and their best attitude to this movie, and I think a lot of that goes from the top down. I mean, Bette's commitment. For her to come in forty-five minutes early to have somebody put on real acrylic nails so that they wouldn't get knocked off and take her out of a shot. When everybody wraps and Doug Jones is coming out of makeup and she's just coming out of her trailer because she's had her acrylic nails removed for the night so she can go to bed and not worry about, you know, slicing her face. I think that that sense of professionalism and commitment, it just trickles down to everyone.

Chapter 4

PUTTING TOGETHER A COVEN

*W*inifred may be the leader of this witchy trio, but her sisters needed to be just as fierce. Bring in pre–Sex and the City *Sarah Jessica Parker* as "Sarah," the most beautiful (and vapid) of the Sandersons, and Kathy Najimy, just off of the Touchstone Pictures hit film Sister Act, as "Mary," the obedient middle sister with a bloodhound's ability to sniff out children. Unlike Bette Midler, Parker and Najimy, who were in the early stages of their Hollywood careers, had to audition for their roles and faced stiff competition. Rosie O'Donnell revealed in a 2023 interview with the Hollywood Reporter that she turned down the role of Mary, while it has long been rumored that Jennifer Lopez was in the running for Sarah. (Lopez has never confirmed or denied those rumors.) Yet it's hard to believe anyone other than Parker and Najimy could have possibly played Midler's hilarious younger-sibling sidekicks. The three actresses managed to create a sisterly bond with help from Kenny Ortega and choreographer Peggy Holmes that turned them into a family you wouldn't mind spending some time with. It helped that Parker and Najimy were life-long Midler fans.

Ilene Starger:

I am always reluctant to discuss who may have been offered a role because it sort of disrespects the actor who did play the role so memorably. And often, rumors are just that: rumors. I will say that, in any casting process, one makes lists of actors and various names are considered, even if there is a clear top choice. Availability is a factor; sometimes filmmakers who are not locked into a schedule can wait for an actor if the actor has conflicting commitments; other times, not. Sometimes one can get one's first choice for a role, and sometimes not, for various reasons.

Jeffrey Katzenberg:

Casting is always a complex process of trying to find the right actor, getting them interested in a part, and then working out the timing to see if they're actually available. Kathy and Sarah were always at the top of our list, and we were lucky we could get all three of these great actors who had such wonderful chemistry together.

Gail Lyon:

We definitely did quote-unquote "cast" them. They were cast in the film as opposed to Bette. It was just the process. We auditioned people and they were great, but, after *Sister Act*, there was a creative belief in Kathy as a crazy comedic talent.

David Hoberman:

Kathy was hilarious in *Sister Act*, so that's kind of a no-brainer. I don't know who came up with the idea of Sarah, but we also thought that she would complement Bette and Kathy.

Gail Lyon:

Sarah Jessica Parker was cast because she was obviously terrific, but it was such a great threesome of three totally different presences. They work individually, but the mix of those three people is everything.

Mary Hidalgo (Casting Assistant):

I'm sure Bette had a say in who they hired for both of those roles. Then the studio had a say in who they hired for both of those roles. That's happening in rooms that I'm not in. It is very typical that the studio wants to be in charge of that casting, you know. Who's got the box office? Who's got *that* thing?

Kathy Najimy, 2022:

When Jeffrey Katzenberg called and said, "Hey, Kathy, do you want to be in a movie called *Hocus Pocus* playing Bette Midler's sister?" That was crazy. That was an unbelievable highlight of my life.

Doug Jones ("Billy Butcherson"):

Kathy Najimy had just come off of *Sister Act* so we were all blubbering idiots over her. I had known Sarah Jessica Parker from her *Annie* days. She was younger than me, but I very much felt like I'd grown up with Sarah.

Sarah Jessica Parker ("Sarah Sanderson"), 2022:

When I was about thirteen, the stage manager for *Annie* took me to see [Midler's revue] *Bette! Divine Madness* on Broadway. I was a great admirer, and the idea of working with her was enormously appealing to me.

Vinessa Shaw:

Sarah Jessica Parker had done this TV show *Square Pegs* that I was obsessed with. She was also in *Footloose* and *L.A. Story*, which I loved as well, so I pretty much died when I first met her. We had the same makeup artist on set and I would come in after she was done so I'd catch her as she was stepping out. The first day of shooting, she asked, "So is this something that you want to do for the rest of your life? You like acting?" And I was like, "Oh my God, are you talking to me?" I just couldn't believe it. She talked about being a child actress, how it was really fun. She was like an older sister to me. She was so sweet.

Mary Vogt:

Sarah Jessica was like a little angel. She was the kind of person that little birds would follow her around. She was just very light and airy, and very sweet, kind of giddy all the time. I wanted to do something ethereal with Sarah's costume, but I ended up doing something a little more sexy for her than the other two girls. They all had corsets on, but hers was just a little more fitted.

Steven Haft:

I worried from time to time that it was really not fun for an actor of Sarah Jessica's thoughtfulness, pedigree, and intellectual horsepower to play the "dumb blond." Although she, in the best *Some Like It Hot* way, managed to always make it fun when the camera was on and was very gracious at all times when it wasn't.

Sarah Jessica Parker, 1993:

I loved the idea of being able to create Sarah. It was liberating. I felt the character wasn't me, it was someone entirely different and so I wasn't at all embarrassed about trying things out. Of course, the Friday before we started shooting arrived and I still hadn't found a voice. For a while I wanted to do an English boy, a take-off on Dana Carvey impersonating George Michael. So I tried it out, but no one was particularly excited about it. I liked the idea of Marilyn Monroe, but that voice was too whispery. I wanted Sarah to be a bit like the Shakespearean nymphs, with a little Lolita and a bit of a half-wit thrown in. I came up with the voice, and once we started shooting there was no going back.

Cheri Minns (Makeup Artist for Sarah Jessica Parker):

I had worked with Sarah Jessica before. I knew her when she was dating Robert Downey Jr. I was doing his makeup at the time and he brought me over to the house and I met her. I wound up working with her after that. I've always been a big fan of old movies. My first apartment in New Orleans was covered in pictures of Rudolph Valentino and Bette Davis. For *Hocus Pocus*, I sent Sarah photos of Bette's makeup in her movie *Of Human Bondage* and she loved the idea. It looked good on her. They wanted her to be sexy and pretty, that's why they hired her. They didn't want me to ugly her up or anything. They wanted her to be the sexy witch and that's what they got.

Tobias Jelinek:

Sarah Jessica Parker was an enigma. She was obviously a little bit older than us [kids] and we were mesmerized. But what I was most impressed by was the fact that, at the time, she was dating Ferris Bueller [Matthew

Broderick]. We were on set and back then they would have a large red set phone so producers, directors, and cast could receive personal calls from time to time. I remember the phone ringing and a production assistant answering the phone who said, "Well, hello, Mr. Broderick. Let me see if Sarah's available." The moment he went to look, I just remember looking at the phone, and I was like, "Ferris Bueller is on that phone right now!"

Sarah Jessica Parker, 2022:

I remember I was living out of a suitcase, knitting all the time, and I had just met Matthew, so I was occupied in ways that were really exciting.

Neil Cuthbert:

My favorite line in the script is "amok, amok, amok." I'm pretty sure that was mine, but Sarah may have added a few more *amok*s than I had in there.

Cheri Minns:

[Sarah Jessica Parker and I] had a good time working on this movie. We were like girlfriends. I had a new niece that I just adored, and Sarah didn't have children at that time. My family lives in New Orleans, so I sent my mom one of those mini recorders with the little tiny tapes. Remember those? My mom used to put it on the table and have my niece sing nursery rhymes and we'd listen to those while Sarah was getting her makeup done. She would just get so excited. "Oh my god, listen to her little voice! Play it again! Play it again!" And people in the trailer would be like, "Don't play it again!" She was happy as a clam every day coming to work and working with that cast and crew.

Sarah Jessica Parker, 1993:

I had this beautiful song that I got to sing that [composer] James Horner wrote. It's this beautiful, seductive, luring ballad but it's just minor enough to be scary and awful when you know who the person is. . . . I'm covertly scary. The rest of the witches—Kathy and Bette—they're very overt and there's no pretense at all. They're just evil, but I'm fundamentally evil. Their evil is calculated. Mine is just who I am, that's why it's really, I think, even more scary. I mean she's awful. I don't respect her, but I love her.

David Kirschner:

James Horner and I had done five films together and one or two TV series, and we were dear, dear, dear friends. James died very tragically [in 2015]. He was flying one of his World War II aircrafts back from Santa Barbara, and the plane fell out of the sky. It still haunts me. But long before that happened, I had asked James to score the film and he was on board to do it. Then another film came up that was an enormous opportunity for him, and he just said, "David, I'm sorry, I can't do this." And I said, "Will you just write one song, just one song for me?" So he wrote a song called "Come Little Children," the song that Sarah Jessica Parker so beautifully sings to lure the children who will have their souls sucked out of them. It was heartbreaking to hear the song because it was so great. I just thought, *Oh my God, what are we going to do now?* I mean, it's nowhere but downhill from here.

Brock Walsh (Lyrics and Incantations):

James wrote the music first and I wrote the lyrics to it. I think it was called "Garden of Magic" then. Sarah Jessica Parker's character was clearly trying to shepherd children away from their caregivers and into jeopardy. It's done in a very innocent childlike fashion, but it's no less predatory. I remember seeing a clip of Sarah singing it on YouTube and people going, "Oh my God, is this Edgar Allan Poe?" The lyrics have no connection to Edgar Allan Poe so I waded into the discussion. Suddenly there were two hundred comments and I thought, *You know, this was the wrong move.*

Vinessa Shaw:

Listening to Sarah Jessica Parker's song "Come Little Children" recently, I realized it has a similar flavor to the song in *Mary Poppins*, "Chim Chim Cher-ee." It's totally a classic Disney song.

Omri Katz:

Kathy was kind of a newcomer. She wasn't a megastar yet and, to be honest, she was probably the most genuine, sweetest, nicest person. She really got to know us kids on a more personal level. My dad threw this event at our house and Kathy attended; she didn't have to, but she did. She was just extremely genuine and extremely personable.

Amanda Shepherd:

While we were shooting, if Kathy Najimy saw me, she would pick me up any chance she got. She'd take me around the Disney lot and then back to set. She was just so funny and so sweet, but for whatever reason, anytime she saw me, she'd just pick me up.

Neil Cuthbert:

I had one interesting meeting with Kathy Najimy. She came in, sat across from me, and said she didn't mind playing a greedy, evil, deceitful, duplicitous middle sister, but she didn't want to be the butt of fat jokes. I said, "No problem."

Rosemary Brandenburg:

There was a feminist side to this whole story, just the vilification of witches and women and the distortion of the history of these people. It was really interesting. Kathy Najimy was really vocal about all that stuff.

While promoting the film on the Today *show in 1993, Najimy revealed that she almost didn't take the role. "I'm not a witch. I don't know any personally," she said. "But when I read the script, I thought, 'This is really perpetuating a stereotype about an evil, ugly witch.'" It was only after speaking with journalist and social activist Gloria Steinem about the early history of witches being midwives that she felt comfortable taking the role. In 2023, the interview went viral, with many commending Najimy for her support for the witch community.*

Mat Auryn (Author, *Psychic Witch: A Metaphysical Guide to Meditation, Magick & Manifestation* and *Mastering Magick: A Course in Spellcasting for the Psychic Witch*):

The warmth exuded by Kathy Najimy in that *Today* show clip is absolutely palpable. She astutely points out the antiquated notion of witches consuming infants. Women accused of witchcraft were often midwives [and] played crucial roles in managing miscarriages and possessed knowledge of herbal remedies that could induce abortions. In addressing these misconceptions, Najimy urges us to approach witches and pagans with a greater sense of empathy and inclusivity, fostering a sense of community beyond outdated expectations.

Amanda Yates Garcia (Author, *Initiated: Memoir of a Witch*):

Witches love to play with popular culture, so it doesn't bother me that witches eat children in movies. Films like *Hocus Pocus* don't convert people to witchcraft. I mean, it's hard to imagine looking at Bette Midler, with her buckteeth and red hair, like, *Oh yeah, that's what inspired me to be a witch*. But movies like this make it possible for people to feel more comfortable saying that they do identify that way.

Rachel Christ-Doane (Director of Education, Salem Witch Museum):

I think it's Pam Grossman, who wrote *Waking the Witch*, who said something along the lines of, "If you want to look at society's views on women, look at how they talk about their witches." When you see changing depictions of witches, you're also oftentimes in culture seeing changes [in] conversations about women and women's autonomy and power. Today witches are kind of this very empowering symbol for women.

Doug Jones:

Kathy is fascinating to watch at work. She has such a background in comedic improv. She had a stage production in New York that ran for years with her friend Mo Gaffney. It was *The Kathy and Mo Show*. Her fearlessness in trying something new while the camera's rolling was fascinating to watch. I always thought, *Oh my gosh, maybe I should take more chances*. She would throw a line out that was hilarious, like, *How did she think of that?*

Jessie Wolfson:

Kathy Najimy is just so funny. Kenny would let Kathy do her thing and she would do a bunch of takes because she would like to find her groove. She was great to watch.

Neil Cuthbert:

You got to understand, with this kind of comedy, there's so much improvising that goes on once the cameras start rolling.

David Kirschner:

I always want to give credit to the three actresses. They just added so much to the movie that wasn't in any of the scripts. One of my favorites is after they've come back from the dead and they go back to the Sanderson house that's a museum now, and the kids are hiding in there, Kathy says, "I smell children," and she's sniffing and sniffing and she says, "It's a little girl, seven, maybe seven and a half." I just love that! It still makes me laugh thirty years later.

Mary Vogt:

Mary was more like an apothecary than a baker. She had an apron on because she was mixing these herbs and things. She had these little circles that I thought kind of looked like something you would have in an herb shop, like you could hang herbs from them. I should have hung some herbs from it, right? She had great hair, like a cornucopia, which I had nothing to do with.

Kathy Najimy, 1993:

My idea for Mary was to make her immediately identifiable. Sarah's hair is long and blond, and Winifred had a great big pile of red hair. Because of the character's keen sense of smell, there had to be something distinguished about my face, so we put an extension on my nose to make it more pronounced. But I wanted the audience to see Mary's shadow and know it was her. One day during rehearsals, I saw a pumpkin that someone in the art department had made. It had a great stem that was big on the bottom and curled up like a decrepit branch at the top, ending with a twist. I thought, *There's my hair!* Now I have a great twisting purple wig that looks like it's a branch growing out of my head with spiders and dirt.

Kenny Ortega, 2018:

What I really, really remember [is] observing Bette and Kathy and Sarah really finding their characters, in the mirror with makeup, hair, prosthetics, and I just burst out laughing. Looking at one another, you saw this chemistry come into play, and I knew we were going to have a lot of fun.

Brock Walsh:

I wrote the incantations that the witches speak, the spells. It was a really fun part of the gig, sitting in a circle with those three comedians, practicing incantations. I wish someone had been rolling a camera. That's as different of an experience as I have ever had. I would sit with Kathy, Bette, and Sarah and play and invent and be childlike. We'd talk about a scene and the rhythm of it. We'd come back the next day and recite it and crack up. It's the most ridiculous thing, but it sounds like it's in the witch vernacular. I fought for "incantations" as my film credit because I thought, who knows, there may be a side gig in this for me. Like, "He's eighty, but he's still got a few incantations in him." Somebody agreed to the title, which is the funniest part to me.

Kevin Haney:

Kenny Ortega really worked on getting that camaraderie between the three ladies. I remember one makeup test where they were dancing to Vivaldi's *The Four Seasons*, the Storm and the Summer parts. I wish that footage still existed in the Disney archive somewhere; I would love to see it.

Peggy Holmes:

It was super important for us that they each had their own unique way of moving and a unique silhouette as a trio. You've got three characters that are going to be on camera together all the time and you don't want those scenes to feel stiff. We worked a lot in rehearsal about sculpting shapes that looked good for all three of them. We actually worked on making them feel as if they were familiar with each other so that they could move around each other seamlessly, as if they were sisters cooking in a kitchen together.

Neil Cuthbert:

I think it was really [about] developing the sisterly relationship. You have Bette's character who's power crazy. She's the number one witch, don't get in her way. Then you have Sarah Jessica Parker, who's the seducer and a bit of a flake who drives her sisters crazy. Then you have Kathy Najimy, who's stuck in the middle playing one against the other; that was fun to work that out. The actresses played the shit out of it so that was great, too.

Nancy Patton (Art Director), 2013:

They all wanted scary noses and warts, and the studio was saying, "Bette, we love your face; Sarah, you're sexy; Kathy, you're fantastic. We want you to be recognizable." We went the whole gamut in terms of their look and then pulled back. That's part of the design process. We ended up with a storybook approach. The women are themselves, but with a tweak.

Amanda Yates Garcia:

It just underscores, for me, the way that people think about witches; they think of it like a costume. It hasn't quite penetrated into popular culture to such a degree that people think, *Oh, this is something that people really do.* They think of it as these cultural references, and not as a way of life.

Peggy Holmes:

Kenny would never say, "I want them to move this way" because it's a matter of working with the actors and finding this specific unique nature of each one of their characters. Obviously, Bette, Sarah, and Kathy all came to the table with ideas, but we didn't want them to be what everyone knows as a stereotypical witch.

Vinessa Shaw:

I just remember coming in to rehearse and watching Peggy Holmes work with the three witches on their character and what each character embodied and how they moved in unison. She was the choreographer, but was also acting as a movement coordinator, helping them embody a character through movement. They felt very unified to me.

Doug Jones:

I'm driving to work my first night on this huge studio movie and I heard Bette Midler singing "From a Distance" on the radio. It was a night shoot outdoors on a scene that was deleted from the movie. It took place after Bette magically awakened me and I chased the kids through the sewer and came out of the manhole cover and got my fingers cut off. We head to a park somewhere where she wants an update about the kids. Bette Midler, as Winnie, gets in my face and is yelling. Then Sarah comes up going, "Hi, Billy!" I kind of stroke her face and, and I take a strand of her hair and I put it against my cheek. This is my first night of work. I'm inches away from Bette and Sarah and Kathy! At the end of the scene, they all storm away, but because I'm now so enamored with Sarah I stumble after them. I'm not going to catch up with them, but my arms are out and I get caught on a light post and I just kind of go, *clunk* and slump on down. Well, they watched the playback of that on the monitor, and Kathy Najimy pointed at the screen and said, "He's good." It was the greatest compliment, like, "Oh my gosh, Kathy Najimy thinks I'm good!" On the way home. I heard "Wind Beneath My Wings" on the radio. I thought, *Okay, this is how huge this is!*

Bette Midler, 1993:

We'd laugh when we felt we'd hit it, you know, we got a lot of satisfaction out of really nailing the little bit that we had set out to do. I laughed all the time. I was always like, "Girl, you are so funny!" to Kathy or to Sarah or to myself.

Cheri Minns:

Bette was really cool. She'd get on the set and it all got real businesslike. You did the work when she arrived. Not that anybody else was not there to do the work, but when she got to the set, it's like, "Let's do it. I'm ready. Let's get this party started!" You don't let Bette down. She brings it, so you better bring it, too.

Mary Vogt:

I remember Bette was walking onstage with a dresser and I think she tripped on a cable and she fell. She got up and went back to her trailer.

When she came back, her dresser was walking in front of her and Bette said, "We're back and we're meaner than ever." That really stuck with me. It was funny, but she came back so serious. I wouldn't say mean, but she meant business.

Pamela Alch:

In *Hocus Pocus*, the language for the witches was archaic. There were a couple of words here and there that Bette didn't pronounce properly. I corrected her once and she looked at me and said, "No, you are wrong," and I said, "I think you'll find that I'm right." So finally, we were shooting in a house somewhere, and I pulled a dictionary out and took it to her and said, "You see that?" pointing to the word, and she said, "Oh, you're right!" After that, she was like, "Any questions go to Pam. She knows!" It was very sweet. She had great respect for me and the crew. She didn't have an ego. She was absolutely approachable. She was no big star that you had to be afraid of.

William Sandell:

One of my fondest memories is being onstage back at Disney and seeing the girls all practicing their walk.

Peggy Holmes:

It wasn't, "Oh, we should come up with a funny walk." It came out of the reality of what their characters were going through. They were brought into a time period that they didn't know, and it was scary and intimidating. The idea was they would want to stay close together. In a way, it was our version of, "Lions and tigers and bears, oh my!" [from *The Wizard of Oz*] or [the vaudeville act] "Slowly I Turned," you know?

Jason Marsden:

They're like the Three Stooges. They might as well be Moe, Larry, and Curly. The sisters are performed so wonderfully by those gals. My favorite part of the movie is just watching their synergy. You can't get tired of watching it. Some husbands have corrected me on that, but I don't get tired of watching it.

Bette Midler, 2022:

I always thought I was the star of the picture, and then I saw what the other two girls were doing. They were so funny! I realized, "Oh, my gosh, it's all about the trio! We're like the Three Stooges in skirts!"

Mary Vogt:

I don't remember them being friends or palling around. They all had their own trailer. I don't think they hung out together. They were all really different and that helped.

Omri Katz:

I never got any of that big star attitude from any of them. Everybody was always so genuine and sweet to me personally. I've heard other stories about other productions and other actors where it's like they're difficult to work with. I never experienced that. It really was a great time to be had.

Thora Birch:

There are about four or five times where [the kids and witches] commingle [on set] so the days when we all knew that that was gonna happen were probably the most exciting. "Bette's going to be here!" Then the day would come and it would be like, "Oh, this is what it's like when they're around." It was still great because the energy was there, but it's a funny thing, the dynamic that you share with your other characters often becomes the dynamic that takes place with the actors. It bleeds into the experience of it all and it takes hold. So all the dynamics you see in the film were heightened 100 percent in reality.

Vinessa Shaw:

I remember one scene where I got to act with all three of them, the salt scene. I was sort of nervous because that is my scene, my strong moment all by myself. This is my second movie and I was super nervous. I remember the energy of the three of them being just explosive. It's such a different energy than when the three of us [kids] were acting together. I thought, *Gosh, they're just like on fire.* Everyone's focused on me at that moment and I'm trying to hold my ground with these iconic actors. It was a little bit of a scary moment.

Mary Vogt:

The only thing I remember about the fittings with the actresses, and I only remember it because I have a photograph of it somewhere, is at a fitting with Sarah, she's looking pained, like, "Ah!" because I stuck a pin in her back by mistake. It's funny because with Bette, I took a costume of hers from another movie to make a pattern for her corset and she kept complaining about that costume. She said, "I kept getting these stabbing pains from it." We took the costume apart and when we did, we found a straight pin in the bust cup. No wonder she was getting stabbing pains, she was being stabbed! That's why it's good for actors to keep up their tetanus shots. They're constantly being stabbed with pins.

Peggy Holmes:

Honestly, we just lucked out because we got three amazing actors who had to fly, sing, do physical comedy, act, and create an unbelievable trio that ended up being unforgettable. They're like quadruple threats. They're really able to do it all and that allowed us to kind of really push the boundaries.

Neil Cuthbert:

They're the reason the movie succeeded. I mean, they're what everybody remembers. They're what everybody wants to see on Halloween. I think that's pretty obvious.

Chapter 5

CASTING THE RIGHT KIDS

*B*ette *Midler, Sarah Jessica Parker, and Kathy Najimy are so good in* Hocus Pocus *that it's easy to forget that the Sanderson sisters aren't the heroes of this story, they're the villains. The witches have returned to Salem on this Halloween night, three hundred years after they were hanged, to suck the souls out of children in hopes of earning eternal youth and beauty. It's up to three kids—angsty teen Max, his precocious little sister Dani, and his crush, the smart and capable Allison—to stop them because, like most kids' movies of the eighties and nineties, their parents are absolutely useless. (To be fair, Max is the one who, by lighting the Black Flame Candle, unleashes the Sandersons on the world again, so it is kind of his mess to clean up.) The film's casting directors, Mary Gail Artz and Barbara Cohen, knew that finding the right young actors for these pivotal roles was key to making the movie work.*

Mary Hidalgo:

Having cast a lot of kids in my career, you can feel it when somebody walks in the room whether or not they're good. Thora Birch, who played Dani, was this special little thing. Mary Gail Artz and Barbara Cohen loved Thora, but everybody was like, "Thora is it!" It was her confidence. She was so young, but she understood the process of acting and what we were asking of her. When you were that young could you do that? I couldn't. She really had it together and really knew what she was doing. It was so natural. To me, it felt like she was the driving force behind the movie.

Ilene Starger:

Thora is very gifted; she was and is smart, beautiful, sensitive, funny. She had done a prior film, [1991's] *Paradise,* at the studio. There was a strong ethos at Disney of wanting to work again with terrific actors and filmmakers, if possible.

Thora Birch:

I was under contract for Disney, which was a thing back then, but my parents pitched me about the project and I was already hooked. Halloween was my favorite holiday. Then they handed me this three-hundred-page script to read because I was already at that level where I could read my own scripts. I read it and I just remember thinking, *Man, this is really dense. There is just too much information in this script!* I've never read a script so full of backstory and world-building. I thought, *This is not even a script. It's a freaking book!* But it was detailed to the point where I could imagine everything.

Doug Jones:

Thora, at eleven years old, had quite a résumé. I mean, she was playing Harrison Ford's daughter in *Patriot Games* a year earlier. I was in the presence of a lot of talent.

Omri Katz:

Thora and I got along really well, but she was a little bit of a brat; a little bit of a diva at the time. I think I would check her on some stuff. I'd be like, "All right, quit being annoying!"

Thora Birch:

I had a natural connection with Omri and I remember just instantly falling in love with Vinessa Shaw. I was like, "She needs to be my older sister." I just demanded it. I think I actually went up to Vinessa—by the way, I call her Vinny—and I was like, "You're my older sister, right?!" And she laughed and was like, "Yeah, sure, why not?"

Vinessa Shaw:

She was like a little sister to me. She even joked that she was a little jealous when my actual sister would come on set.

Amanda Shepherd:

Thora was doing her own makeup, going into the makeup trailer and saying, "I can do this myself, thank you." The way she was talking about her character and the film, I thought, *This girl's brilliant!* She was so young, but she was so experienced. She was a little older than me, but she was just well beyond me. I just thought I could learn a lot from her, so I would try to hang around her.

Thora Birch:

I couldn't handle people putting mascara on me. It's a little bit of maybe a controlling personality that was popping up, but I did my makeup off and on [throughout my career].

Michael McGrady:

Thora was just a little tiny squirt, but when you work with kids in the industry, [you know] they're not your typical garden-variety kids. They're precocious, very smart, and very trained. They bring a lot to the table. You never feel like you have to patronize these kids. Usually, it's, "Wow, that's better than any adult I've worked with in the last two years." They just don't have any inhibitions, no hang-ups. They just let it go.

Steven Haft:

You had to believe that these kids were leading the revolt against [the witches], and it was easy to see Thora in that way. Little Thora was a leader; a kind of large-screen hero for a pint-sized person. Dani was written as a sort of sidekick, but Thora's personality was so strong, Dani ended up being the leader of the kid team.

Mary Vogt:

She had a personality as big as Bette's, probably even bigger. She was a really spunky kid and I just thought, *Wow, this kid could take a lot of color.* So I found this fabric and I made her a little blouse and then we gave her a witch's hat. We put some orange around it and just tried to match her personality.

William Sandell:

Every day in the screening room, we were in shock over Thora. Every delivery was different and magnificent. We were like, "Who is this little thing that's delivering these lines better than anybody in the movie?"

Vinessa Shaw:

My favorite thing to do was to go see dailies during lunch. I remember being in the screening room, watching dailies when we all saw Thora pulling the hat back on her head after Max lights the candle and he says, "What happened?" She puts the hat on her head and goes, "A virgin lit the candle." We all just roared with laughter in the screening room. It was, "That's the one!" In other takes she put the hat on her head a little more correctly. You could see her face. But that one was so funny because she pulled it way down over her eyes. She didn't mean to, and it just became so funny.

Thora Birch, 2018:

I hated dealing with the hat so much because it was always flying off my head and they would have to stick more and more pins in there to hold it down. I had such an attitude when we wrapped, but looking back on it now, I probably should have grabbed one of those hats. We did a twenty-year screening and they had some of the artifacts there [on display], including my hat, so I did get a chance to try it on one more time. The freaking thing still fit!

Casting Thora Birch, who at ten years old had already starred alongside Melanie Griffith, Don Johnson, and Harrison Ford, was a no-brainer. It took a bit longer for the casting department to find the right teens to play Max and Allison.

Neil Cuthbert:
When we were auditioning kids for the parts, the little kids were great. They'd come in and they were just totally committed. The teenagers were all very self-conscious. It was a challenge casting those parts.

Ilene Starger:
It's always a challenge casting young performers, not just because of the intelligence and talent required, but also because of curtailed work hours (minors must be schooled on set, and, due to labor laws, must work less hours than adults). Also, if a performer has never acted before, there is a lack of experience; however, with a lack of experience comes freshness, a sense of discovery. The best acting, from young actors or actors of any age, seems like lived behavior, not acting. For Disney films, a certain intelligence, freshness, likeability, charm (quirky or otherwise) is important. When I was at the studio, we worked with some incredibly gifted young performers, such as Thora Birch, Elijah Wood, Charlie Korsmo, Reese Witherspoon, and many others.

Mary Hidalgo:
For the main character of Max we saw a lot of kids who were really interesting. Oliver Hudson came in, [his mom] Goldie [Hawn] brought him. He had a different energy and ultimately didn't get it, but Goldie had in tow [her youngest son] Wyatt Russell when he was just a little blond-haired thing. He was so cute. But, for Max, we had really wanted Leonardo DiCaprio.

Kenny Ortega, 2017:
The [casting] ladies called me up and they said, "We're sending you an actor today, but he's not available, but you're going to fall in love with him, but you can't have him." I'm like, "Why are you teasing me?" They were like, "You need to see this guy because he'll inspire you and if nothing else, he'll help you find the right guy to play Max." And they

send in a young Leonardo DiCaprio, who I completely and absolutely fall in love with.

Mary Hidalgo:

Leo was so good, and he was the right age. He had a presence. At that age, especially with teenage boys, they're not usually that good. They haven't formed yet. There's nothing there. When you find a kid that has presence at that age, it's remarkable—and he did. Kenny gives him the pitch and we're talking to him and he's just, "Yeah, I don't know. I'm up for this other movie where I play Johnny Depp's brother."

Kenny Ortega, 2017:

He was like, "I just feel really bad being here because I'm up for two other movies and I really want them both and I don't want to lead you on." I was like, "That's okay, I was already warned. What are the movies?" One of them was *This Boy's Life* and the other one was *What's Eating Gilbert Grape*.

Omri Katz:

I remember there being rumors that Leonardo DiCaprio had auditioned for the role. It was definitely a small pool of young actors that were working at that time: me, Leo, Tobey Maguire, Jonathan Brandis. I auditioned for *This Boy's Life* and I remember reading with Robert De Niro in the casting room. I was pretty starstruck, so I was probably extremely nervous. I didn't book that role. Later I tested for *Basketball Diaries,* but my nerves are probably why I didn't get that either. Leonardo and I had a pretty good relationship. We auditioned a lot together. It wasn't ever extremely competitive, like, "I'm going to get this role and you're gonna sit and spin." It was never that. At least from my perspective, we all got along.

Mary Hidalgo:

We all thought, "Ah, Leo's not gonna get that part in *Gilbert Grape*. Look at him, he's a blond kid!" He doesn't look anything like Johnny Depp. We thought for sure he wouldn't do that movie because, as talented as he was, he wouldn't even get it. We were wrong. He would've been great [in *Hocus Pocus*], but it would've been a different movie.

Kenny Ortega, 2017:

Obviously, he left and incredible things happened for that young man . . . but meeting him awakened me to the kind of spirit and fun and sincerity that I was looking for in an actor. When Omri Katz came around, I fell in love again and he was our Max.

Omri Katz:

From what I remember it was the typical auditioning process with *Hocus Pocus*. We did a screen test and then I didn't hear back from them for months. I kind of just brushed it off and said, "Okay, I guess I didn't get it." I'm always humble about my acting abilities. I never really considered myself a real talented actor, but then they called me out of the blue and said, "Would you come in and screen test again?" I screen tested with Vinessa [Shaw] and we hit it off.

Vinessa Shaw:

I believe my first audition was with Kenny Ortega. I don't recall the actual audition itself, but what I do remember is leaving the audition at Disney Animation Studios. Kenny comes running out to the parking lot, which is not what directors do, and is like, "Vinessa, could you please come back and do it one more time? I had another thought." I went back in and I must have done something different. I don't recall what, but I remember it feeling better than what I had initially done. After I left, I got the call that I was going to have a chemistry test with two actors,

Leonardo DiCaprio and Omri Katz. I already knew Leo from doing this TV show called *Great Scott* with Tobey Maguire. I had never met Omri Katz but had heard of him. The world of acting at the time for young actors was very small and I really liked his TV show *Eerie, Indiana*. At the screen test, it was only me there with Omri in the waiting room area; I don't remember any other girls. The casting director said, "Well, at the last minute, Leonardo decided not to come."

Thora Birch:

I was so excited [about Leonardo DiCaprio possibly auditioning] because I had already worked with him on [the short-lived early '90s TV show] *Parenthood* and I had a developing crush on him. I was like, "Yes, let's get him in here! That's my older brother!" But he didn't audition; he just flat out turned it down. Honestly, for a young man his age, it was a ballsy move.

Leonardo DiCaprio (Actor), 2014:

I don't know where the hell I got the nerve [to turn down *Hocus Pocus*]. You live in an environment where you're influenced by people telling you to make a lot of money and strike while the iron's hot. But if there's one thing I'm very proud of, it's being a young man who was sticking to my guns.

Vinessa Shaw:

After Omri and I did the screen test I think they told us we got it right away because I was jumping around the parking lot with my mom. I was so excited. Growing up, I watched The *Wizard of Oz* over and over again. That's my favorite movie of all time and here I was a sixteen-year-old girl, the same age as Judy Garland in *The Wizard of Oz*, starring in a big-huge movie with witches. It just was too much for me, like, *Did I really manifest this?*

Omri Katz:

I was like, "Sweet, guess I got a job for the next few months!" I didn't take any of it seriously. I never truly had a passion for acting. It was just kind of something I grew up doing. I was kind of naturally animated and my parents thought it would be a good opportunity; maybe I could use it in the future. Here we are thirty years later and it's the gift that keeps on giving.

With the young leads now in place, the casting team set their sights on filling the supporting roles of seventeenth-century Salem boy Thackery Binx and his little sister, Emily Binx, as well as the teen bullies (and soon to be fan favorites) Jay and Ernie, better known as "Ice."

Tobias Jelinek:

Hocus Pocus was my first audition. Casting set me up with [legendary children's agent] Iris Burton, who worked with River and Joaquin Phoenix, because I showed up to the casting and I didn't have an agent or anything. A Disney scout had seen me in a community theater production in Santa Barbara and sometime later I was called in for a cattle call. I just remember there were a bunch of kids and, initially, they had me read for Max. Then the casting agent asked me to read for Jay. I do remember that the script I read had Jay and Ernie riding motorcycles, and Jay was an avid fan of Guns N' Roses. It took a long time to hear back after the audition, but I remember listening to Guns N' Roses' "November Rain" on my Walkman, because there was still a chance this film was going to happen.

Mary Hidalgo:

Jake Busey came in for the role of Ernie. He looked like his dad and his energy was just like his dad's. He was turning twenty-one, it was his birthday when he came in, and he was just so excited. He was like, "It's my birthday today! I'm twenty-one! I'm gonna go get drunk!" We were all like, "Okay, see you later!" He would've been great; he had a great look, but I don't think we could have handled that energy. Larry Bagby had such a great face, a perfect face for a bully, I just remember how cute Tobias was with that blond hair. He was a little skater kid. I think it was just the combination of their faces. The beauty of those small roles is they're like cartoons, so when you cast those kinds of small roles, it's all about their looks, you know?

Larry Bagby ("Ernie 'Ice'"):

I'd been acting professionally since I was twelve years old, so I started pretty early. I'd done some TV and film, but mostly TV commercials and some guest-star stuff. I remember reading for *Hocus Pocus* and really having a lot of fun with the character. I based him on *Grease.* I had done the play for my senior year and played Sonny, who's basically Ice, just a sarcastic and playful bully-type guy. I felt good about my audition, but I didn't hear anything for weeks. When I eventually got a callback I went in and Tobias was there. They matched us up. They saw the chemistry.

Tobias Jelinek:

I do remember Larry and I waiting in the lobby for our callback and immediately we were joking around. They brought us into the casting room where they had an old Hi8 camera and the casting directors left the room for a few minutes. We were in there together and it's very exciting when you're finally in the moment, and this guy suddenly gets down on the ground and starts doing a head spin. That's when I was like, "Oh, I love this guy!"

Amanda Shepherd:

I'll never forget seeing a rush of girls leaving the audition for Emily. For a second, I thought, *Oh, maybe I'm late?* But when I got called into the room, Kenny said, "Well, you're the last one for today." I said to him, "Oh, I'm so sorry. You must be so tired." He said, "Nope. We always save the best for last." Coming from somebody else, that might sound fake, but coming from him, you could tell he was genuinely saying that from a place of love. That immediately made me relax. I said the lines, there's very few of them so it was easy for me, and all of a sudden his eyes lit up. I'll never forget that, *his eyes lit up.* I knew right at that moment that I got the job. I think it was two or three days later I got a call from my agent giving us a heads-up that they wanted to talk to me. This is so embarrassing, I've never said this to anyone, but when I heard my mom pick up the phone, I went into the corner of my living room and, no joke, I started praying, like, hands together, "Dear God, please let me get this role." My mom got off the phone and she told me I booked the job. That was the only thing that I ever prayed for.

Those who have worked with Kenny Ortega say he has a skill for bringing the best out of young actors. He started his film career choreographing members of the Brat Pack in St. Elmo's Fire *and* Pretty in Pink *before going on to direct Zac Efron, Vanessa Hudgens, and Ashley Tisdale in the High School Musical trilogy, pushing the young stars to inhabit their roles. Many in the teen cast of* Hocus Pocus *took that advice to heart, turning their characters into reflections of themselves.*

Tobias Jelinek:
Like Max, Omri Katz was really into the Grateful Dead. He drove a VW bus. I think he bought it while we were shooting. I remember he was very proud of it.

Omri Katz:
I had a '79 VW bus, puke green. At the time, I was a pseudo hippie who wished I had lived back in the late '60s. I wore Birkenstocks, corduroys, and tie-dye. My hair just got longer and started smelling like patchouli. It was a time. I would say back then, any part that I did, no matter the role, was just basically an extension of myself. I was a huge

Grateful Dead fan. Kenny knew that and was like, "I've got these tie-dye tapestries and, you know, maybe you should wear a tie-dye shirt." I brought a lot of myself into that character and Kenny wanted me to as well.

Mary Vogt:

I would not have come up with the idea of tie-dye for Max. I don't particularly like tie-dye. I wouldn't have associated it with this kid from California that goes to Salem. Why is he wearing this stupid T-shirt? He's trying to fit in! Like, this kid is really asking for it, wearing a tie-dye T-shirt on the East Coast. What are you, crazy? He may have wanted a Grateful Dead T-shirt, but it's really hard to get approval from the Grateful Dead. So we may have said, "We may as well do tie-dye." We had this dye left over from the witches, so it's just a coincidence that it's the colors of the witches. There was no big plan there.

Aaron Wallace:

Early in the film, Max is doodling "Grateful Dead" in his notebook. What never occurred to me until I began researching it for my book is that "Grateful Dead," in addition to being the name of a band, also refers to, in literature, an out-of-towner who is traveling or who is visiting a place that is new to him. He comes across a dead body that has not been properly buried and so he rights that wrong. He gives the body its proper burial and then that person's ghost appears to thank the visitor for giving him his final resting place. We see that happen in *Hocus Pocus*; Max is a newcomer to Salem who discovers Thackery Binx, who has not been given his proper final resting place. Max is able to give it to him and immediately after which Thackery appears as a ghost and says, "Thank you." So, early in the film, when Max is drawing the "Grateful Dead," not only is it a very effective characterization device for him, but we learn later that it was also foreshadowing.

Thora Birch:

I was encouraged to bring Thora to [the role] and I was fighting to be a little bit more conservative with the character. I wanted to rein it in. I thought they were directing me to be outlandish and preposterous. I was like, "No, this is going to seem absurdist." Where this really came to the forefront was the "Mom" scream when Max won't take Dani trick-or-treating. I remember when I was doing that specific shot, they were like, "No, more! More!" And I'm like, "No, no, no, people are going to think that I'm doing a Macaulay Culkin impersonation." This was after *Home Alone*. But once they realized that was my thought process, they figured out how to talk to me. Reverse psychology completely worked on me.

Vinessa Shaw:

Mary Vogt was really instrumental in encouraging me to see the magic behind Allison's look. She would say, "Allison wears this because she has such knowledge and history that her mother taught her about the witches." There's leather twining that is laced through the trim of the sweater, which gives it an old-world feel. The necklace that I wear throughout the whole movie looks like a pentacle if you connect all the jeweled dots. Now there are articles on Allison that I just cannot believe, like "Seven Reasons Why Allison is a Witch." I feel like maybe the magic dust was kind of sprinkled by the costume designer. No one directly said Allison is an awakening witch or a witch in training or knows about white magic, but I think we all feel that she had something more than just knowledge.

Mary Vogt:

Even though her family had been there during the witch trials, I just thought she was into it, I never thought that she herself was a witch.

Neil Cuthbert:

That's not something that I have any memory of thinking about or of anybody talking to me about it. But, you know what, people are having fun.

Tobias Jelinek:

It was a lot of fun as actors to be able to show up and see the level of detail with the costume and the wardrobe. The rings, the jewelry, the spiked leather jacket [that Jay wears], having the flannel flipped around to the front. Originally, they were talking about [Jay wearing] a kilt, that's how far they were going to go. Then the idea was to show how a kid who was maybe interested in wearing a kilt would do it back then. I think Kenny worked very hard to keep that whimsy, that sense of imagination that kids have to utilize when they're finding their identity. That attention to detail really is how I think Kenny approached not only this film, but *High School Musical* and *Newsies*. He always paid attention to that adolescent detail and imagination.

Larry Bagby:

I was a church-going boy when I had the "ICE" shaved in the back of my head. I went down to Wilshire and 6th [in Santa Monica], like a legit barbershop. . . I had that for over a year. I'd wear a backwards hat anywhere else I would go, but no hats in church. I remember there were some whispers [about my hair at my church]. Later we found out that some of the members were like, "What is happening with that Bagby kid? It seems like he must have gotten into some kind of rap group or is becoming some kind of gangster." There was concern.

Mary Vogt:

At that time you could rent clothes from other studios and the *Dangerous Liaisons* costumes had just come in to Warner Bros. One of the dresses that Michelle Pfeiffer had worn in *Dangerous Liaisons* was in the costume house. I thought that would look great on Vinessa. So the dress Allison wears at the party at her house is actually a dress that Michelle Pfeiffer wore in *Dangerous Liaisons*.

Vinessa Shaw:

This was interesting because I did not know this until about two or three years ago. Somebody did a split screen on Instagram and put me side by side with Michelle Pfeiffer in the same dress and did a silly "Who wore it better?" I flipped out because I'm a huge Michelle Pfeiffer fan. You know, in the script, I was supposed to be in that period outfit the whole time. I don't know if it was Kenny or Mary, but someone saved my life. It would've been very awkward to run through all of Salem, the brambles of the graveyard and all that, in that corseted outfit.

Chapter 6

A Zombie Fit for a Disney Movie

A contortionist and mime by trade, Doug Jones has become known for the many monsters he's played in director Guillermo del Toro's films, but his most beloved role might be his first big screen one: Billy Butcherson. The seventeenth-century zombie was poisoned to death by Winifred Sanderson, who was jealous of his bond with her sister, Sarah. Jones created the character in collaboration with special makeup effects artist Tony Gardner, who knew the spindly six foot four actor was right for the role seemingly before anyone else did.

Tony Gardner:

My company Alterian had done *The Addams Family* and a couple of films that were sort of in the genre before we were contacted about this film. I'd done a couple things for Disney Theme Parks prior, including "Honey, I Shrunk the Audience!" so we knew some people there. I just remember going in and having a meeting and being excited that it was Disney and that it was Halloween related. There was a zombie and they said, "You know, he's from a couple of hundred years ago and he gets his head knocked off and his fingers cut off and his mouth is stitched shut, but you have to figure out a way to do this and make it kid-friendly because this is a Disney film." That was the challenge right off the bat.

Doug Jones:

Tony had never met me before, but I had done an awful lot of commercials by that point, and guest starred on a couple of shows as monsters. The creature-effects people were starting to whisper my name around the industry. Two years before we filmed *Hocus Pocus,* I was working on my "Mac Tonight" campaign for McDonald's, which was one of my very first jobs in Hollywood.

Tony Gardner:

I had seen the "Mac Tonight" commercials and there was this tall skinny guy with this giant moon head singing and sliding down a piano

bench. I remember thinking whoever that is has to be literally misera-
ble because that head has to weigh so much, but their body language is
amazing. This would be the perfect person to build a character like Billy
on. I sort of became a little obsessed [with the "Mac Tonight" commer-
cial] and I hunted down Steve Neill, the person who had done the Mac
Tonight moon head. It was a lot harder to hunt people down back then.
You had to go find a phone book and start calling people with the same
last name. You have to bring a lot of quarters, but I found him. He was
gracious enough to invite me to his house. He had a shop in his garage
and we talked about the moon head and this guy that he had built it on,
who was so kind and patient and tolerant, named Doug Jones. I asked
if he still had a head or any sort of cast of Doug to figure out the design
proportions so that we could design Billy. He said, "Well, to be honest
with you, behind my garage, there's an old head cast of him." I went out
back and it had been in the rain for years. It was just this very sad-looking
Doug Jones, but to me that was jackpot city. I asked if I could borrow it
and he was like, "Oh, you can have it."

Doug Jones:

Tony, bless his heart, had taken some clay and had thrown it on a life
cast of me, a plaster version of me that one of Tony's sculptors, Chet
Zar, then sculpted into a bust for Kenny's approval. Kenny was like,
"Oh, I love it!" Tony then said, "Well, by the way, just so you know,
underneath that makeup is Doug Jones, an actor that I think would be
great for this." That was happening simultaneously with my audition.

Tony Gardner:

I wanted to keep Billy as thin as possible because I wanted all his
emoting to come through it. I didn't want his performance to be lost
inside it. So when I was showing the bust, I was like, "See this design
that we sculpted? If you all like this design as much as you say, then this
design can only be done on this guy because it's so thin, it literally is

this guy." I found out later Doug was under consideration for the part because of the clown that he had played in *Batman Returns*. Everything came at them from all these directions and it's just this big flashing "Doug Jones" sign.

Doug Jones:

This is 1992 so this is early in my career. Getting an audition for anything was, "Thank heaven," you know? The *Hocus Pocus* audition was not in a typical casting office with a desk and someone reading lines with you. At this point, the script didn't have any lines for Billy, but he was a presence in the film. I got to the dance studio where the audition was being held and Kenny Ortega, casting director Greg Smith, and choreographer Peggy Holmes were there. Kenny then told me who Billy was and said, "So what I want to see is you waking up from the grave and stumbling. I want you to get across the room, wake up, and look up in the sky and there's a witch hovering above, and I want you to be angry with her." He had a boom box with him, and this music started playing. It wasn't the "Monster Mash," but it was like a soundtrack for old bones waking up from the grave. It was kind of groovy. I remember feeling so inspired. I made my body as creaky as I could and as stiff as I could. When I finally sat up, the minute I started moving, the laughter started. I'm not sure what I was doing, but I thought, *Whatever it is, it's working.* By the time I got home from the audition, the call had come in already. I could not have been more excited.

With Doug Jones officially cast, the next step was creating Billy Butcherson's look. Tony Gardner and costume designer Mary Vogt created a lovable zombie that would appeal to Disney fans and goths.

Tony Gardner:

Billy was a sympathetic character. You needed to be able to relate to him and I didn't want him to get too far away from being human. I imagined him as Ichabod Crane, a sort of tall, gangly guy with a pony-tail, and just a little offbeat. I always saw him as a little punk rock. I was looking at pictures of Siouxsie and the Banshees, Adam Ant, the Cure. It was, "How do you come up with that cool Adam Ant sort of vibe with a dead guy?"

Mary Vogt:

When they cast Doug, I thought, *Oh my God, he looks exactly like Ichabod Crane!* He's very tall, super skinny. He's got an incredibly long backbone. He would look amazing in that sort of seventeenth-century outfit. Also, he's like the nicest guy in the world.

Doug Jones:

This movie is not that long after the Michael Jackson "Thriller" video. We all fell in love with that, so that was kind of the beacon of light that we were all guided by. When I saw the makeup, the cheekbones they'd added to me and the hair, I saw Michael Jackson once he turned into a zombie. I wanted to channel that.

Tony Gardner:

I think the fact that I worked on "Thriller" shows up in regards to my foundation colors for Billy. To be honest, they're [legendary special makeup effects artist] Rick Baker's foundation colors for Michael's zombie makeup in the "Thriller" video.

Mick Garris:

I was also one of the zombies in "Thriller," and that very much played a part in creating Billy. I didn't imagine the fright wig, and he's a little more comical than what was originally written, but he's definitely from my imagination. Stitching his lips together? That's pretty dark. One of my favorite parts about having written this movie was coming up with Billy Butcherson.

Chet Zar (Special Makeup Effects Artist):
I got into the effects business pretty early. I started working in high school, which is like '85. The remake of *The Blob* in '87 is how I met my boss, Tony Gardner. I was at his shop, which was pretty successful at that point. I was a sculptor and a painter. *Hocus Pocus* was just a job that came in. I had been a zombie freak since I was a kid, so I was excited to get a chance to do a single zombie's makeup and just make it as good as I possibly could. I like the old-school zombies; I loved carving wrinkles, which is a super nerdy thing. If you look at certain mummies, the wrinkle kind of goes out to form crepey skin and I remember doing that on the neck. As I went further in my career, I learned all these detailing techniques that are better than what I knew back then. I always think, "Man, I wish I would've known these techniques back when I was doing Billy." Not that anybody would have noticed, because it looked good in the movie. I think it still holds up.

Tony Gardner:
I wanted to do the prosthetic piece that Doug wears as one piece so there wasn't a glue line or anywhere where those skinny little wrinkles didn't line up. I really wanted it to all work as a believable, sunken face, so it's one giant foam piece wrapped around his head. It takes two people to get it right because it's so big.

Chet Zar:
There were gloves for his hands and there was a facial prosthetic. What I did was sculpt and paint the prosthetics. Margaret Prentice did the application on Doug. These kinds of pieces are always a challenge because you have to try and make the actor look thin, but you're adding bulk that you can't take away. With Doug, he's so thin that he's kind of the ideal subject in that way. He doesn't have any body fat really.

Margaret Prentice (Special Makeup Effects Artist):

Doug had to put up with a few things between the stitches on his mouth and having those foam gloves for his hands. Tony designed the face prosthetic so it was one piece, but it's a little tricky when you're first placing it on. You have to make sure that the eyes, nose, and mouth are all lined up in the right place. The tricky part is getting it centered. Then it's Tony on one side and me on the other and we have to kind of flip it up and start gluing little by little till it reaches over to the ear. The prosthetic piece is pre-painted to a certain extent, but we have to blend any edges, especially around the eyes and the mouth. The full foam gloves we wouldn't put on until he was ready to work. He couldn't really do anything once he got into those. It took a few hours to apply all of this, but Doug was excited and wanted to really do a good job. He wanted to be as helpful as possible, so he always gave us all his attention and his time. He was never demanding of anything. He has such a gentle personality that he's able to tolerate a lot more than some actors. Whether Doug is comfortable or not, he doesn't let you know.

Tony Gardner:

We really wanted Billy to look like his clothing was hanging in tatters. That's why Doug's wearing a full bodysuit underneath his wardrobe with all the skin sculpted on it so that we could tear literally a whole elbow away or the knee and not worry about it. We knew his face would be a prosthetic and take a lot of time from the collarbone up, but we made everything else so he could slip in and out of it. It was all built for speed really.

Doug Jones:

Once my look was all put together—the hair, makeup, and costume—I walked onto the studio lot to do a camera test. Kenny told me later that he was getting whispers from some of our lady crew members saying, "He's a zombie, but he's kind of hot." That's exactly what we were going for. We wanted Billy to be charming enough and dateable enough that the audience could connect with him as well as be slightly frightened of him until you know his story.

Tony Gardner:

I was just really hung up on him being an attractive zombie. It's funny, now when I think of Jack Skellington, Billy has that same sort of vibe. He's dressed nicely and he is supposed to be attractive. There had to be sort of an elegance to him.

Karyn Malchus ("Headless Billy Butcherson"):

Doug and I had a conversation about how brittle Billy's bones had to be so that his head would fall off or his hand would go flying. We wanted to make sure that the audience understood how fragile he was, but also wanted to make sure it didn't come off as scary because this is a family movie. To do that, we had to get the comic timing right. When I was doing the scene where Billy loses his head, I remember Kenny saying, "Karyn, when you get up again, you've got to remember that this happens all the time. It's not that big of a deal. It's just like, *Where's my dang head?* And you gotta put it back on."

Kevin Haney:

I didn't like that they made it clear that he was friendly at first, but I know they did that for the kids because he's pretty gruesome-looking, you know?

Chet Zar:

When Doug is wearing all this makeup and glue and costumes, he's always totally sweet and nice to everybody. It's so weird. He's like a different kind of human being, because I've worn that stuff. I had a little part in [Tim Burton's 2001 remake of] *Planet of the Apes* as a background ape and they put all that stuff on me and I became such an asshole. I'm a nice guy, but it just made me so grumpy. It's so uncomfortable. It made me really appreciate suit performers.

Doug Jones:

A misconception can be that someone who has played lots of characters under rubber bits is all about throwing the limbs around and having talented elbows. The thing is, those elbows won't do what you want them to do if the actor *schmactor* part of you has not ingested that character into your heart and your soul. You need to know that character's wants, needs, loves, and fears.

Vinessa Shaw:

I felt like the character he is playing is very *Wizard of Oz*, very like the Scarecrow in nature. That made me adore him more. I just feel like Doug is like Ray Bolger.

Doug Jones:

Ray Bolger as the Scarecrow was my hero as a kid. I'm not playing a scarecrow, I'm a zombie, but being long and lanky, I was just living my Ray Bolger dream.

Tony Gardner:

Hocus Pocus is the first film where I was given so much creative freedom. The design of character, that was what I wanted it to be, and I was trusted. That was super unique. I was never doing makeup on Doug. I always felt like I was collaborating with Doug to create a character.

Doug Jones:

My career has had a certain look to it. A certain glued-on costumed look to it. Tony Gardner and I worked together so well and got along so well. We giggled and laughed, and we became real friends, and because of that, he referred me again and again for anything that came through his shop that needed a creature in it. "We need someone who is rotund and four foot eleven," Tony would say. "Doug Jones is perfect for that!" He was so good to me. I would say we've done at least fifteen projects together. His referral process got me in front of new directors and other creature-effects people. I owe Tony Gardner a lot for that, and *Hocus Pocus* was the project that sparked it.

Chapter 7

RUNNING AMOK-AMOK-AMOK IN SALEM

Hocus Pocus *is set in Salem, Massachusetts, a historic coastal city known for being the site of the 1692 witch trials, during which nineteen innocent people were executed for allegedly practicing witchcraft. The cast spent less than a month filming on location in Salem, but it was a memorable shoot for everyone involved, including the locals.*

William Sandell:

I was living in Burbank, California, and flying back and forth to Salem scouting locations. I put, like, a hundred thousand miles on my American Airlines and Delta cards waiting for the trees to change. I was in heaven. It was actually the happiest time of my life.

Steve Voboril ("Elijah"):

When I got the part of Elijah, I had just worked with Kenny on *Newsies*. I was twenty-one. I was barely making ends meet. I was living in Venice Beach, California. I've been clean and sober for twenty-nine years now, [but] at that time, I was just a hot little mess. They sent me a first-class ticket to fly on an airplane to Salem, and a limousine to pick me up. I think we had a per diem of twenty or thirty bucks a day, which was a bit of money at the time. I blew nearly all that money on a phone call from the airplane. I still remember, I spent a hundred and eight dollars to make a call from first class. I think I called my mom.

Neil Cuthbert:

My wife and I drove up to Salem, Massachusetts, just to check on the place since that's where the film was set. It was really fun because we got there and realized this is a town that is in fact insane for Halloween. I mean, they go crazy there. I thought, *Oh, this is just great!*

Omri Katz:

We filmed in October and saw the change of seasons. Being from California, it was the first time I'd ever really witnessed that in real life.

I have fond memories of visiting Walden Pond and taking all that in, the beauty of the landscape and how different it was from a Southern California desert, which was all I knew then.

Mick Garris:

Taking a trip to Salem was the thing that exploded my imagination. I'd never been there before, and I went right before Halloween. They celebrate the eleven days leading up to Halloween, and it climaxes with a candlelight vigil to Gallows Hill, where the witches were stoned and pressed to death. There is so much of the city that has given over to the wicked history of Salem, Massachusetts, in 1692. That trip was probably the biggest influence of all [on my script]. It's why the movie, in my head, had a lot more shadows.

William Sandell:

We were in Salem on Halloween shooting on the tercentenary anniversary of the witch trials. They were building the Salem witchcraft victims' memorial while we were there. They inscribed on each of the stones the last words that they said on the gallows.

Rachel Christ-Doane:

In the '90s, there was quite a large tourism industry emerging in Salem really focusing on its witch-related past. That was also the time of the tercentenary, the three hundredth anniversary of the trials, so there were some really important conversations going on in Salem about how we engage with modern witchcraft and what all of that means to people today.

Kate Fox (Executive Director, Destination Salem, 2007–2023):

We estimate that about 85 to 90 percent of the visitors who come to Salem as tourists say that they're coming for "the witchy things." A lot of them don't know what that means so we will often break it down for them and say, "This is what happened in 1692. This is the historical fact of the witch trials." Then we also have a modern witch community and then we have the pop-culture witches like the Sanderson sisters. I do think more people are coming because of *Hocus Pocus*, whereas at one point people were coming because they wanted to do the Salem Witch thing, whatever that means to them.

Lt. Governor Kim Driscoll (Mayor of Salem, 2006–2023):
Ever since the three hundredth anniversary of the witch trials in 1992, the city has had a steady drumbeat of recognition for what our history means to tourism and hospitality. We could tell all of our stories, right? The witch trials, the golden age of Salem, and *Hocus Pocus*. That more pop-culture piece of what was filmed here and filmed in other places, but was about here. Give the people what they want, so to speak.

David Kirschner:
I remember soaking in the vibe of Salem. All of this history was really exciting and just the feeling of fall and what could be created from that.

Ralph Winter:
We were worried that we were going to miss the changing of the leaves. That we'd show up in New England and all the leaves would be gone or everything is still green. It was hard to predict. Now it's become more of a thing to watch the colors, but we wanted to be sure we had the right materials, so we brought our own leaves. We filled a five-ton truck full of orange-painted leaves. That's a lot of leaves, but we used them.

William Sandell:
If you look at some of the scenes in Salem, you'll see it's pretty green up [near the top of the trees], but a little more colorful down lower when the camera pans down. Everywhere I went people were laughing their heads off because I had bags and bags of fall leaves and branches. I had my greensman running around sticking them into trees and throwing

'em all in front of the kids and in front of the camera. Good old-fashioned movie making, right?

Rosemary Brandenburg:

It wouldn't have been as cool a project if we'd done the whole thing in LA. It was just really cool that we were able to go to New England; that set the tone. It set the stage for a lot of really good historical discovery and layering. It just gave it a richness that I might not have been able to achieve by being able to go there and see things personally.

Steve Voboril:

The locals in Salem were literally on set walking around like, "Hi! How's it going?" I remember standing with Sean [Murray] before shooting a scene and a little girl, she had to be like five years old, brought me this little stick of wood. She says, "This is your wand to protect you from the witches." I still have it.

Russell Bobbitt:

We're shooting in Salem. I think it's the scene where Max is riding his bicycle through town and he gets his shoes stolen. This little boy walks up to me, he's got to be eight years old. He goes, "I know who you are. You're Russell Bobbitt." I was like, "Okay, this is weird. Who are you? What's your deal?" He goes, "I just love movies. I pay attention to everything and I'm just really into it." I was like, "Okay, weird," but he was just a nice little kid. He had no fear. He goes, "I want to give you my phone number. Can I have your phone number? I'm gonna stay pen pals with you." He was really legit, so I said, "Of course, we'll stay in touch. It'll be great." I get back home and the kid calls me and goes, "Hey, my parents said I could come out for the summer and I was wondering if it's okay if I come and visit you and your wife?" I'm married, I have kids, and I was like, "Well, okay." Weird moment number two. I called the parents and they're free-spirited people. They explain, "He met you on set and he met a bunch of people and he is going to stay a week with this person, a week with that person. If you want to have him, great. We appreciate it." The kid comes out, we have a great time. He comes to the set with me. He goes back home. Next year, he calls me again. It's summer vacation. "I'm spending a week with Ivan Reitman and another week with Al Pacino. I'd like to spend a week with you." I was like, "Okay, Jeremy, come and visit." He did this for many years. He ends up getting a degree at Yale because he said in his essay, "If you let me into this school, I'll get Al Pacino to come here and talk to your class at graduation." And he did. He went to school for law, but now he's [*Succession* star] Jeremy Strong. When I see him now, I'm like, "Oh my God, that's Jeremy, my little friend from *Hocus Pocus*."

William Sandell:
I stayed at the Hawthorne Hotel right in the middle of town by the Salem Common, which, by the way, is a very haunted hotel. There are a couple of floors that are very active. Laurie Cabot, the official witch of Salem, had her crystal shop right by. At the end of the day, I would see Laurie and her girlfriends sitting by their Chevys smoking, all in their witch dresses, which were all kinds of chiffon. I'd always wonder where they were going. I would walk in the cemeteries at night and you could peek into these old crypts. For a guy who had been doing a spook show on his front lawn, I was seeing the real thing. I really did a lot of research on Salem witches. It took me a long time after this movie, which was a very happy experience, to sort of shake the horrible images from that time. The horrible ways these women were treated. I wish it wasn't in my head. Accuracy wasn't that important to Kenny, but it was important to the art department.

Rosemary Brandenburg:
I'm definitely a research maven. My father was a historian and professor of history. My mother was an art historian. I was dragged around to

every museum in the world. I love the process of finding historic detail. Sometimes it puts me at odds with a director. For example, when I worked with Quentin Tarantino on *The Hateful Eight*, which was another period project, he was really into looking at old movies and using that as reference. It may be cool for shots, but as far as the dressing, those old Westerns are kind of primitive. They were working strictly from what was available in the prop houses at the studios. You can see the same stove over and over again. I just prefer primary references, as historians say; really going to the historical documents. On *Hocus Pocus*, everybody did their research: the windows and doors, the size of the stairs, the weight of the beams. I would go into a store for those reenactments of the Civil War or Revolutionary War and buy beautiful period nails and hooks. You rust them up and you stick them in the set. Whether you see all these details in the movie or not, I don't know, but I don't care. We just really took it seriously.

Mary Vogt:

In order to exaggerate, you have to start with realism. When you start doing any kind of research, the best thing to do is to read people's diaries. That is the closest to the truth. It's not an interpretation, it's actually there. They usually mention the clothes and things they packed and things they did during the day. In the museums they have a lot of patterns for period clothes, and *Hocus Pocus* wasn't set that long ago so we stayed pretty close to the patterns of the original 1600s clothes. Once I've gotten a good feeling for what was happening then, the politics and the culture, then I start to exaggerate and hope that some of that realism comes through.

Kate Fox:

People don't realize *Hocus Pocus* is fiction, which boggles my mind. We have lots of requests for, "Where's the Sanderson sisters' house?" In LA on a soundstage. It doesn't exist, which was great until Disney made the

Airbnb for *Hocus Pocus 2*. Every day we tell people the Sanderson house doesn't exist, and then they make it exist.

For one night only in October 2022, fans were able to stay in a re-creation of the Sanderson sisters' home via Airbnb. The cottage may not be an actual Salem landmark, but the movie turned several of the city's real historic locations into photo opportunities for fans, including Pioneer Village, America's first living-history museum.

William Sandell:
Pioneer Village is the wildest thing of all. I went there and no one told me that it's a replica of Salem as it was in the seventeenth century where people pretend to be living in that era. It was a rainy, drizzly day. No one was there. I poke my head into one of the buildings and there's this woman sitting there darning something. She says, "Hello, good sir, come on in. Is the weather so bad?" I'm getting goose bumps right now just telling this story. She says, "Where are you from?" I said, "Well, I'm from California." She says, "Oh, I don't know where that is. Where would that be?" I said, "Well, it's a bit far away." I go outside and I see a guy hoeing behind his little house and I say, "Boy that looks like a lot of work." He says, "Oh, it's God's work," and keeps on hoeing. I take pictures of everything. I go back to the studio and I say, "I gotta see Kenny right away." I go into his office in LA and I'm still in shock. He says, "What's the matter with you? Your eyes are all bugged out." I'm like, "I just got back from the East Coast on a scout. We gotta go right away." When we went back it wasn't as magical as the day I saw it; there were more people there, but that aerial shot in the beginning of the movie, that's Pioneer Village. It really was the coolest thing I ever saw.

The exterior of Allison's house in the film was filmed at the Ropes Mansion, which is owned by the Peabody Essex Museum, one of the oldest continuously operating museums in the United States. The location is the third-most-googled home of all time, according to TheStreet *in 2023, with searches for "hocus pocus house" averaging 12,000 searches per month.* (*The houses in* Home Alone *and* Twilight *came in first and second, respectively.*)

Paula Richter (Curator, Peabody Essex Museum):

[The Ropes Mansion] was built in the late 1720s and it's on Essex Street in Salem, a really main thoroughfare through the downtown of Salem, one of the historic districts. I think it is one of the most recognizable sites in the film, in part because of how it was decorated. The fence outside was completely surrounded with carved pumpkins, really large pumpkins, all beautifully lit, the cornstalks and hay bales and all the trappings of Halloween and fall in New England. I think it's a very memorable moment in the film because of all of the decoration and the attention that went into it.

Rosemary Brandenburg:

We made a pact that we wouldn't buy one store-bought Halloween decoration, that we would make everything ourselves whether it was corn husks or red devil tridents. We had a really fun crew that really got into it.

Paula Richter:

I have worked at the Peabody Essex Museum for many years and I was present during the filming. It was a very dramatic experience. The furnishings of the historic house actually represent four generations of belongings of a single family, the Ropes family of Salem, who originally lived in the house from the eighteenth century until 1907. Some of the front rooms had to be emptied of their content because there were actors and actresses who were stationed in the house and appeared as shadowy silhouettes in the windows during that party scene, which was filmed from the street. I remember looking out from the house, at this vast crew with large pieces of equipment. The cameraman could move seamlessly without any distortion or extraneous movement, one slow steady pan of the front of the house. That was very interesting to watch. They took up most of what is usually a very busy street, but beyond them were folks from the neighborhood who were kind of standing out in the periphery, staying up very late or very early into the next morning to watch the filming take place. The last couple of years, the museum actually partnered with a Disney fan club to decorate the historic house like it was in the film during Halloween; it really became a favorite spot for selfies.

The movie also turned a private residence into one of the city's most Instagrammed sites.

William Sandell:

I was looking for Max Dennison's house in Salem. I picked that one because it's so charming. That house was actually right on the water on this beautiful little bay. There was a big long scene where Max and his father have this heart-to-heart down on the beach. I wanted to put them by the water because Salem is surrounded with water. It was a huge important shipping port. Everybody was a captain who was living in these marvelous homes. Everything has a plaque, "Captain so-and-so, 1801." There's just so much history there. You just get a vibe.

Rachel Christ-Doane:

I don't mean to speak for everyone in Salem, but I think that nobody really expected *Hocus Pocus* to become as popular as it's become. That's an important part of this conversation. The feelings around *Hocus Pocus* I think have changed in recent years because it's driving so many people here who are coming with this kind of different perception of the witch history here. They're coming because they want to see the Sanderson sisters' house, which doesn't exist. They want to see the house where Max lived in the film, which is a real house that's privately owned. That's actually becoming a problem because so many visitors are going there.

Kimmy Blankenburg (@KimmyBlanksHocusPocusLife; *Hocus Pocus* Devotee):

I've been lucky enough to go to Salem every year since 2008 and have created my own personal "Kimmy's *Hocus Pocus* Tour" for my family. We hit all the filming locations. I tend to get emotional whenever we pull up to Max and Dani's house, properly known as the Balcomb Cottage. During one of my yearly visits, I was fortunate enough to meet the adorable owner of the home, sitting in a rocker on her porch, enjoying the view of the water. She actually lived in the house while Disney was filming and told me all of the wonderful experiences she had with the cast and crew, and how respectful they were.

Lt. Governor Kim Driscoll:

Everybody wants a picture in front of that house, that's for sure. That's probably the place most people go. We now have to put up a police detail in front of the house.

Kate Fox:

I've had tour buses filled with fifty people from Canada who just drive right up to that house. Picture a bus just stopping in the middle of the road and letting everybody get out to take a picture. That's a huge problem for the entire neighborhood. It impacts not just that house, but all the neighbors, and the neighbors complain more than the people in that house.

Brian Sims (Author/Performer, BORAH! Brewington Snaggletooth XIII; Registered Respiratory Therapist, Brigham and Women's Hospital):

I moved to Salem in 2016, and every year more and more people will tell me they're here for *Hocus Pocus*. Those fans are over the top—in a good way! The Sanderson sisters are the most popular costumes every year. My witch character, BORAH!, can be sarcastic and kind of rude in a fun, positive way so I'll see an older person dressed as Winifred and be, like, "You better go light another candle!" But I look at it this way: this is a tourist town and with tourism comes some negativity. In October, sometimes it can feel like thirty-one days of headaches, but, for me, the positive outweighs the negative.

William Sandell:

This was a couple of years ago, but I got Dot, the little old lady who owns the Max Dennison house, on the phone. I said, "So do you hate me for picking your house for this thing?" She says, "No, Bill. It was fun. I remember when I saw you down by the water in front of our house and you were looking for sea glass for your mother." I said, "I remember you invited me in and made me coffee and offered me some of your cookies." We had the nicest talk, but I always wonder about that poor street. It's just loaded with people getting their picture taken in front of their house. She said, "Everybody's pretty nice. Nobody bangs on our door. Nobody's disrespectful. They just stand in the street and take a picture." We painted a portrait of the Max Dennison house. You see our painting in the movie, hanging in the hallway. The owners still have that picture and it's hanging in that same spot. That was my gift to them.

Chapter 8

"THE PLAYGROUND FOR ALL OF US TO PLAY IN"

*S*alem *may have been where* Hocus Pocus *took place, but the majority of the movie was actually filmed across multiple locations in Los Angeles. Many of the film's key sets were custom built on Stage 2, the largest soundstage on the Walt Disney Studios lot, where only thirty years earlier,* Mary Poppins *was filmed.*

William Sandell:

I read things all the time: "They shot for two months in Salem." I don't want to ruin somebody's day, but we shot most of the trick-or-treating around LA. We shot the cemetery with the big gates in the big backlot of Warner Bros. on Hollywood Way. We shot some scenes where the kids are running through Old Salem, like the moment with the cop, on the sets that have been up at Warner's for years and years. I remember people were shocked to see the *Friends* fountain in *Hocus Pocus,* and it is the same fountain, because they thought *Friends* was shot in New York. We built this giant set over on the big stage at Disney. Going to work every day was a treat. For many years I had a clause in my contract that I would get Halloween off. We had Halloween for months on *Hocus Pocus.*

Vinessa Shaw:

Soundstage 1 [on the Disney lot] was Billy's graveyard and the Sanderson house. The final battle scene with the witches was contained on Soundstage 2, and then Soundstage 3 was Max and Dani's house. It just felt so magical every day on set.

Amanda Shepherd:

People would be riding bicycles on the [Disney] lot and the squirrels would be riding on the handles, it was hilarious. Most people would be a little bit taken back and scared, like, "Oh God, I don't want to get rabies!" I was just like, "Oh, look at these friendly squirrels!" I would be petting one and my mom would be like, "No, no, don't touch that!"

Jason Marsden:

The soundstages—that is Hollywood to me. That is the glitz and glamour of Hollywood. *Hocus Pocus* was definitely that. At night, I walked onto the set and it was like being somewhere in the backwoods on the East Coast with a kind of creepy "Hansel and Gretel" sort of house. It was just fabulous.

Doug Jones:

The backdrop in the studio on the Disney lot could do sunrise or nightfall. It was really magical. I felt like I was at Disneyland on a ride that was Salem-based. It was, "Wow, I get to play in this make-believe world." It was so beautiful.

William Sandell:

Hiro Narita, the cinematographer on *Hocus Pocus*, did a wonderful job. He's a very magical man. We collaborated on the fantasy backings behind these witch houses and gave them this light and this glow.

Kevin Haney:

I just remember Kenny Ortega always talking about his acid-green sky. If you watch the film, when you're going up to the cabin, it's an acid-green sky. He got his vision.

Tony Gardner:

It was like going onto the *Pirates of the Caribbean* ride where all of a sudden, you're in the dark and you're in a completely different world. You couldn't see the walls because they were using every foot of stage space to get distance and depth. Days where I didn't have to work, I would go hang out because it was literally beautiful. Bill [Sandell] built the playground for all of us to play in.

William Sandell:

My crew is filled with a lot of people that have their architectural credentials and their masters in art. This has been true for the studios since the '20s when they used to grab people from USC, architectural students mainly, and throw them into the art department at companies like Universal or Paramount. That's why these movies look so incredible from that era. Sure, they're monster movies, but these architectural graduates were happy to be working in the art department for a monster movie because they'd be stuck designing condominiums for the rest of their life otherwise. In the movie business, one day you're designing a flying saucer, the next, you're designing a volcano. Here you just build it as fantasy without all the fire codes and load codes, then you throw it away, and start on another thing.

Russell Bobbitt:

We made some fun things. We had our vacuum cleaner brooms and things like that, but the Book is the most iconic prop for me at least—and for many of the fans. When they find out I worked on *Hocus Pocus*, the first word they say to me is, "BooOOOook" like Bette Midler does. I was personally running the remote control for the book to move the eye, so I was kind of the personality of the book. I would decide when the book blinked or moved. I would pay attention to the actors doing their dialogue and I would move the eye over to who was talking. A young person heard that explanation from me and said, "So you are Book?" And I've never thought of it that way, but I guess I was sort of Book.

Don Yesso ("Mortal Bus Boy"):

In the movie, when Allison reads the plaque on the book, she says, "Made of human skin," but on a plaque that [leadman] Chris [L. Spellman] made, it said it was "made from the skin of a child," and they made her change the line. The reason why I know this is because I had the plaque.

Chris gave it to me. We sold it at auction and we had to get confirmation that it was really in the movie. You don't see it in the film, but I found a behind-the-scenes clip of them passing the book and there it was.

David Kirschner:

My first day on set, I can remember it and I can smell it so well. I brought Liz and our two girls and they were building the Sanderson cottage. I remember walking onto the set and the smell of lumber, which is always wonderful, stood out. Now I cannot smell lumber without associating it with the brilliant Disney artists creating that set.

Liz Kirschner:

The smell really did equate to happiness.

Jessie Wolfson:

Walking through those stage doors was like being in Salem. You were fully transported. You felt like you could do a potion in that house and something may happen. It was almost like a state building. You almost wanted to whisper inside because you felt the magnitude of that building when you walked in. It had a dark eerie feeling and a musty smell that was super exciting.

William Sandell:

It's Smell-o-Vision, really. If we're doing a set, say a hamburger joint, after we get done making it, painting it, dressing it, I'd get the effects department to hook up the stoves in the kitchen. I'd tell everybody to come in and eat lunch here. Cook your hamburgers in here so the place doesn't smell like latex paint. I really did that on *The Perfect Storm*. I had people drinking in the bar we built. We had a crew party there. The studio said, "What if they wreck it?" I said, "I want them to carve their initials and throw up in there." With *Hocus Pocus*, we had real water hookups so there was really this stream running. Inside everything was oil and candle wax so everything kind of smelled great. We brought in trees from the East Coast, real trees and dirt, so when you walked in, the whole place smelled like earth.

Vinessa Shaw:

The trees and foliage had to be wet down before we did the scenes so the leaves would stick on the ground and not fly around with the wind. It had this dirty mulchy smell that I think only an East Coaster would know about. I'm a Californian and so was Thora, so we just equate that smell with *Hocus Pocus*.

Thora Birch:

It's true. It was a very distinct mixture of mulch and dying and decaying leaves. Once in a great while, I'll be in a certain area, maybe right after it rains, and think, *Oh, that's that smell from the* Hocus Pocus *set.*

Rosemary Brandenburg:

They used a lot of organic material for the ground, peat moss or whatever, and there was so much water on the stage it ended up getting all moldy. It was terrible. We had to air out the stage every day and try to have fans and heaters around to kind of mitigate the humidity. We did a lot of dirt on a stage when we did the third *Guardians of the Galaxy*. I was like, "Watch out guys. I don't want it to start rotting!" They ended up using a very new inorganic mix. I think everybody learned a lesson from those *Hocus Pocus* days.

David Kirschner:

I was reduced to tears when I saw the witches' house in my story. I just wrote, "The witches' house." It was very easy to write that phrase. Well, Bill Sandell created it.

William Sandell:

There was no false facade or walls that pulled away. It was really built like a real house. Every nail was a square nail. All the lead is real lead in the windows. It had been polished and aged. You could take the camera anywhere in there and there was never any phony wood. Everywhere you went, it was real.

Rosemary Brandenburg:

The Sanderson house was so beautifully designed and beautifully built. It was such a rich canvas to work with and add on top of. Bill Sandell is renowned for a term that he made up called "phlegm-wagu." "I need some *phlegm-wagu* on that." By that he means, asphaltum and aging, you know, some physical grime, toning, and transparent stains that are used so the details don't all get obscured.

William Sandell:

I did use the phrase "phlegm-wagu" all the time. Where and how I started using it I can't remember. It was sort of code for "let's keep giving it more." In my set painters' case, it would mean "let's keep aging the set," that type of thing, in Rosemary's case it might mean "it just needs a little more." Sort of a poor man's *je ne sais quoi*, perhaps.

David Kirschner:

When Liz and I were somewhere on the East Coast, I bought a broomstick that had two brooms coming out of it. Kind of a dual-exhaust broom, if you will. I brought it in to show Disney, but I never got it back because they put it in the movie. It's in the Sanderson Sisters Museum. It's not part of the Sanderson sisters' original lore, but it's for whatever reason hanging there. Every time I look at it, I just say, "I want my broom back!" but they think it's theirs.

Allison Dubrosky (@HocusPocusCollector; Cohost, *The Black Flame Society* Podcast):
The Black Flame Candle that you see in the film was the one that David created to pitch the movie. He went to CVS, bought a candle, wrapped some black paper around it, put it in his oven, and that's the one that you see on screen.

William Sandell:
I ended up with [one of Winifred's spell books] from *Hocus Pocus*. The effects company that built it wrote a nice plaque inside to me and gave it to me as a gift because I got them the job to build the books. I'm the only one that has a Book, which David didn't know. No one knew. It was the stand-in Book that was used in the background. Not the Book with the working eyeball, supposedly Florida Disney has that one, but I think it's a replica, so I have the only Book used on-screen. I keep it at the SugarMynt Gallery in South Pasadena.

SaraRose Orlandini (Founder, SugarMynt Gallery):
The gallery is next door to the Michael Myers house [from *Halloween*]. It's the number-one thing we're known for, but we also have the original Book used in *Hocus Pocus* and original concept drawings from the film's illustrator, Giacomo Ghiazza. People can purchase the prints for twenty-five dollars, which are only sold here. Fans all get so excited when they find out we have the Book; it's a whole next level. I got a case dedicated specifically for the Book. You can tap it with your fingernails and go "BooOOOook" like Bette Midler does. Right now I don't have the Book, Bill took it back and he deserves to have it back once in a while, but when I see him I go, "I want my Book back!" When I held the Book, I mean, it was incredible.

Neil Cuthbert:

What's impressive about Hollywood is the incredible competence of all the people that make things and design things. You go into a room full of executives and it's a mixed bag, you know what I mean? But then when things really start getting made and all the people who actually make things show up, and you're sitting in a room full of incredible competence and talent, you feel like, "Wow, this is really something."

Cheri Minns:

The movie was a lot of work for a lot of people. There was a lot going on all the time. There was a lot of production value to the movie. . . . Kenny Ortega was a certain type of taskmaster, so you wanted to just do everything right so he didn't turn around and look at you, you know?

Omri Katz:

I think some of the coolest moments of filming *Hocus Pocus* were working in the Sanderson house. I wish they didn't tear it down. I wish they made it an attraction at one of the Disney parks. I'm sure people are kicking themselves now, but back then it was kind of, "Destroy it, on to the next one." Like, holy moly, man, you guys built all that and just to tear it all down? How sad.

William Sandell:

I have a funny story about that house. I was working at Universal on *The Flintstones*, which was Elizabeth Taylor's last film. One day, I'm standing on the set ready to hit the lights and get out of there and I hear screaming. Michael Jackson had arrived to see his friend Elizabeth Taylor, but she had just left. I'm the only one around so a completely shocked publicist from Universal asks if I could take Michael, his big bodyguard, and his little niece on a tour of the set. I say yes and Michael comes over to me and goes, "Bill, I'm really good friends with Kenny. I love *Hocus Pocus*. They're going to give me your *Hocus Pocus* house. I'm going to take the *Hocus Pocus* house to Neverland." Like, excuse me? I'm about to go into shock because here's Michael Jackson. I showed him around the set for an hour; he had a ball. Later on, I wondered what happened to the *Hocus Pocus* house because I never really knew, so I asked David Kirschner. I said, "Did Michael Jackson ever get the *Hocus Pocus* house?" David said, "No, he wanted it and we were going to send him the blueprints so he could build a *Hocus Pocus* house out on his ranch." Michael said he had the house, but no, he just wanted it.

Tony Gardner:

They offered David the house and he didn't say no right away. He thought about it. He's like, "Hmm, if I get rid of my swimming pool, it'll go all the way out to the walls of my yard, but maybe it'd be worth it." I have a feeling if he could have, he would've kept it.

David Kirschner:

It was an enormous discussion for Liz and I, and I think I made the mistake of saying this in front of our daughters, who would've been around twelve and ten at that point. I just remember them screaming and jumping up and down. The yard just wasn't big enough to house this giant thing.

Liz Kirschner:

We tried, but there was no way we were going to be able to put that in our yard with everything else we had in our yard. It was so upsetting. We would have kept it in a heartbeat if we could. It was like getting rid of a child, "What's gonna happen to it? They're gonna dismantle it and then it will be gone?"

Allison Dubrosky:

I have one of the blueprints from *Hocus Pocus* for the Sanderson sisters' house. It's one of the first things I added to my collection. It was actually an eBay find and I paid, like, sixty dollars for it. I verified it with Bill Sandell, whose name is on it. He said it was indeed one of the actual ones just based on how old it was and how it was rolled. He said, "Oh my God, I haven't seen that in twenty-six years!" The seller who sold it to me is probably kicking themselves. I'm sure that would go for a lot more these days, but I'm very glad to have it.

William Sandell:

We shot the trick-or-treating scenes in Whittier, home of Richard Nixon. It's an old town here outside of Los Angeles that has a kind of a historic district of older homes built at the turn of the twentieth century. When we had gotten back from shooting in Salem, it was late November, so when we went to Whittier it was almost Christmas. Everybody had their Christmas lights up. We had to pay them to take down their Christmas lights and put up Halloween decorations.

Rosemary Brandenburg:

I mean, some of them hire professionals to put their Christmas decorations up in those kinds of neighborhoods. So, it's, "Okay guys, we want to take them down just for a week or so." You know, they don't really have faith that you're going to get 'em back up the way they were, but that's the massaging that those location guys do. They massage the community to work with us and we manage to make it work.

William Sandell:

People come to historic Whittier to drive up the streets and see the holiday decorations. People were driving around the neighborhood seeing all these trick-or-treaters, orange lights, and pumpkins. We had a liaison at the Chamber of Commerce who was telling me they were getting calls like, "What's going on over there in Whittier?!"

Mary Vogt:

With *Hocus Pocus*, we got a lot of kids to play the trick-or-treaters who weren't movie kids, they were locals. The thing with kids is sometimes they will agree to wear something that you put on them, but they may not like it. They don't want to say anything because they're shy. What I would do is I would pick out four or five costumes and say, "Okay, you pick, which one do you like?" They really got into it. They would pick a hat from one costume or shoes from another and they would put it together better than I could! It worked out much better because no one looked like they were in a costume from Amazon.

Bonnie Bruckheimer:

My son is in a scene where they're trick-or-treating. He wanted to wear a ninja costume and wore a hood over his face. I said, "Honey, take off the hood." Nobody would ever see him in the movie because he insisted on wearing it, but he was five.

William Sandell:

My niece is in the film. She's the red-haired trick-or-treater who comes bustling out of a house in a shiny lavender skirt. Now, she's a doctor at Stanford. My sister saved all this money to put her through college.

Of course, these weren't the only family members who show up in the movie's trick-or-treating scenes. The late acclaimed directors and siblings Garry and Penny Marshall make uncredited cameos in the movie as a bickering couple whom the Sanderson sisters mistake for the Devil and his wife.

Kenny Ortega:

The idea of Garry and Penny coming in and playing these roles was so farfetched to me. I was an enormous fan of both of theirs, but, right off the bat, my casting folks were saying, "Don't get caught up on [casting them in the film], but why don't we try it?" Garry and Penny are just fun, good people, and they saw a good humor opportunity. We were very fortunate that their schedules and their interests made them available, and they were absolutely beyond wonderful to work with. The fun they had moving into the roles, getting into costume, and working with the other performers. I mean, they [were] just geniuses, both of them. It was just really an honor to be there. I didn't have to do much; I blocked the scenes and threw in a few bits of guidance and direction, but when you're working with talent like that it kind of happens all by itself. You just point the camera in the right place.

Rosemary Brandenburg:

All the pumpkins in those scenes were real. We had a lot of them because we needed them in New England and then in LA and Whittier. We bought a big raft of them and then carved them up as we needed them. Then we put them in a concrete room, but the shoot went on longer than expected or the schedule changed and they just started going. You'd pick one up and it would just fall to mush. It was just gross; they smelled horrible. Thank goodness we figured out that some people were freeze-drying pumpkins, but we had a big dumpster full of rotten pumpkins. It was pretty rough, but those are the little twists and turns and problem-solving that we ended up having to do. It's why I'm addicted to the work; I want to solve the problem. There's a lot of joy in it, but there's a lot of being a bit afraid of not getting it done. That hasn't left me, I can tell you that. I still work with plenty of anxiety trying to get it all done.

As stressful as the rotting pumpkins may have been for the crew, Kenny Ortega and the film's producers were dealing with bigger issues. Composer James Horner, who went on to score Titanic, *was forced to drop out of the project weeks before they were set to start recording. In came John Debney, a young composer who, in 1993, was looking for his big break. Now he's considered one of the most prolific and most successful composers in Hollywood.*

John Debney (Composer):

About two weeks before they were going to start recording [the score], James Horner had to leave the project, and Disney didn't know what to do. I had been working for the studio for a number of years doing a lot of television and theme park stuff, so they knew who I was. I met with the people in the music department at Disney, and one other person met with them, who is a friend of mine, actually. I went into the meeting, and they were kind of in a panic and said, "Would you be willing to do this project with someone else?" I said, "Yes, I would," which only made sense with the time constraints. Then, lo and behold, the other chap went into the meeting, and they asked him the same question. He said, "No, I don't want to work with anybody else. I can do it all myself." I guess they liked my answer, because I got the job.

David Kirschner:

I went to Jeffrey Katzenberg, and I said, "Look, as you know, James has bowed out. I'd definitely like John to do it." He said, "Who is that?" I said, "He works with me at Hanna-Barbera," thinking that might impress him. He said, "He does music for Saturday-morning cartoons? Not a chance." . . . He looked in my eyes when he said no. He was very honest about that stuff. But I wouldn't let this go. Finally, I had the support of the Disney music department, and that changed everything. Very reluctantly, Jeffrey said yes to this, and then, after hearing the score, Disney signed John to a three-picture deal.

John Debney:

Hocus Pocus basically launched my career. Two or three weeks [after I was hired], we were on the scoring stage. We recorded at night because I had to write during the day. I don't think I slept for two weeks. I got it done with a lot of coffee and a lot of prayer. I listened to "The Sorcerer's Apprentice" [scene in *Fantasia*] and a lot of John Williams scores that were in that magical vein. Kenny is just a dream to work with, but we didn't have a lot of time [to talk]. The one thing he told me—"John, remember this is really a musical. The ladies are dancing in every scene." I had to find the cadence and the rhythm; it was really a ballet. This was the first time I had personally been on the stage with an orchestra that big. It was ninety plus, and it was phenomenal from start to finish.

While the crew might have felt the stress of the big-budget production, the cast say Kenny Ortega made work fun.

Doug Jones:

Kenny was the popular kid in high school and invited all of us to join him at the lunch table. That's what it felt like. We were playing games, hanging out, and having fun. It was not a work environment, it was a play environment. He encouraged off-the-cuff singing and dancing around and tomfoolery.

Vinessa Shaw:

It definitely was like summer camp. In between takes, I just remember giggling so much and singing songs with Thora. We were singing [Charles & Eddie's] "Would I Lie to You?" and Jane's Addiction with the video playback guy.

Larry Bagby:

Thora was a lot of fun and so smart. She would be playing Hacky Sack with everybody and telling us what lenses the director was shooting. "Larry, this is your close-up, the money shot." She's like, "Is that a thirty-five-millimeter lens, Kenny?"

Doug Jones:

I was old enough to be Thora's dad. I was thirty-two when we were filming and she was ten or eleven. I think Vinessa and Omri were both just shy of eighteen. I felt like the weird uncle that they love when he comes to visit because he is not quite right. When you're dressed up in a big fluffy zombie costume and makeup, you're fun for kids to be around. But I loved the youthful exuberance they brought to the set. You can't be a jaded old actor when you're around that kind of fun-loving energy. I didn't feel like I was one of the kids, but I felt like I was certainly loved by the kids.

Thora Birch:

We were always so happy to see Doug. I remember feeling so bad for him because of all the things that he had to go through. They tortured this poor guy, but he had such a great personality and he was like a crazy uncle. We all loved him. Every time I see him, I always want to run up and give him a hug, but I still think he's going to break [like Billy].

Amanda Shepherd:

Kenny made it like a family. That was something that I wasn't used to. I had worked on many sets as a child, and I never experienced anything like that. I think that family environment translated into the film. He really set the tone. He made everyone feel special. It wasn't that he was trying to make somebody feel special for the sake of getting the best out of them. It was, "We're making a movie and we're going to have a great time."

Omri Katz:

We just had fun on set, like kids would normally do. *Home Improvement* was filming on the same lot, so I would go and play basketball with some of the *Home Improvement* kids. Sarah Jessica Parker had a puppy at the time, so I got to play with her pup a lot.

Vinessa Shaw:

We were right next door to the *Home Improvement* soundstage. I just remember Thora and I having a little bit of an ego, "We're on *Hocus Pocus*. It's a really cool movie with Bette Midler, Sarah Jessica Parker, and Kathy Najimy!" We felt like these three kids on *Home Improvement* were scrubs. Of course, we were just dissing-them-slash-flirting with them.

Thora Birch:

Every teen magazine at that time, it was always the same seven guys on the cover. JTT [Jonathan Taylor Thomas] and [*Boy Meets World* star] Rider Strong were in there somewhere. [The *Home Improvement* guys] ran around like they owned the fucking studio. I'm like, "We're in movies!"

Amanda Shepherd:

They gave tickets to Disneyland to all of the people that were shooting on the Disney lot and that included Elijah Wood, who was shooting *The Adventures of Huck Finn* in the studio next door. I had developed a big crush on him. I don't think he was into me at all, but we ended up becoming friends for a little while after that. I invited him to Disneyland and he and his sister rode with me and my mother. That's one of my best memories, going to Disneyland and hanging out with Elijah Wood.

Vinessa Shaw:

Elijah Wood was a peer and he was friendly. I thought, "Oh cool, he's a nice guy." I just remember us—Amanda, Omri, Larry, Tobias, me, I believe [actor who played Thackery Binx] Sean Murray, and Elijah Wood and his brother—eating a huge lunch together in the big pizzeria there. I kept dissing my mom for taking all these pictures and now I'm so forever grateful that she did.

Tobias Jelinek:
I remember Omri invited me to a Grateful Dead concert and I didn't go and that's my one regret of *Hocus Pocus.*

Larry Bagby:
I didn't get an invitation. I don't think I was cool enough. I think he was embarrassed of me showing up with my Vanilla Ice haircut.

Omri Katz:
Kenny was the choreographer of the Tubes, a band from the '70s. One of the members, Vince Welnick, was the keyboardist for the Grateful Dead at the time we were filming. Kenny knew what a big, huge fan I was and he was like, "Did you know, I know Vince well?" And I'm like, "Shut up. No way, man! This is insane!" And he's like, "Let's go stay with Vince and go to some shows and have some fun." Honestly, still today I'm a little in shock that I got to experience that and meet all the band members and be backstage and just get that VIP treatment. I really connected with Kenny a lot. I probably spent more time with him than anybody else on set.

Vinessa Shaw:
I went to public school at the time when I was doing *Hocus Pocus.* I had a class that was career-planning-slash-driver's-ed. The semester that I was doing *Hocus Pocus* was the career-planning section and I got a lesser grade in my class because my class participation was low. I was like, "But I'm doing my career?" It was the weirdest thing, but it was also the moment when I realized, "Oh dang, I'm making more money than my teacher and he is a little pissed," you know?

Tobias Jelinek:
I was still fifteen when we were shooting in Los Angeles. Larry and my birthdays are close, both Pisces, but he had turned eighteen. We were

really hitting it off and my mother had taken time off work and it was starting to get a little tricky because we had to come up from Santa Barbara. At a certain point, Larry and I came up with the brilliant idea that since he was now eighteen and legally an adult, she could sign guardianship over to Larry.

Larry Bagby:
I was his guardian. It was like the blind leading the blind.

Omri Katz:
I'm not shy or embarrassed or going to fake the truth. I was high, I want to say, 99 percent of the time [while filming]. Unless I said something, most people couldn't tell. I definitely drew the pot leaf in Max's notebook. That was really what was going on in my life. I was experimenting with cannabis at the time. That was an instant love affair that I had with cannabis and I'm still a cannabis user and have my own cannabis business.

Vinessa Shaw:
I'm his age so I knew he was high most of the time. I remember I hadn't gotten my driver's license yet so my mother was driving me. Omri's a month older than me so he'd already gotten his and he's driving down the freeway in a VW bus with Grateful Dead stickers all over it. He was wearing a tie-dye shirt, kind of à la Max. Anyway, I look over and he is taking a big old puff, so even if I had only an inkling, it was kind of hard to deny what I saw. He was getting ready to go to work, having his morning toke. My mom and I were like, "Hello, we can see you!" and he was just like, thumbs-up, "It's a good day!"

Tobias Jelinek:
I would never go to set stoned, are you kidding me? *Never.* But one day Omri convinced me in his trailer to smoke some weed before we went to

a rehearsal with Kenny Ortega. I could not hang, I could not handle it. I remember showing up to this rehearsal and I couldn't remember lines.

Larry Bagby:

I was not aware of this, but I was very innocent growing up. I grew up Mormon. I didn't even feel comfortable smoking a cigarette in the film. We changed it to "Do you have any smokes?" which I appreciate Kenny understanding. I think Disney probably appreciates that now, too.

Omri Katz:

There was one occasion where I was high and I was just not hitting my marks and Kenny called me out in front of everybody. That definitely was extremely embarrassing and it was a wake-up call 100 percent. . . . I've always had a really good work ethic. I want to make sure that I'm not the person that's messing everything up.

Larry Bagby:

I always had a video camera around, but I didn't know I wasn't supposed to be filming on set. One time we got caught while we were waiting to film the cage scenes.

Tobias Jelinek:

I just remember it was a semi-traumatic experience for Larry. He had, for those days, a very high-tech large and oversized camera. It was an ungodly sight. He would bring it on set, which I'm glad he did because now there's all this behind-the-scenes footage, but we were in the witches' lair. We were at the cauldron and I remember we showed up one day to watch Bette work and it was fantastic. I think this was actually the moment where they were casting the initial spell and it was the three of them. After a take, Larry whips out his camera and he's going around and I think he was mesmerized by Bette so he just kind of held the camera on her and she sensed it. You know, when you're driving a car and you can sense someone looking at you a lane over? She sensed that there was a camera and it was not the right camera. She whipped her head around, which by the way has been recorded, and she stares at the camera and she's like, "Who's that and what are you doing?" You see Larry, because again this footage exists, quickly roll the camera and he's suddenly looking down at the ground, just breathing heavily.

Larry Bagby:

Kenny's like, "What are you doing, Larry? You can't film without permission." We hadn't done our scenes with the witches yet so I felt like I might have been on her bad side from the get-go. She was kind of intimidating. I mean, that was the biggest film in my career at that point and it was huge.

Mary Vogt:

One day I said to Bette's dresser, "I want to play a joke on Bette." Her dresser goes, "This is not the day for jokes. She's in a really bad mood. Do not play any jokes on Bette today." I said, "I have to, I can't stop myself." She goes, "Okay, well, you're going in on your own." We had these little puppets [of the Sanderson sisters] that were re-created for the flying scenes. I had someone re-create the costumes for them, small little costumes, and they did a beautiful job. I went into Bette's trailer and I was hiding this little costume behind my back and she was getting made up and everyone was walking on eggshells around her because she was in a really bad mood. I said, "Hi Bette. I have some bad news for you." She goes, "What? What bad news?" I said, "Well, we sent your costume out to the dry cleaner and unfortunately it shrunk." I showed her the tiny dress and she laughed so hard she literally fell off her makeup stool.

Kevin Haney:

There was an incident where Kathy and Sarah Jessica had gone to a spa for the weekend. They had facial peels, and they came in on Monday and we did the [old-age makeup] stipple. Sarah says, "Is this supposed to burn?" It's not supposed to burn. Bette looked at me and went, "Well, I'm fine. I must be a tough old bird." Because of the facials Sarah Jessica didn't have any protective layer for the stipple. The next day, she came back after recuperating and everything was fine.

Tony Gardner:

Doug always wore this horrible velour tracksuit for us to do his makeup in because it was comfortable and easy to get on and off. He didn't care if he got stuff on it so it had all these, like, makeup stains on it from different projects he'd worked on. One day they wrapped Billy at around lunchtime, so we said goodbye to everybody and we went into our little trailer and took Doug out of the makeup. They're still filming so he says, "I want to go watch people shoot. I want to watch the rest of the scene. This will be really fun." Doug's hair is shorter [than Billy's] and now it's greasier because it has makeup remover in it. His face has been scrubbed so he looks a little raw and a little blotchy and he's wearing this horrible velour tracksuit and he's on set trying to talk to the kids. They eventually key into who he is, but all these adults on the crew were like, "Who's that creepy dude trying to talk to the kids?" They're trying to call security and stuff 'cause nobody's ever seen Doug out of makeup and he doesn't look good. They're trying to get him booted off set and Kenny Ortega looks at him and goes, "Oh, that's Doug Jones!" It was so funny; he went to say hi and he almost got arrested.

Doug Jones:

I have a 1980s jogging suit that is white polyester with black sleeves and a gold stripe that connects the black to the white. Very '80s! The elastic in the white pants wore out quickly so I replaced the bottoms with a pair of gray sweatpants from Kmart, while still wearing the original zippered top to every acting job I worked on that involved a creature makeup or costume. This became my getting-ready-for-work outfit starting in the late 1980s when I was still doing those original "Mac Tonight" commercials for McDonald's. As the years wore on, that jogging suit looked more and more weathered. Even with frequent laundering, those stains will never come out. So when I am going to and from work with my human face showing, I get looks from people in my dilapidated clothes. That would include the story Tony Gardner told about me stopping by the set one day to say hi as myself. Most of the crew had only seen me as Billy, so there I was looking like some random tall, skinny guy who had just snuck in off the street in an old, ill-fitted sweat suit.

Omri Katz:

I want to say, while filming the movie, Vinessa and I had a somewhat flirtatious relationship or an attraction to each other. There wasn't really much work involved behind the scenes in order to create that on-screen chemistry. I think her and I just naturally had that bond right from the get-go. I think we both had mini crushes on each other.

Vinessa Shaw:

Omri and I both had boyfriends and girlfriends at the time, but we had good chemistry. There's a scene where I talk about salt being a way to protect yourself from a zombie or an old boyfriend. Omri and I did a screening together and I noticed that I was blushing in that scene. I turned to him and said, "That's so funny. I was blushing. I think I had a crush on you!" He's like, "I think I had a crush on you too!" So it finally came out.

Omri Katz:

Even now, she's a really easy person to talk to that gets me and I feel like I get her. Our lives have taken completely different paths, but it's still there. The bond and the magic is still there between us. It's a beautiful thing.

Chapter 9

TALKING CATS, TRAINED MOTHS, AND FLYING WITCHES, OH MY!

*T*o create a talking cat and a flying vacuum, the film's special effects team had to use every trick they had up their sleeves—and then create some new ones. In 1992, computer-generated graphics, better known as CGI, was still in its infancy, so most of the effects in Hocus Pocus were practical effects or effects created on set without the use of computers. The witches really flew and Billy really coughed up those moths, but Binx was quite a cinematic feat. To create the talking cat, the special effects team used a combination of live cats trained by Gary Gero and Larry Madrid, animatronic cats made by Tony Gardner and his team, and early CGI technology, which led to Disney animator Chris Bailey earning the singular title of "Cat Animation Supervisor."

Chris Bailey (Cat Animation Supervisor):

[Executive producer] Ralph Winter was really the one that I dealt with the most and he explained to me how we were making our cat. "We have the cat animation wranglers, the real cat wranglers, then we have these guys making an animatronic puppet and the stuffies, and then we have our CG cat." He sort of drew them as three little boxes on a piece of paper and then he put me in the middle and he said, "We see you being here, so you'll be working with all these people to pull them all together into one performance."

Ralph Winter:

We had trained cats, which I think is an oxymoron, but they were trained to do different things. It was a bit more than maybe what the studio had anticipated, but Disney has a history of movies about kids and animals, so they were willing to go along with it.

Larry Madrid (Head Animal Trainer):

In '92, I was the manager at the animal show at Universal Studios Hollywood, and I was training animals for movies and television. I was just kind of starting out in Hollywood, so my boss went and secured the movie. He told me that the black cats that I had were going to be the stars.

I had already started training them so we had the advantage. However, we only had two cats, so we had to put a team of cats together. I think we ended up with six or eight cats total. With any kind of acting you need somebody that has talent and then you need to mold that talent.

Vinessa Shaw:
You can only teach a cat one trick. Dogs you can teach many, but there was only one cat for one thing that Binx would do. Binx is literally a piecing together of many cats. There's a jumping cat, a jumping-on-your-shoulder cat, a sleeping cat, a cat that would jump on the book, and a cat that would just meow and sit.

Chris Bailey:
There was the cat that would heel, the cat that would walk with the gang, the cat that would sit perfectly still, the cat that would paw, and there was the one that would hiss. To make an animal hiss they have to be scared and you don't want to be traumatizing the cats, so [*Hocus Pocus*'s animal trainer] Gary Gero said, "You know, I always wanted to just put a hiss [sound] over a cat meowing and see if that would work." I just went back to my office one day and said, "Hey, could you take this little piece of video with the cat meowing and put a cat hiss on it." Of course it looked brilliant. Gary saw it and was like, "Oh my God, this is perfect!" I trust that he used that tool in the future to convince people that you don't have to terrorize the cat to get a nice hiss.

Larry Madrid:
I always tell everybody, if you want to train an animal, make a simple list, start with five basic behaviors that you want to teach them. Don't move on to the next one until you finish the first one. In the process of doing that, you learn lots of things about your animal and your animal learns lots of things about you. . . . You use a buzzer to mean "food." Then you use a clicker, and the clicker means "good." You can feed them for

all their good tricks and they'll learn to associate those sounds and your mannerisms with the trick. They'll learn to come here and go get on a mark like a dog. But you have to remember, they're not dogs, they're cats.

Vinessa Shaw:

Thora didn't really like the cats, but I liked the cats. I didn't grow up with cats in the house, so I found it fascinating. The cats were trained by their trainer, but then we would come in and have to rehearse the scene with the cats. We would have a buzzer and we'd buzz through the scene and give them treats. There was a clicker, too, depending on which one that cat responded to. I'm sure the sound department hated that.

Thora Birch:

I just hated the cat. First of all, there were four or five different cats we were working with. Then there were the puppeteer cats and then there was the non-cat, the X on the light stand that we were looking at for the CGI. I preferred the CGI cat to the animatronic one. Every time the cat was in a scene, it was a big fucking deal. It really killed my vibe, man. You're dealing with on-set trainers who are getting their actors to perform, which involves a lot of buzzing and clicking and treat-giving. It messes up the flow of the scene. Dani had to be the most in love with it and I'm not even a cat person, I'm a dog person, but I had to love this cat.

Vinessa Shaw:

I can't imagine what this trainer went through. I would've been pulling my hair out. You're working with teenagers and a ten-year-old and the ten-year-old's like, "Do I have to do it?" It's a lot for a child to remember their lines and then train this cat. But I was like, "I'll do it!" I was always the one that volunteered to work with the cats.

Larry Madrid:

All of those cats featured in the movie, we got from the pound. We went and rescued them so that they could have a good life and a good home.

Amanda Shepherd:

For years and years, I thought that I owned the cat that played Binx. I told everybody, "This is Binx!" I didn't find out until years later that my mom totally tricked me.

Chris Bailey:

I remember shooting the scene right when the witches come to life and Omri's running along, he slips and falls and Binx jumps on his chest, hits him in the face, and says, "Hey, snap out of it!" I storyboarded that and Kenny liked it, but he said, "Well, it looks kind of cartoony." I said "Yeah, I'm a Disney animator, sorry, but the guys say the cat can do it." He said, "Well, can you show me?" So I took my personal video camera and worked with the cat wranglers and we just staged the shot with the cat. It gave Kenny confidence that the gag would work. At that point, I stopped drawing boards and I would just shoot these little scenes with the real cat to stage these bits.

Larry Madrid:

You have to have a certain look for your actor. It's the same thing for an animal actor. It's a certain look that you want to represent. Finding the double for the cat is really difficult. None of the cats, if you put them side by side, except for their color, actually looked alike. But you could never tell because you never shoot 'em in the movie together.

Thora Birch, 2018:

I think *Hocus Pocus* was where I first heard the W. C. Fields saying "Never work with children or animals." Then I kept hearing it, like,

"You know what W. C. Fields says?" Yeah, I know what W. C. Fields says, thanks. Just throw us in with the animals.

Omri Katz:

There was a moment in the beginning of the movie where Vinessa and I open the spell book and then Binx jumps on the book to close it. That cat had a really difficult time doing the trick. I think we did ten-plus takes. We had these clickers and these cat treats and we're just trying to get this cat to do this one trick and it just didn't want to cooperate.

Vinessa Shaw:

The cat was supposed to jump on the book and close it and also bat our face and kind of wag its finger at us even though it doesn't have one. So the cat had two things to do, which was challenging: jump on the book and then paw at us. That took multiple takes. I remember at the time, Binx had to say, "Nothing good can come from this book." I just remember us doing it over and over again. The cat would jump, do too much batting and then Sean Murray [who initially voiced Binx] would go, "Nothing good can come from this book." We finally got it and cut for lunch. I just remember repeating that line over and over again to my mom at lunchtime, "Nothing good can come from this book. Nothing good can come from this book. Nothing good can come from this book." My mom was laughing, but I was entranced. It became seared in my brain. Now that's the one line I remember more than any other in the movie.

Larry Madrid:

We had the cat jump on Bette Midler's shoulder for one scene and [then she would] spin around with the cat. I had to make sure that the cat was going to do it every time the same way no matter what was going on. We'd rehearsed it with our trainers and we'd rehearsed it with the stunt doubles. Bette came in and she was a trooper. She did a great job—and the cats did their job, too! We showed her how to hold on to them to give them confidence when she's spinning around so they'd stay up on her shoulder and not freak out and fly off. That was a big challenge, but a lot of fun. She was really a trooper.

Chris Bailey:

There was one day where the editor was cutting the scene after Binx had been turned into the cat. I said, "Can I ask a question?" This is like an old, seasoned Hollywood guy and he's listening to this stupid animator guy. I said, "Well, I'm curious, why didn't you cut to a shot of the cat trying to get his dad's attention? Like pawing at him or running around his legs?" He said, "Well, I don't have one," and I said, "Well, I'm shooting a second unit tonight, I can get one for you." We talked with wardrobe about who would fit in the pilgrim shoes and be a good match for [Thackery Binx's] dad and it turned out that was me. It was my on-screen debut, a close-up of my leg, kind of pushing Binx out of the way. I had a framed picture of that on my wall for a number of years.

Tony Gardner:

I remember the day that we were filming the bus running over the cat. They wanted a cat to sit there as the bus approached so we had our animatronic one ready for the shot. All the cables came out of its rear end and went into a hole in the asphalt so that we could operate it. The cat is looking around and then it sees the bus and its ears go up and it sort of backs up a little bit. Larry Madrid, the animal trainer, said, "Well, I've trained one to sit there and let a tire come up on it. Let's try it." It was amazing. The cat sat there and the bus came straight up to it and stopped right in front of it. I was like, "You don't need us if you have Larry Madrid!"

Larry Madrid:

I remember that I was challenged by that scene, but I knew I could do it and I wanted to do it. Of course, it was totally safe. The big thing is the cat has to trust you and you have to train him to make sure that he knows what you're asking him to do. Buses make a lot of scary sounds and you can't have any of those noises when you're filming. The movement of the bus and the size of it, the lights, it didn't really affect the cat. He didn't really care because we had trained him to stay. That's why I love my job. If you do your homework and you train the animals and they get used to these situations, they can do things that people don't expect them to do. I think they ended up using the animatronic cat in the movie, but that's okay, we still did it.

Chris Bailey:

I think maybe we don't give the cats enough credit. I think there's a frustration that can come with working with an animal, but really we got most of our cat scenes in three or four takes. It very rarely took longer than that. The big thing that I learned with training a cat is that it's about repetition. They're not as smart as a dog. You have to kind of train this behavior and then keep working it to get them to repeat it.

William Sandell:

It's not dogs and children that are difficult to work with, like W. C. Fields once said, it's animatronic puppets. There is so much downtime. I worked with [director] Joe Dante on *Gremlins* and I remember him just sitting in his chair as they set things up. I said, "God, how do you do it, Joe?" He said, "This is the nature of the beast. I'm gonna sit here for maybe forty-five minutes while everybody rigs the next little gremlin to do its next little gremlin thing." It really is the nature of the beast. You're sitting there waiting for things to happen, but boy, when they do, it can be magical.

Tony Gardner:

From the very beginning, all the talks about animatronic Binx were, "Besides all the talking Binx stuff, we're going to need opposable Binxes and inflatable Binxes." It was an army of fake cats and some of them only did one thing. We had to match the animatronic cat to the real cat and then we were told there were probably going to be about twenty cats used in the film because each one of those cats would literally only do one thing really well. We kind of had to come up with sort of an amalgam of all those cats to figure out what one particular close-up of the cat would look like.

Larry Madrid:

If Tony needed the cats to come down to set so he could take measurements of their fur, their skeletons, their heads, anything he needed to do to make the animatronic animal, we were there to help him achieve that. For what he could do with the animatronic cats, they looked amazing. I ended up keeping one of the animatronic cats that doubled my cat. For many years after that movie, I'd just bring my Binx cat in and I'd set him up in front of the camera to use as a stand-in for a real cat. They'd light him and set it all up, and then I'd take him back and put him in my truck, and then I'd bring the real cat out and we'd do the shot.

Chris Bailey:

No matter how good the animatronic stuff looked, I felt like I could hear the servos inside it, like, *vroom, vroom.* The animatronic cat talking or acting didn't have quite the same feel. I think ultimately there aren't many shots left of it in the film because it really stuck out, but Tony Gardner and his team made the cat that blew up on the ground when Binx was run over by the truck. It was a wonderful cat and those guys were great.

Jessie Wolfson:

I remember watching the bus go over Binx while visiting the set with my dad and being scared. My dad said, "No, no, no." He was always trying to explain how everything works. I saw how Chucky was fake and the animatronics of it, but when you're watching it as a kid, it kind of looks real. Even though we were seeing the cameras and the dollies, I remember being concerned about Binx.

Tony Gardner:

The design concept for the animatronic cat in the beginning was to embrace the fact that Binx had been a human boy. They really wanted him to be able to articulate and talk with his hands and be very human in his body language. It was really cool as a robot when it didn't have fur on it. Once fur went on it, and it was obviously a cat, some people had problems seeing a cat being very expressive with its arms and pointing in different directions. They felt like it got a little too fantastical, which is funny because we're talking about a talking cat that used to be a boy.

While working on the army of animatronic Binxes, Gardner's team was also working on a practical effect that would make it look as if the cat was talking.

Tony Gardner:

We had sort of borrowed a page from the effects work on the movie *Gremlins*. All the gremlins had these really tiny heads, but then when they wanted to shoot close-ups of them they had a head that was like three feet across so that all the detail would hold up in camera in close-up. We built this one Binx head that had eyeballs that were a foot across. It was this giant head. We realized that we could build it as a suit and one of the other mechanical designers, Bill Sturgeon, built it on himself. We shot all this great stuff in the shop, like, forced perspective à la *Lord of the Rings* and you could see the face in extreme close-up making really subtle expressions. We shot a bunch of video tests in our shop, which were super successful and really cool, really simple, and, the key word, really cheap. The studio asked us to bring it in for a camera test when we were doing Billy's first camera test, but the cat head wasn't finished. We didn't have ears on it so we cut out pieces of cardboard in the shape of his ears and stuck those on it just to fill it out. I remember a couple of executives saying, "The ears really don't look very realistic. Are they gonna be that color? It almost looks like cardboard." Everything just derailed at that point. They're like, "We don't know how we could use this. What would we have as the background?" Nobody really had that much experience in this yet so we kept saying, "Well, the background would be blown out of focus. It could just be a green screen and it could be a photo you take on set." We're trying to bring people up to speed, but it was very daunting. It was an interesting process because everything was being figured out while we were filming. CG technology sort of came into being while we were making the movie. *Terminator 2* came out in 1991 and the liquid-metal guy all of a sudden had everybody saying, "Oh my God, we could do really cool stuff!" CG then became a larger part of what we were doing.

Chris Bailey, then an animator at Disney, was tasked with figuring out the best solution for Hocus Pocus*'s talking cat problem, which led him to Rhythm & Hues Studios, the visual effects and animation company that would go on to win an Academy Award for making farm animals talk in the 1995 film* Babe.

Chris Bailey:
Peter Schneider, who was president of Walt Disney Feature Animation, said that some producers wanted to talk with me about *Hocus Pocus*. They were doing tests about how to make the cat talk and they weren't confident on which way to go. He knew I had a little bit of CGI background and when I met with them, they showed me three tests that were done by three different special effects houses. One was that technique of painting talking mouths on the footage. Another was using the live cat's footage, warping it, and then putting a 3-D mouth on there, which we've seen a lot of in the years since. Then there was a third test that entailed putting a CG cat's head on the real cat's head. I came in and just gave my opinion, which was that painting talking mouths, no matter how well they were

done, would feel old-fashioned because we saw it, like, a hundred years ago. The CG one was personally my favorite because you can actually tilt the head and you can turn it when you want. Not that you can't get the real cat to do those things, but when you're locked into that timing you don't have a lot of flexibility later on. They asked me to work with each of the three houses, which included Rhythm & Hues, who were on the forefront of CGI, and had done the 3-D head.

Colin Brady (Animator: Binx the Cat):

I went to CalArts, which was Walt Disney's school of animation, and my dream was to work at Pixar. They weren't quite ready to launch their first feature film when I graduated, which, of course, became *Toy Story*. But Rhythm & Hues, then just a local computer-animation company, was hiring. John Hughes, different from the one who did *Ferris Bueller's Day Off*, was the founder of Rhythm & Hues. I had so much respect for him and grew a lot from working with him. Every Friday he would be very open with the financial situation of the company; we always knew exactly how much money we had in the bank. He was also a big believer in vitamins, so there was all the vitamins you ever wanted in the office, as well as peanut butter and jelly sandwiches. That year [working at Rhythm & Hues] became a graduate year for me in computer animation. We were already talking about creating talking animals. When *Hocus Pocus* came up as a possible thing, it was just a really, really good fit.

Steven Haft:

Rhythm & Hues were a sort of start-up at the time, doing TV commercials and things. The decision we made [to use Rhythm & Hues instead of Disney's in-house effects team] had some significant financial consequences. It freed up money to do other things. If we had done the CGI at Disney, it would have been much more costly. I authorized that we gamble on Rhythm & Hues, which saved some of the money that I knew was going to go into overshoots because Kenny wouldn't finish on time. We were taking a chance on Rhythm & Hues. They were less proven, but they did an amazing job.

Ralph Winter:

Getting the cat right was something we had to fight for. It was sort of new ground and no one had really done what we were doing with a talking cat. *Babe* would come out after us and so we were testing and trying things along with Rhythm & Hues. I don't think the cat had that many speaking lines, but it was a complicated process between animatronics, CGI, and real cats. We had to make you believe that the cat could talk. That was probably one of our biggest challenges. No one at the studio that I was in touch with cared about advancing technology.

Chris Bailey:

I remember when we presented the new footage there were a bunch of producers there. I forget who the brain trust was, but we showed the 2-D mouth test first, and it was all the same piece of dialogue for all three tests, and they weren't thrilled. Then there was the 2-D test with the 3-D mouth and it was like, "Oh!" It got everybody's attention. Then when the Rhythm & Hues test came up, the cat was actually turning his head and squinting his eyes. They were all like, "Ooh!" I could tell that there was enthusiasm there and they felt good about that approach.

Creating a realistic looking cat face using computer animation proved to be quite tricky.

Chris Bailey:

We had an issue at the beginning with the cat's mouth and his teeth, it wasn't working for anybody. The conversation became very circular: Are the fangs too sharp? Are they too long? Are they not long enough? Are they not sharp enough? Are they too wide? Are they too white? Not white enough? Once I got into it a little deeper and took a look at the

CG model, I saw that they were modeled more like really nice werewolf fangs. After looking at a real cat's mouth, I realized they weren't fitting together the way a real cat's teeth do.

Tony Gardner:

I think one of the things realized early on was that a cat's mouth is designed with a permanent sort of smile to it. The teeth that become visible were super scary to people. So we had to go in and literally file the canines down on the animatronic one. They would do a lot of mouth replacement on the CG cat and would actually almost eliminate those teeth entirely.

Chris Bailey:

No one would have made the comment that the teeth were too scary if they were actually more natural to the cat. The cat's head told you it was a real cat. The cat's body told you it was a real cat. Then the teeth said, "Oh, that's a CG model of a cat." Once we realized this, it was, "Oh my God, we can't go back. It's too much money," which you hear on every movie. But this cat is arguably the star of the movie, so they cracked open their wallets and they remodeled the teeth so his mouth looked just fine.

Larry Madrid:

Chris was from the CGI world. He had to make the cats because we were pioneering a new technology in '92. I didn't realize the scope of it then, but I was interested in the process. I would do anything I could to help him make the best cat that he could make for the movie. If he needed me to come down and take pictures of the cat or videotape the cat, that's what I did. I think the end result is pretty amazing. We fought a lot to make sure that the real cat could work as much as possible, but when they write things that we can't do, then we need help and that's what CGI is there for. The effects teams do a great job and they got better at it since then. I can still tell when CGI animals are on camera, but they've done so much better with it over the course of these thirty years. *Hocus Pocus* was the early stage of CGI animals and Chris was a big part of that.

Neil Cuthbert:

One of the notes that came down while we were doing the rewrites: "Not so much talking cat. Cut back on the talking cat." I was like, "What do you mean? The talking cat's great!" Well, it turns out that CGI back in 1992 was really expensive. Now it's lunch money, it's nothing, but then a talking cat was a major expense so it was "less talking cat."

Chris Bailey:

People wanted to see more of the cat in the film. I remember that. We'd have dailies and people were very excited to see the finished shots. When you show the early shots, everyone's like, "Is this gonna stink?" It's so raw when you see the CG and then when you all of a sudden throw a couple finals in there, they're like, "Oh wait. This is gonna be all right!"

Tony Gardner:

I think the notoriety of the digital cat face was a big deal at the time because the *T2* liquid guy is walking through flame and doing amazing stuff, but this was the first time something was carrying sustained dialogue. It was a great place for this technology to sort of get its trial run. It's cool that it worked so well. They took a real cat and an animatronic cat and this budding digital effects concept, pulled those three things together, and not only made it work, but also built a character out of it. I think the choice of casting for the voice was really key to making him a real character.

Sean Murray played the human version of Thackery Binx in the film, but it's Jason Marsden's voice that is heard throughout the movie. Marsden voiced both Binx the cat and the human version of the character, dubbing over all of Murray's dialogue.

Jason Marsden:

I remember reading for Max and being introduced to what the story was. We didn't get a full script, of course, but it sounded intriguing. I didn't get very far with that role because it was cast with my friend Omri, who I knew from working on *Eerie, Indiana* together. A couple months after they wrapped the film, I got a call to audition for *Hocus Pocus* again. This time for the voice of Thackery. I don't think it was explained to me that I was replacing anybody or filling in for Sean Murray. It was just an audition. I read for it, got a callback, and next thing I knew I was on the Disney soundstage looping the cat.

Omri Katz:

He and I had just worked on *Eerie, Indiana* together. However, I don't think I had any influence in him getting the part. He came on board after the movie was filmed. I think they just realized that Sean Murray's voice didn't seem to fit the timeline of the movie, which was the 1600s. They wanted a more English type of accent, and Jason, being a voice actor, just nailed things like that.

Jason Marsden:

Sean was hired to play human Thackery and voice Binx, so they animated most of Binx around his performance, which is traditionally how it's done. I had to just put my voice where Sean's voice would be. It was explained to me before the audition that Binx is a teenage boy from colonial Salem, so I'm sure he's freshly immigrated, probably from Ireland or Britain. Not too heavy of an accent, so I pitched him up a little bit to have that sort of youthful sound and gave him sort of an English lilt. In hindsight, I wish I had maybe done a little bit more work on it. Sometimes the accent falls short, like, "Am I Australian? What the heck am I doing?"

But it's kind of a game. They show you the clip so you get a feel for it, and then the engineer places three beeps in to help you keep time. Where the fourth beep should be is your cue to go. You're kind of prompted so it's like beep, beep, beep, "Max, get away from that spell book!" Chris Bailey, the gentleman who is in charge of Binx's animation, was such an important part of the process. Sometimes I thought I would nail it, but I was like half a frame off. Only his eyes saw it, not mine.

Chris Bailey:

You play it back and you go, "Ah, it looks like he opened his mouth a frame too early." The animator is actually sitting at their computer and within their file they've got the film of the real cat. They have their CG heads sitting in front of that screen that's in the computer and then they can scrub through the dialogue so they know exactly when the cat says, "Halloween night," when to pop its eyes for "night." Their rhythm is really driven by the dialogue.

Jason Marsden:

Some people thought that I was doing the voice because Sean Murray couldn't do the accent. That wasn't true. I've seen that reported and I hope I didn't spread that erroneously somehow because that's not the case at all. It wasn't because he was doing anything wrong; Sean's a great actor. It was a sound they were looking for and the only way to marry the two was to have another actor do it. This kind of thing does happen more often than you would think. If you remember the Tim Burton movie *Ed Wood*, there's a scene where Ed meets Orson Welles, played by Vincent D'Onofrio, who is an amazing actor, but he was dubbed by Maurice LaMarche, most notably the Brain of *Pinky and the Brain*. So it happens.

Steve Voboril:

I remember Kenny telling me, "Well, the producers think his voice sounds too young for an elderly cat." I don't know if they even brought

Sean in to try to do an English accent, but, at the time, I felt bad. I thought, *Well, there goes his career!* Little did I know, thirty years later, he'd be on *NCIS*.

Sean Murray ("Thackery Binx"), 2018:

They weren't exactly sure what they wanted to do with Binx. They originally wanted a sort of California vibe with the voice, and then at some point thought [they] should do it Olde English. I'm not a voice actor; I couldn't do an English accent, I'd never been trained to do that, and I was young. [Jason Marsden] is a great guy! So it's never bothered me.

Jason Marsden:

I did feel a little uneasy at the time. I actually haven't spoken to Sean since [*Hocus Pocus*] . . . I hope that they told him before the movie came out. I've always thought that he and I both collaborated on one role, what a gift.

As impressive as Binx may be, many of the film's most memorable stunts were achieved without CGI.

Peggy Holmes:

The flying is all practical. It's all in camera. [Special effects coordinator] Terry Frazee and his special effects team did such a great job sort of creating these unique rigs to use on this movie.

Carolyn Soper (Visual Effects Producer):

Terry Frazee's job, that's a different kind of stress. You not only have the timing and the crew waiting for you, but you have to make sure that Bette Midler doesn't fall on her ass.

Mary Vogt:

The actresses wore harnesses, and back then, the harnesses were not very comfortable. Cirque du Soleil really revolutionized harnesses. Now they're super sleek corsets, but back then we had harnesses that were made by the special effects department. They didn't care about how it looked, they cared about safety. I don't know how this evolved, but they took a pair of blue jeans, the old-style heavy Levi's jeans because blue jeans are very strong, and cut off the legs. They kept the waist exactly the same and they put metal plates on either side with bolts that came out. Then they hook the wires onto the bolts and when you pull up, it goes up in the crotch. That's why they put lambswool in there. I mean, it's very uncomfortable. I think we gave the girls padded bike shorts to try to give them something under their skirts, but they were really bulky.

Peggy Holmes:

You don't want to ever notice that you have a harness on so we worked a lot at the beginning on takeoffs and landings. I'm super proud of the girls and of us because we show that on camera and that's really hard to do. Part of it was just learning how to lift your body so that we don't see you get lifted. It takes an intense amount of strength in your core and it takes an intense amount of timing. It's coordinating with your handler and you two getting in lockstep about how it should go. There's always a little lag time on the wind of the wire, so it's really this very intense rhythmic rehearsal. You just need to do it over and over, but you can only be in the harness for so long because it really starts to hurt your rib cage and your hips.

Bette Midler, 1993:

I can't say it was a blast. It hurt like hell, but there were certain things that were kind of fabulous. The director was having a fight with someone and he was way over on the other side of the stage, so I had the fly man pull me up so I could look over and see who was fighting. I was spying on my broom. It was great.

Steven Haft:

She's talking about me and Kenny, so if you're asking how the job got done, the answer was, it was every day and it was occasionally bloody. The role of inglorious bastard fell to me. I was trying to keep it on time, which was impossible. One realized in a matter of minutes that "on time" was not something that Kenny Ortega could do. But within budget? If it's not on time, then how else do you do it?

Carolyn Soper:

I worked at BVVE, which was Buena Vista Visual Effects, the Disney in-house visual effects company. We had been awarded *Hocus Pocus*, which was great for us. It was definitely of an ilk, mostly because of Bette Midler, but it felt like it was under-budgeted. Ralph Winter will not like to hear this, but, at that point in time, we were able to charge [for] wire removal. The actors were hung on wires on the set and sometimes you could see the wires, and it needed to be removed. Well, in the old days, that was an incredibly labor-intensive process. You would have to take physical photographs of every single frame and then a person would have to go and draw a matte to cut out where the wire was and then you'd have to re-photograph it again without creating any kind of line. It was very, very, very difficult. It didn't end up looking perfect and it was very laborious. So we, along with everybody else, started to charge for wire removal by the second. I think it was like a thousand dollars a second or something like that. So let's say you had a twenty-four second shot, that was $24,000, it was money in the bank. This did not last very long.

Ralph Winter:

I think the flying was rudimentary, but we tried to make the most of that.

Kathy Najimy, 1993:

After I was cast, they told me I would fly, but I hadn't really given it much thought. I guess I thought they'd do it with animation. When it came time to actually fly, I was really excited. I loved it. There's a danger but it's really fun. It feels like swimming or sailing or being weightless. Everyone dreams of flying, and this was a great feeling of going fast and being free.

Mary Vogt:

I remember Sarah [Jessica Parker] up there reading the *New York Times*, which was surprising because it couldn't have been comfortable.

Sarah Jessica Parker, 2018:

I could fit an entire *New York Times* up the back of the corset. And I found that the harness was comfortable, so I would just sit up there and read the *Times* while people took their breaks or changed the camera and sometimes went to lunch.

Doug Jones:

Watching these three grown women acting like kids flying around the room, it added a whole new element of fun. They were all loving the flying experience so much.

Kenny Ortega:

It was a hoot, but it was hard and demanding. We didn't have the visual effects and the wire rigs that exist in filmmaking today. A lot of this was [done with] pulleys and ropes and erasing things later. It was tough. It required a lot of effort from those women and they were just so pro in the way that they attacked it with great strength and good humor.

Rosemary Brandenburg:

I remember that flying was really a challenge. There were all these trees on the stage, which would hide some of the ropes and stuff, but they also kept having to be adjusted to create the path of travel. There were some times when they didn't make their days because it was really hard.

Thora Birch:

When you get in the harness and they fly you around, it's like a roller-coaster ride. But when you're shooting, [it's] *Stop, go, action, cut, reset! The light's too high! No, lower it. Now that light's messed up! We got to go fix that one. Now the wires need to be lubricated.* You start to say, "Okay, are we going to roll soon? We've been sitting here for like forty minutes clenching our butts and it's really hurting."

Peggy Holmes:

I feel like there was a lot of pressure on the actors to . . . get those shots in a minimal amount of takes. Everyone's in harnesses and it takes a really long time for us to get them all in their wardrobe, get them hooked up, then get the flight people ready, get the lighting ready, and the camera ready. You know, it just took a really long time. But we also wanted to make sure that the actors knew that they could at any time say, "I need to come down" because you can forget. You just get busy wanting to get the shots that you forget that they've been in their harness for a certain amount of time. I hope the actors feel like we tried really hard to make sure we didn't lose sight of that, but I'm sure it happened.

Stephanie Faracy ("Jenny"), 2018:

There are moments when you're shooting something when you realize, "This is the best of Hollywood!" Seeing Bette and Sarah and Kathy flying around in a harness on broomsticks, it was really kind of dazzling.

Bette Midler, 2018:

[Flying is] joyful, it's also a dance, and there's a lot of trying to be graceful while not being sure you weren't going to be turned upside down.

Peggy Holmes:

Bette has one shot where Winifred goes diving down toward the kids. That was such an intense shot. She was so good. I mean, they're really flying through trees and they are really heading from however high up they were down like four feet. It takes so much physical strength to do that. When you're on a flying rig, your natural position is upright so anytime you're tipped at all it is the actors that are forcing that.

Thora Birch:

We were shooting the scene at the end of the movie, and it had been a long day. I think everybody was just about over it. The crew, the cast, everybody was like, "You know, I think we quit." I was sitting there [with Bette Midler on the broom] and we're both insanely uncomfortable. I'm just about to crack and I guess she could tell, and she just started singing "Wind Beneath My Wings" and everybody stopped. The whole stage went silent and it was just a beautiful, uplifting moment that got everybody back on track. It takes true grit to know that, in that moment, that's what was needed and to provide it. I'll forever love her for that.

Jessie Wolfson:

One of my biggest life regrets was that I was offered [a chance] to go up on one of the brooms and I was too shy. So I tell my kids, "When you get an amazing opportunity, do it." This is like one of their life lessons that they get to hear through the movie because I watch them go on those brooms and I think, "Why did I not do that?"

Don Yesso:

Sarah was really driving the bus in our scene together. She was driving a four-ton bus down Burbank Drive somewhere. The director did a disclaimer before we started, "Listen, Sarah's really driving the bus. If anybody's uncomfortable, get off the bus now" — and you have all these makeup people going "Sarah's driving the bus?!" but everybody's got a job to do. Nobody was going to leave, so she's driving and I'm pushing the gas and I don't know when to hit the brake because I can't see and she's jumping up and down. The director's shouting, "You brake at the end of the road," but I couldn't see a goddamn thing.

For all the movie's practical magic, the most notable stunt comes in the final act of the film when Billy Butcherson slices through the stitches that have kept his mouth closed for three hundred years. Not only do words, his very first, fly out, but moths, too.

Doug Jones:

In this day and age, they would probably CG that whole thing with [the] moths and dust coming out of my mouth, but back then it was practical. I had a whole contraption in my mouth, which was an upper and lower retainer that held a latex sheath in place to protect me from the moths and the moths from me. We shouldn't be intermingling in my mouth, so the latex was there to make sure that didn't happen. I was still able to breathe because at the back of this retainer was a fiberglass cup with three air holes at the back. In that cup sat what they called Fuller's Earth, a kind of purified dirt. That's the first thing that came out of my mouth. Then the moths were sitting below that on my tongue with latex over it. The tedious part of this was that the moths could only be in my mouth for so long before they would start to moisten up.

Omri Katz:

The fact that he had real moths in his mouth was already so impressive. You couldn't pay me enough to do that, like, that's disgusting.

Margaret Prentice:

Doug was all into it. He just always kept a really good attitude. He is very low-key and always wants to hug everybody. That's why he's gone so far, he has the patience it takes to go through these stressful kinds of makeup setups.

Doug Jones:

There was a moth trainer that was on set. He brought the moths in little cages and knew their behaviors. He said, "A moth has to stay dry or it won't fly." If they get moist at all, they don't have the capability to fly. That's why putting the moths into my mouth had to be the last thing that happened before we filmed those takes.

Tony Gardner:

When we would shoot, we would give Doug mouthwash mixed with black food coloring to stain his teeth and his tongue. We would wait till the camera was rolling and then we would put those drops in his mouth because it dissipates fairly quickly, so we were in this habit of, "We need to shoot right away when we're doing that kind of stuff." When we were doing this scene, there were all these additional layers to it. We had built essentially an Invisalign retainer that fit on his upper teeth and his lower teeth and had a collapsible latex cup connected to it that had some holes punched in the back of it so he could blow air through it. We would put Fuller's Earth in it so he gets a decent amount of air to blow out through that hole and form a cloud of dust in front of him. It's real dust, not digital. We have to light it so you can see it, otherwise it's almost not there.

Omri Katz:

We had to do a few different takes because the moths wouldn't fly out of his mouth.

Tony Gardner:

We did two takes. The first one, we put the mouth retainer in and spooned in some Fuller's Earth. That made a nice soft little bed for the American Humane Society moth wrangler, who would hold them with tweezers and lay them sideways. Then he would stack them in Doug's mouth on top of each other.

Doug Jones:

This moth trainer, with tweezers, would put three moths into my mouth. Then the makeup artist had to quickly glue on the stitches that were precut in the middle to shut my mouth. They were very lightly glued together so that I could run the knife over them and they would pop open. That all had to happen on the fly with the camera rolling so we could get those moths out of my mouth quickly enough to stay dry. The first take, we had the system down. We knew what we were doing. The moths go in and a light on set bursts. Shards of glass fall to the ground, they stop the camera, and I'm sitting there with these three moths in my mouth. I could feel them flipping around and I could feel the water table in my mouth and throat rising because I have an intruder in my mouth and my saliva glands are reacting. I could tell this is going to be ugly by the time they get this thing fixed up. The light is replaced and now the camera's rolling again. I'm still ready to go, but I don't know what's happening there. I cut my mouth open, and I coughed out a string of drool and there was a moth kind of just surfing on it. It was a total dud of a take. We had to clean up, dry up, change out, and do it again. We got it on take two and that's what you saw in the movie.

Omri Katz:

In the movie, I looked disgusted and I really was disgusted. They totally captured my natural reaction.

Doug Jones:

In the first script that I was given, I had one word to say. I cut my mouth open and look up at the hovering Winifred and call her a "bitch." I didn't feel quite so comfortable saying such an unsavory word in a Disney kids' film. I wanted Billy to be charming and to win the kids over. I'm not sure that just spitting out that one word was going to do that. On the spot, I pitched the idea to Kenny Ortega. "Ken, what if I went on a more of a rant that was a bit softer verbiage?" So that's when "Wench! Trollop! You bucktoothed mop-riding firefly from hell!" came in, all while I have Max by the neck. I've just wrestled the knife away from him, cut my mouth open. He's not sure whose team I'm on right now and I'm spitting out three hundred years of pent-up anger. After wrestling with Omri, I looked at him and said, "I've waited centuries to say that." Then he ad-libbed, "Say whatever you want, just don't breathe on me." It created a really great moment that we came up with that night.

Vinessa Shaw:

Hearing that he added those insults that he shouts at Winifred, I feel like he definitely brought more to the character than any other person could have. He just really embodied Billy from head to toe.

Surprisingly, the moths were not the most difficult stunt that Doug Jones performed in the film.

Doug Jones:

My final scene in the movie, where I'm saying goodbye to the kids standing in my grave, I have to flop backward and I have to do it confidently without killing myself. This is before CGI was what it is today so there was a kind of a mattress pad of sorts that you couldn't see in the grave that I was going to land on. It was covered with dirt and lightly packed dust so that when I hit it, this puff of dust would come up. I wanted to fall backward, not looking like a guy who was scared to fall backward. It was a bit of a mind trick, *You're safe. You're safe. It's gonna work out fine!* But my open grave had shards of wood around it where my coffin had burst open. I had my arms spread wide when I leaned back and on my first take, it didn't go so well because my right hand caught a shard of wood that kind of splintered off, went airborne and a little piece of wood landed in my eye. I came up out of that grave real quick going, "Ah, is the set nurse here?" She was so sweet; she came over and quickly flushed my eye out. No damage done, and we were ready to go for take two, but I could have put an eye out.

While Doug Jones did his own stunts, it was Karyn Malchus, an actress and dancer half his size, who played the headless version of Billy Butcherson.

Karyn Malchus:
There was a scene where Billy Butcherson was going to have to lose his head. Tony [Gardner], who I had worked with before, called me and told me that the role was pratfalls and shtick. As a dancer, you have that skill in your back pocket.

Tony Gardner:
Karyn was really good at throwing her center of gravity and giving you the impression that she weighed a lot more than she did. We did this movie, *Freaked*, directed by Alex Winter, and there's a character in it called Sockhead, played by Bobcat Goldthwait, who goes through some weird science experiment and ends up with a sock puppet for a head. She wore a fiberglass skullcap with this animatronic sock on the top of it for

that movie. For *Hocus Pocus,* we used a similar rig that went over her shoulders so that she looked like a headless man. Karyn stood at about Doug's shoulder height. From her waist up, we built Billy's torso so her head fell where Billy's neck stump was. We built rare earth magnets into the stump so Billy's head literally clicked right into place and could fall off. Billy wore a knitted neck scarf so the knot of the scarf went literally right in front of Karyn's eyes.

Karyn Malchus:

The tricky part about wearing a rig, you can't really see, so you're kind of going at it blind. You have to have really good muscle memory. You have to be able to remember, *I take three steps and I fall. Then I get back up and there's a slope, and I gotta make sure I go down the hill and don't fall again.* The rig has to be fiberglass so it will look real, like bones. They pad it out, but it was quite heavy. It really digs into the shoulder. When you're shooting sixteen-hour days, that can get real old, real quick. But Tony's team is amazing at making the actor and whatever they have to put on as comfortable as can be. I've worn full-length latex suits where you're covered from head to toe, so this one was not the worst for sure. The funniest part was, if they brought in a seat for me between takes, they'd kind of forget about me because they can't see me. I just looked like the body of a headless dude.

The special effects in Hocus Pocus *were inventive and in many ways ahead of their time, but the work was overshadowed by 1993's biggest hit,* Jurassic Park, *which used a combination of CGI and animatronic puppetry to bring a T. rex to life.*

Chris Bailey:

Oh, how could *Jurassic Park* not steal our thunder? My God. We made a cat talk and then the dinosaur came and stepped on it. I remember seeing *Jurassic Park* and thought, *Oh my God.* I can't think of a big enough adjective that would do it justice. That was just wonderful work.

Carolyn Soper:
Jurassic Park was brand-new [technology]. We were doing the same kind of effects that had been done for years just in maybe slightly different ways, so no, I don't feel like *Jurassic Park* overshadowed us.

Ralph Winter:
We didn't have the same budget or ambitions that *Jurassic Park* did, so it's easy to be overshadowed by that, but I think the effort was to do what's good enough. It wasn't about getting an Academy Award nomination. I thought what we accomplished was kind of remarkable for not much of a budget.

Chris Bailey:
I remember Charlie Gibson, one of the co-founders of Rhythm & Hues, and I were talking about how in *Hocus Pocus* the scenes where there was interactivity were the ones that really came to life. If you just look at a shot of a cat talking, it's a visual effect, as good as it is, but you stick a human being in it and they're turning their heads looking at each other and reacting and it just sings. When they went into *Babe*, they were like, "Okay, we got to do more of this." They studied the work that we did in *Hocus Pocus* and said, "Okay, how can we improve upon that? How can we improve upon that with the filmmaking and bringing the actors in and having more interactivity?" They had done a test to sell director George Miller on that film while we were working on *Hocus Pocus*. *Babe* was actually more CG faces on realistic animals, the technique that we chose not to do on *Hocus Pocus*. They showed it to me and I thought, *Damn, that's amazing.* There was nothing wrong with it. I couldn't pick it apart.

Ralph Winter:

We were sort of a guinea pig in some ways. The flying stuff has become far more elegant, and with computers visual effects have become a lot fancier. I mean, we used puppets in the first movie for some [flying] shots, and those I kind of cringe at now.

Rick Lazzarini (Miniature Flying Witch Puppets Creator):

They needed miniature likenesses of the actresses, in full costume, riding their broom, mop, and vacuum cleaner. They would have the real actresses on flying rigs for many shots, but having the miniatures of them just gave them more variety and flexibility in terms of the shots they needed. I remembered an old BTS video of *Return of the Jedi* in which a Stormtrooper is atop an Imperial speeder bike in the famous forest-chase scene. In the making-of sequence, they revealed that it was a very detailed one-quarter-scale puppet, mounted on a gimbal, and the head operated from above via rod. It moved so smoothly, so realistically. I thought this would work perfectly for the three witches.

Carolyn Soper:

What Rick Lazzarini and his team did was really amazing. Even in the movie, they weren't as great as when we would go and check the progress. He'd be moving them and you'd think, *Oh my God, that's incredible.*

Tony Gardner:

In the beginning there are those three shots of the witches flying over the water. Those are miniature puppets and they were beautifully done. The wardrobe was scaled down and the fabric scaled down so that it takes wind the same way. It's just so well executed and that's kind of a good example of the way things worked back then. If you do your job well, nobody knows you did anything.

Rick Lazzarini:

Duplicating [the witches'] hairstyles proved to be a fun challenge. Of course the costume work, always a demanding task because, in miniature, scaled-down fabrics don't move the same as their larger scale counterparts. It took a good amount of research—and shopping! Lots of shopping downtown!—to find fabric equivalents that would look right and move properly at scale. For some reason, the Winifred and Mary face likenesses were easier to achieve, because they were somewhat caricatured and silly. But the Sarah puppet was eluding us. I initially used a sculptor who does very good work, but he wasn't quite getting it; her face always seemed too "chiseled." I made the decision to switch up sculptors, and that's when [sculptor] Michelle Millay added just the right amount of softness and femininity to really nail SJP's likeness to a spellbinding extent. Everyone forever afterward would comment on how realistic the likeness ended up being; it was like a tiny Sarah Jessica Parker–Sarah figure come to life.

Chet Zar:

Now some kid in their bedroom could do that stunt with the moths in a matter of hours. We spent weeks developing that technology, but it adds to the charm of the film. I think people really do appreciate practical effects.

Omri Katz:

When I lit the candle and the floorboards started to move [in the Sanderson house] and smoke started coming out, all that was real. We didn't really have to act, all we had to do was just react. We didn't have a green screen so we didn't have to imagine it. It was literally happening.

Carolyn Soper:

All of the glows and the [powers] shooting out from Bette's hands, all of that is hand drawn. That was not computer generated. We would have to project down onto a piece of paper the scene and on one piece of paper per frame, the effects animator would draw the "glow" with a hard-edged pencil. Each one of those film pieces was then scanned into the computer and now existed as layers. It was complicated. You've got to remember, how you did that stuff was not by dragging and dropping it with a mouse, it was all code.

Rosemary Brandenburg:

There are sort of silly parts; the visual effects now look a little primitive. The flying scenes are fun, but it's done better now. Yet *Hocus Pocus* is not looked down upon, people still love the movie. I mean, they made the sequel. They wouldn't have made the sequel if the original hadn't been so powerful.

David Kirschner:

To watch the witches flying over the cemetery and bringing Billy Butcherson to life, stuff that came right out of the original story, I wish there were words that convey properly just what runs through my body when I think of those things. It was very magical.

Russell Bobbitt:

We were old-school filmmakers making an old-school movie that plays just as well as the big CGI movies do today. That's cool.

Chapter 10

THE MAKING OF THE "I PUT A SPELL ON YOU" SCENE

The most iconic moment in the whole movie may be when Winifred Sanderson steals the mic to perform her own version of Screamin' Jay Hawkins's "I Put a Spell on You" in hopes of enchanting the parents of Salem so she and her sisters can steal their kids' souls. The scene, which included nearly two hundred extras, was filmed over the course of a week at the ballroom in the MacArthur, formerly known as the Park Plaza Hotel, in Los Angeles, which was standing in for Salem's Old Town Hall. It's hard to even fathom, but the showstopping song break almost didn't happen.

Neil Cuthbert:

The song "I Put a Spell on You" wasn't in the script initially. The scene of the parents being enchanted was in the script, but Kenny came up with the idea to have Bette Midler sing the song.

Kenny Ortega:

I don't remember whose specific idea it was. I think we were all fans of Bette Midler's musicality and theatricality and wanted to do something to take advantage of it. We felt that if there was a way to slide in a musical number in an organic capacity that it would be wonderfully right for the film. In the end, it wasn't an elaborate musical number; it was actually a tiny sort of cabaret performance.

David Kirschner:

I was very concerned about "I Put a Spell on You." I knew the song by Screamin' Jay Hawkins, but stopping the movie in the middle to do a dance number? I remember Jeffrey Katzenberg being a bit sarcastic to me, saying, "We're gonna do a movie with Bette Midler and not take the moment to have her sing a song in the course of it?" I understood that, but this was my story, and I was so worried we were going to damage it.

Liz Kirschner:

Dave just didn't care for it. He just thought it was not going to be good for the movie. I just said, "But it's fun!"

Mick Garris:

David hated the idea, and I didn't like the idea, either. But if you've got Bette Midler, and you don't have her belt out a song, you are missing something. Whether it's as organic as the rest of the movie is open to debate, but I know the audience is happy that it's there.

Kenny Ortega:

I don't remember any pushback. David Kirschner was so great to work with. We had a good thing going.

David Kirschner:

Kenny sat with me and as opposed to saying, "No, this is what we're doing," he explained to me why that scene made sense. He's just someone you really can't even disagree with. He has the patience of Job. He is the sweetest human being on the face of the earth. He really just seemed to know what he was talking about and clearly he was right and I was dead wrong, but I still wasn't sure, honestly. I really thought, *We can edit it out if it doesn't work.*

Thora Birch, 2018:

I think it was the most stressed-out I had seen Kenny. He was running around with a bullhorn, trying to keep it all together. That was the only time that I saw him not in a great mood. If you were to ask him about that scene, he'd probably be like, "I don't even want to talk about that!"

Kenny Ortega:

We had one day to shoot that musical number—and not even a whole day. I think that we had that ballroom for two days, but we also had all of the other stuff that we had to shoot. So we had to accomplish all of the scene work *and* the musical number within two days. I just wanted to do it right and I wanted to serve Bette and the other actresses, and the wonderful crew, which was a great, great overall crew. I also wanted to serve the story and the moment so I was up against a lot.

Mary Vogt:
The musical scene was filmed at the end of the movie shoot and by that point I had completely run out of money. I spent all my money on the witches and on Billy so I went to the executive on the film and I said, "I have this big party to do and I'm out of money. Can I have some more money?" They said, "Uh, no. That's what 'out of money means,'" and left. The only plan B was to ask people to come in their own costumes, but then I remembered because we were a Disney film we had paid like $5,000 or something to use their wardrobe department to take as many clothes as we wanted. Since we had this deal with them, I thought, we'll just get all the clothes [for this scene] from there. In the end, that's why they're all so elaborate, we dressed two hundred people in costumes from *Tron, Treasure Island*, these three Supremes-looking girls, an Elvis guy, and there was a newsboy, I think, from *Newsies*. If you look close, you can see the history of Disney movies that came out before 1992.

Peggy Holmes:
Kenny is so, so, so, so good at creating this bigger-than-life scene. We worked with our actors that were in the crowd to create special moments for each of them. I don't think we could actually choreograph them, but we could direct them to react a certain way. Kenny's really good at finding certain people in the crowd that are doing their own really special thing.

Doug Jones, 2018:
Teda Bracci, who played Calamity Jane, was a friend of Bette Midler's. We all had so much fun hanging out between camera setups. That was a

night shoot until the sun came up, as we had to vacate this private club in downtown Los Angeles before the next business day started.

Thora Birch, 2018:

Sometimes when you're doing those kinds of party scenes, people get fatigued and they lose their energy. They never lost their energy on this one. Kenny had them all dancing, he had them all into it. I think people felt like they were really at a Halloween party.

Vinessa Shaw:

The background people were all sweaty and I thought, *Oh my God. People are actually loving this!* I know it's because of Kenny; he just had that kind of presence. No one was treated as a background player. Kenny understood that everyone is important in a dance number and he needed to have an audience that was dance till you die–type people. I feel like every person was embodying their character, from Diana Ross and the Supremes to the guy dressed as Frankenstein. Even Charlie Rocket and Stephanie Faracy as Dad-cula and Madonna; that scene just felt so alive.

Stephanie Faracy, 2018:

I loved filling Madonna's bra. It was the first prop I ever wanted to steal. I didn't, but I really should have!

Mary Vogt:

The fake Madonna outfit has a very homemade look because we needed to do a cheap version of it since we had run out of money. It's the kitchen version of Jean Paul Gaultier. She had to look like she made it herself from stuff in her kitchen, so the bra was made out of plastic funnels for baking. Stephanie wasn't embarrassed to wear it, which was great; she pulled it off.

Stephanie Faracy, 2018:

Early morning when you're ordering a burrito and you have the bra on, that's when you feel a little ridiculous. When you're like, "Take the cones off me, I have to eat!" But I thought, *Wow, this is the best outfit for Halloween this year and I'm in it!*

Thora Birch, 2018:

There were times in that scene when Vinessa, Omri, and I were split up from one another. We would get back together and we could compare notes about the extras that we were around, "Oh, I'm by the mummy" or "I'm by the green dinosaur." We'd also get together and be like, "Can you believe what these guys are saying?" There were a lot of inappropriate conversations that were being had between the Madonna outfit and some of the other more risqué outfits that some of the ladies had on. You wouldn't talk like that around kids today, let's put it that way, but we loved it.

Omri Katz:

Just imagine being a spectator at a rehearsal of a Broadway musical. That's really what it was. It didn't seem like there were cameras even present. It seemed like we were rehearsing to do a live show. I never did theater, but after *Hocus Pocus* I had a whole new respect for how much time and effort was involved in capturing that magic.

Doug Jones:

One of my favorite moments while filming *Hocus Pocus* was reminiscing with Bette about a moment that I had before I ever met her. This was about two years before we filmed *Hocus Pocus*, I was working on my "Mac Tonight" campaign for McDonald's. By then, the campaign had been running for a few years and the advertising agency and the director were butting heads. I was stressed-out and thinking maybe I should stop acting. That week, I saw a Barbara Walters interview with Bette Midler. Barbara digs deep, you know? She said, "Bette, a number of years ago I interviewed you after you had done *The Rose*. You took yourself off the grid for a minute to recoup. What makes you a different Bette Midler today than you were back then?" Without missing a beat, Bette looked at Barbara and said, "Barbara, I don't care anymore. I used to be so worried about everyone else's job around me. I'd think, *What can I do to make it all—this whole thing—run better and smoother?*" She says, "Now I realize what I'm responsible for, and I do the best I can do with that. I stand where they tell me to stand. I wear what they tell me to wear. I say what they tell me to say, and I do all that to the best of my ability. Outside of that, *I don't* care anymore." I watched this and I thought, *I am free, I am free to not care.* I went back to work with this whole new attitude of, "That's their problem, not mine." Cut to 1992, we were filming the party scene and we're taking a break. I'm talking to Bette through the stitches. She said, "I'm worried that your stitches are gonna pop. Should you be talking this much?" And I said, "Oh no, they're gonna stay on, but that does not sound like the 'I don't care' attitude that I've come to love from you so much!" She's like, "Hmm?" So I told her about the Barbara Walters interview and she said, "Really? I said that?" I said, "Yes, you did and it was life changing." She said, "Yeah, that was pretty good, wasn't it?" I loved it!

The cast had a front-row seat to a one-of-a-kind Bette Midler performance, but no one was closer to the action then Joseph Malone, who played the singer whose gig gets interrupted by Winifred and her sisters.

Joseph Malone ("Skeleton Singer"):
I was coming off of *The Tracey Ullman Show* and I got a call to go see Kenny Ortega, who I'd known from my dancing days. I think Screamin' Jay Hawkins was originally cast and he got sick or something so they were

replacing him. I think Kenny and Greg Smith told me that straight up. I went in and I sang "Old Devil Moon" from *Finian's Rainbow*. In my mind, I was playing a singer who thought of himself as the Frank Sinatra guy, the crooner in this town. After I got it, they squeezed me into a unitard with a jacket, gloves, and a hat. Then there was also the fabulous makeup, which I was surprised to find out how many people re-create that for Halloween. I love how many people think that makeup is cool. All the glory goes to the makeup artist. I sat in the chair and they said, "This is what we want to do." It wasn't terribly long to get in and out of the makeup, maybe an hour or two because there was so much detail.

Steve LaPorte (Makeup Artist):

I just ad-libbed that makeup the first day and once it's on, it's on. You don't have a chance to try it a second time and change it up. When you're doing a show like that, where you don't have time for makeup tests, you just have to make sure it works great. There's an old Disney animated film where there are dancing skeletons called *Silly Symphonies—The Skeleton Dance* [from 1929]. It's a classic Disney film and I kept that in mind while designing the makeup. Now you can whip out your phone and google "skeleton face" and find a thousand pictures. Back then you couldn't do it. You just had to just draw on your own memory.

Joseph Malone:

The hardest part was at the very beginning when I spun that top hat on my finger. I had gloves on so I couldn't grab it. It was a really, really, really, really tight shot so Kenny came and put his arm around me and he said, "I really need you to grab the hat, can you?" I said, "Yeah, all right, Kenny. I'm trying." He said, "I know you are, but try extra hard." I eventually got it and it's because Kenny would just create a place where you could trust your own work.

Kenny Ortega:

I knew Joey Malone, who played our skeleton. He was an extraordinary dancer, actor, teacher, and I remember him quickly accepting the role when offered to him. There were a number of actors that auditioned for that role when we realized that we were going into a musical sequence. I don't remember Screamin' Jay Hawkins [originally being cast in the role], but I do remember his song ["I Put a Spell on You"] being played and all of us jumping on it. Then Bette and her incredible longtime collaborator, Marc Shaiman, took it under their wing and came back with this wonderful arrangement.

Marc Shaiman (Composer/Lyricist/Musical Arranger), 2018:

Since I was working on so many films and recordings with Bette at that time, including *Beaches* and *For the Boys*, and am an arranger as well as a composer/lyricist, I guess I was the obvious candidate to help create what they wanted.

Peggy Holmes:

Marc had worked with Bette forever, so he really knew Bette's style and what works well for her and what she likes to do. There was a shorthand between them. I remember seeing a rehearsal where Marc was at the piano, and then all of a sudden I heard Bette start to sing. *"Oh my gosh, it's Bette Midler! Bette Midler is singing right now!"* It's so special when the cameras aren't rolling and you see the sort of raw talent of someone like Bette come to life.

Marc Shaiman, 2018:

There have been many versions of the song to listen to for inspiration, which I did, and then I just went ahead and did what seemed appropriate for the film. Making the first verse more rubato, more orchestral, and then going into a Bette Midler live show kind of groove. It's the kind of groove the opening song of a Bette Midler concert would be, it just fell naturally into that. Since I had worked with Bette and her backup group the Harlettes so often, it was natural to give Kathy and SJP the "Harlette"-style backup parts that they sing and dance to in the movie.

Peggy Holmes:
Sarah and Kathy are going to do backup, so what are you going to do with it? Throwback to the classic girl or guy groups. I thought it would be so funny to just give them this little Supremes throwback feel. That was intentional for sure.

Bette Midler, 1993:
I walked into the studio [to record "I Put a Spell on You"], and [Sarah Jessica Parker and Kathy Najimy] had their microphone and, of course, I had my microphone. . . . Well, I started to sing and I looked over at them and their little knees were [shaking]. They were totally freaked out. They came to me afterward and said, "We couldn't believe we were standing there singing with you!" I was very touched by that.

Thora Birch:
I was super jealous of Omri because he got to go onstage with them. I wanted to be onstage singing backup.

Joseph Malone:
I sing "Witchcraft" and a few bars of "I Put a Spell on You" in the film so we were in the recording studio and I was going to sing it like a crooner, like Frank Sinatra, and Marc said, "You know, that was kind of Bette's idea about how she was going to approach it. I think that's going to be a little too close to what she's doing." He said, "Why don't you do it more like a rockabilly kind of feel." I went, "All right, sure." Marc and I had already worked together on a show called *Leader of the Pack* and he did these fabulous vocal arrangements, so I completely trusted whatever his feelings were. That's not my moment, it's Bette's for heaven's sake.

Omri Katz:

I didn't know about that song before the movie. I never heard the Nina Simone version of that song or the original Screamin' Jay Hawkins version. I thought that song was written for the movie.

Thora Birch, 2018:

I remember there being a lot of stress around whether they could use the original lyrics or even call the song "I Put A Spell on You." I think they were thinking about naming it something else and everyone was very upset about that. I think putting a new interpretation on the song while still paying homage to the original was kind of a stressful thing, but, in the end, it all worked out.

Marc Shaiman, 2018:

I don't know of any concern about the song, I wasn't in that loop, and I don't remember any other song being proposed. We certainly rewrote lyrics. I do believe I did most of them. It all happened very quickly if I recall correctly, on the spot, around the piano.

Brock Walsh:

Well, I rewrote the lyrics to that one. The task was to write parody lyrics that would be appropriate for the witches.

Aaron Wallace:

If you listen to the original recording by Screamin' Jay Hawkins and then immediately thereafter listen to Bette Midler's version [in *Hocus Pocus*], you find that they have almost nothing in common. The song has been largely reworked and rearranged. The genre has been shifted and the lyrics largely rewritten. Yet there is a shared DNA. That song as originally conceived is a song about a man casting a spell of love on his unrequited love. The story goes that Screamin' Jay Hawkins came in ready to record this romantic ballad, got very, very drunk and ended up doing something sort of wild and raucous instead. Who knows how much truth there is to that story, but listening to the recording you can believe it. It's one of the most incredible rock and roll recordings I've ever heard. That sort of unhinged lustiness translates to the unhinged wickedness that we hear in Bette Midler's performance as Winifred Sanderson. You get the sense that those lyrics are spilling out of Winifred and articulating this desire, this need to recapture her life. That this is her one last chance at immortality.

Joseph Malone:

The thing I was a little disappointed about was, when I went to do the ADR [automated dialogue replacement] for the scene, Kenny told me they were thinking about releasing a soundtrack album with Bette's version of "I Put a Spell on You." That didn't happen, but that would've been fun.

Doug Jones:

Kenny shot so much usable footage in that dance party scene that we didn't get to see. Part of that was showing the parents still dancing at the party under Winnie's spell. They did a couple of those cutbacks, and one of them was Billy hopping up on stage. Because I was immortal, I wasn't under the same spell these people were, but I stayed to have some fun with them before I went chasing everybody again. There was a moment where I took center stage to dance, and Kenny just said, "Go for it, improv all you want." I did spins. I did a hurdler split on the floor. I ended up doing a signature move of mine where I'm kind of bouncing up and down, it looks like a jumping crab, and then kicking my legs around before standing up and then waving to the crowd before I exit backstage. It was a really fun moment for Billy.

Kenny Ortega:

Doug is an improvisational genius and he owned that character so full-heartedly. We had to trim back what we did with him in the musical sequence, and that was heartbreaking because everything that Doug contributed was worthy of being on-screen.

Margaret Prentice:

Even though I was hearing the same song for three or four days, it was really fun to watch Bette Midler and the girls up there singing. I am a huge fan of Bette Midler, so watching her work was really special for me. Doug and I were watching her just like, "Oh, this is so cool."

Thora Birch, 2018:

It's the one moment where Bette goes into full-on Bette mode instead of just being in Winifred Sanderson mode. It's, "Oh, there's the Divine Miss M!" She's ripping it up and hitting all the notes and I think everybody was feeling really thrilled to be there and to get to witness it. It was like being at a free Bette Midler concert, you know? It was awesome.

Doug Jones:

Usually they prerecord and have the performer lip-sync those kinds of scenes because there's a lot of cuts involved and they want to keep the sound consistent. Well, Bette was singing out loud from the bottom of her lungs so that the look and the sound matched.

Brock Walsh:

Bette's a wonderful singer. She's instantly recognizable. She manages to convey something with her singing voice that no other singer does.

Omri Katz:

Bette being who she is, she just nails it. I don't even recall her doing too many takes other than being like, "Oh, let me just add this" to change it up and give Kenny some more choices to pick and choose from.

Stephanie Faracy, 2018:

It's one of those days where you come home and say, "Guess what I did today?"

Tony Gardner:

One of my favorite days was standing onstage when they were filming the dance number. I was up there wrangling masks for the band, but I got to stand on that stage every day and watch the three of them. I got to watch Bette do her speech and then do the walk toward the camera. I had that song stuck in my head probably for weeks after that, but those kinds of experiences are kind of magical, you know? Those moments don't come around very often and the older I get the more I appreciate it because I realize just how rare they really are.

Ralph Winter:

She knows where the camera is and she knows how to play to it. That's a movie star skill.

Doug Jones:

The way Bette struts across the stage is unlike anyone I've ever seen before. She does it with such confidence, "I am the most sexy star who has ever walked the earth and you're going to think so too by the time we're done here!" That's the energy she brings. If only I could have that kind of confidence. I'm a goofy character actor, but I think that sexy comes from not just your look, but how you carry it. I learned that from Bette Midler.

Peggy Holmes:

Bette does strut. That's part of her awesome vocabulary, strutting across stage, but we choreographed that whole scene. It's always a bit of a collaboration. If you're choreographing someone like Bette, who is such an accomplished performer, you kind of look and see what are their signature moves that make them who they are as a performer. Then you figure out how to incorporate those into what you're doing. I remember working specifically with Bette on the walk.

Mary Vogt:

I made these crazy shoes for Bette. They look really uncomfortable, but the one thing about performers like Bette, who have done theater, is they're used to wearing really uncomfortable high-heeled shoes. They don't really complain about that stuff, which is great. Sometimes when you're doing movies, the actors say, "Oh, these are so uncomfortable!" I'm always like, "You've obviously never done any theater, have you?!" I don't remember Bette complaining about anything.

Marc Shaiman, 2018:

Since I did not score the film, my name isn't in the front credits in big letters, so it is often a surprise to friends, especially younger ones who grew up on the movie, that I was involved with this one special scene. But when I tell them, they are quite effusive. Any scene that has Bette Midler, not to mention Kathy Najimy and Sarah Jessica Parker, performing is sure to stand out. And it was, I suppose, unexpected within the framework of the movie, so it was twice a delight!

David Kirschner:

The first time I saw the "I Put a Spell on You" scene, it was just like, "Uh, duh. This is so good." It's so funny and so fun. I remember seeing it with an audience and the audience loved it. I remember turning to Liz and saying, "Oh my God, I'm so glad they didn't listen to me!" She said, "Me too. It's one of my favorite moments in the movie!"

Chapter 11

WHO IS THIS MOVIE FOR?

*W*ho *is the audience for* Hocus Pocus? *The answer now is undoubt- edly everyone, but back in 1993, it wasn't clear whether there was an audience for a family film about three hilariously evil witches that steal the souls of children. By all accounts, the multi-genre* Hocus Pocus *was an experiment for Walt Disney Studios, the live-action film branch of the Walt Disney Company, which was looking to entice not just kids, but their parents, too, after the success of the 1989 family adventure* Honey, I Shrunk the Kids.

Gail Lyon:

Hocus Pocus and Newsies were the first two movies out of a sort of reju- venated "Walt Disney Presents" label out of the Touchstone era. Kids have a sense of "this isn't real" in animation, but when you're doing it live action it poses a bunch of questions: *How do we stay universal, but not alienate kids and scare them too much with witchcraft? How do you stay kid friendly and deal with magic and witchcraft and be attractive to more than just kids?* To be honest, Kenny was really a genius with the campy factor, because that in some ways is what appealed to older audiences ultimately.

Steven Haft:

If you notice, the trailers for Disney's animated movies [back then] didn't focus so much on the sweet G-rated stuff, but often found them- selves very much selling the sassy, edgy, or more witty side of some of the animated characters. Why do I bring that up? Because I think that was also the approach here [with *Hocus Pocus*]. Even with a film that might appeal to a YA [young adult] audience, Disney always believed that you had to have adult humor in there in order to get parents to drive to the theater.

Ralph Winter:

I don't think any of us understood until we started shooting how much fun this movie was going to be, but it's definitely dark when you're talking about eating children.

Jason Marsden:

At that time, Disney movies would be a little bit more milquetoast, not so sinister. . . . I would love to know if there was any pushback from the studio. Are they like, "Hey, you know, a little less on the hanging, a little less child murder."

Neil Cuthbert:

We thought we were pushing a certain Disney envelope—and that's a good thing to do. I think a lot of those darker elements were in the original script. . . . I think had [the studio] known what they were going to get, they probably wouldn't have made it. It came out as its own creature. It wasn't what everybody was expecting. It really wasn't.

Mark I. Pinsky:

I didn't find much at all [to be] a menace or threatening in *Hocus Pocus.* They were on the dark side, the wrong side, but there was always a sort of wink and a nod, which sort of defanged the evil.

Heather Greene (Journalist/Editor/Author, *Lights, Camera, Witchcraft: A Critical History of Witches in American Film and Television*):

Hocus Pocus was too scary for children, too silly for adults. You want nine- and ten-year-olds to watch a movie where witches come back from the dead to eat children? Then you have a zombie and this weird talking cat? Adults aren't going to want to watch that.

Neil Cuthbert:

One of the things that was wrong with the original script was the way it was conceived was it was all about the big brother saving the day. The truth is, it should have been about Thora and the cat saving the day. The big brother should have been the comic relief. That's obvious now, but then it wasn't.

Gillian Walters (Cohost, *All Things Cozy* Podcast):
I think what still stands out to me [about *Hocus Pocus*] is the fact that there was a death in the opening scene of a little girl. I don't think you'd see that today. The emotional weight of that hits me harder now as an adult.

Bonnie Bruckheimer:
There was nothing "politically correct" at that time where they'd say, "This isn't good for young kids to see."

Nell Minow (The Movie Mom™; Contributing Editor, *RogerEbert.com*):
Killing a child? That's really the third rail when it comes to movies, particularly movies for kids. Then they turn another child into a cat, damning him to eternal life. That's really rough. In another movie that would be a deal-breaker. Even though I disapprove of that, and in no way am saying that's appropriate, Kenny Ortega does a good job of creating a tone that makes that less devastating than it might otherwise be, but I would say the age group for *Hocus Pocus* is ten to fourteen.

Aaron Wallace:
I'll tell you, as a kid in 1993, I was very spooked by *Hocus Pocus* and I think that's so important. As children, very often the things that stick with us and the things that shape us are the things that challenge us, that scare us, that unsettle us, that reveal some new dimension of life to us. *Hocus Pocus* is very effective at taking an audience of any age to that edge.

Mara Wilson (Actor/Writer):
I don't think I had nightmares [after seeing *Hocus Pocus*], but I do think it scared me. Sometimes late at night I would worry about the Sanderson sisters poking around. I remember my mom saying, "I kind of wish you hadn't seen that movie. I don't think I would've let you watch it." The ironic thing, though, is that my mom was such a cinephile that she

actually let me watch movies that were much scarier, like *Psycho* and *The Twilight Zone.* For some reason, this was the one that really scared me. That feeling stayed with me, but I was also very entertained and very fascinated by it.

Belissa Escobedo ("Izzy," *Hocus Pocus 2*):
I knew a lot of people who were scared of the first one. The Sanderson sisters, especially Winifred, can be a bit scary at times. But I was like, "Don't worry, the second one's not as scary."

Nneka McGuire (Writer):
When I was a kid, my dad worked accounting for the cable company, and so we had free cable and every channel that you could imagine. My parents were probably a little lax about watching what I watched. I did not really have a clear sense of what was acceptable for a kid to watch, so it's pretty surprising that *Hocus Pocus* got my attention. There are not a lot of movies for kids that I think back on and remember enjoying all that much, but with this movie I do remember feeling like I was staring at the screen, super into it, and really curious to see what was going to happen with the cat boy. Even though I was exposed to things that should have predisposed me to not give a damn about *Hocus Pocus*, it still felt really thrilling and tantalizing and titillating.

Megan Townsend (Senior Director Entertainment Research & Analysis, GLAAD):
I watched it as a young kid and it very much fit into this lineup of other movies that I loved at the time: *Nightmare Before Christmas, Addams Family,* and *Addams Family Values,* all these things that are that same kind of spooky creepy, but funny and over-the-top, kind of dark humor, which usually would have some kind of iconic song moment in them. I remember thinking, *Oh, this is my personality. These are my movies.*

Tina Burner (Creator/Star, *Witch Perfect*):

Hocus Pocus couldn't have been campier, but for some reason it was still terrifying. I was talking to a friend about it not too long ago, and they said, "My parents wouldn't let me watch it because of the finger getting ripped off in the pothole." It was scary, it was dark, and I liked that as a kid.

Kahmora Hall ("Drag Queen Sarah," *Hocus Pocus 2*; *RuPaul's Drag Race*, Season 13):

Hocus Pocus was one of the few American traditions in my family. My parents are immigrants from Vietnam and we don't really sit down and watch TV shows together, except for *Hocus Pocus*. Strange, right? These three supernatural witches who eat children are what brought our family together.

A. W. Jantha (Author, *Hocus Pocus and the All-New Sequel*):

My parents were strict about the visual media my sister and I were allowed to consume growing up, and *Hocus Pocus* didn't make the cut; by the time I was staying at friends' houses, I'd missed the boat. Because of that, I didn't watch the film until Disney approached me with the opportunity to work on the novelization and sequel. I feel sheepish admitting this, because I know this film has such a passionate fan base. I watched it before accepting the audition, and fell in love. Halloween is hands down my favorite day of the year, and the movie is a wonderful encapsulation of what is great about the holiday: It's clever, playful, campy, spooky, and full of heart and charm. *Hocus Pocus* shows both kids and adults stepping out of their comfort zones, leaning into adventure—and, yes, even ambition—and learning not to take themselves too seriously. That's something we could all benefit from doing more of.

Tanya Pai (Director of Newsroom Standards and Ethics, *Vox*):
A lot of Halloween movies are very scary and gory or a little too saccharine and sweet. I think *Hocus Pocus* strikes the balance between the tones. It's quirky in a way that maybe movies that are made now are not because they're kind of serving the algorithm. It reminds me a little bit of another one of my favorite Halloween movies, *Practical Magic*. It was kind of a flop when it first came out. They didn't understand what the tone was supposed to be or who the audience was supposed to be, but it had this kind of cultural staying power because that mashup of tones and vibes just makes it unique.

Gillian Walters:
The movie doesn't dumb anything down, doesn't force anything. It has hokey moments and jokes that don't necessarily land, but it talks to children as if they're on the ride. It invites audiences in in a way that I just don't see today. I think sometimes we underestimate the imagination and just the creativity of kids and what they can appreciate. I think it's one of the biggest reasons why it has lasted this long, because you can enjoy it as a kid and you can enjoy it as an adult.

Larry Bagby:
Kenny told Tobias and I, when they were screening the movie initially to get feedback, there was a version where they cut our roles out completely. All of our scenes were gone to try to save time and see if it still flowed. He said it didn't test as well. In fact, he said, people just didn't like it as much. I think we brought in elements of comedy and relief in between this fairly scary story of kids being chased by zombies and witches.

Doug Jones:
In post-production, Kenny Ortega told me that the challenge he was up against was keeping this movie to ninety minutes. I'm not sure what the rules are now, but back then a kid-friendly Disney movie with the

Disney label on it, not Touchstone, but Disney, needed to be ninety minutes for attention span. Because of that, he had to snip and cut and condense. So that's why the film might be missing moments where we were like, "Oh, that would've been fun!" but not necessary to the story.

Kenny Ortega:

Most of what we shot ended up in the movie—we didn't waste much. But there were a couple of things here and there that we had to cut for timing. It was really peripheral stuff. Most of it's in there, folks.

Steven Haft:

What turned out to be the last day of filming was the last day because I insisted it was the last day. Kenny wanted to come back and keep shooting. A decision was made not to because, clearly, there was enough footage to make a tremendously engaging film. I would say the proof is in the pudding, which was tasty and yummy, but nevertheless, some hard decisions had to be made.

Tony Gardner:

There were a couple of things, a lot of really scary stuff, that didn't make it into the final film, like Emily shriveling into a husk and dying on camera, and the boys in the cage aging into old men at the end.

Another thing that didn't make the final cut: a more unnerving ending in which the camera pans to the Sanderson house where Jay and Ice are still being kept. As the screen fades to black, you hear the boys' muffled screams.

Tobias Jelinek:

That is dark! We're screaming like they're torturing us. That's a horror movie. They changed it so we would be singing, but they didn't know what we were going to sing. "Row Your Boat" is public domain so it became, "Yeah, just sing that."

David Kirschner:

In my original pitch, there's a scene where Emily Binx gets buried. Disney thought it was just too morose and it didn't further the story, but I thought it was an important character moment. In my mind, I thought that really gave the importance of why this cat was so hell-bent on sending these women back to where they belong.

Jason Marsden:

When they captured the witches and put the noose around their necks, the most terrifying part to me is how they just don't care. They're laughing at everybody and then they do that spell in front of everyone. It's like, "What's going on? This is out of control!"

Aaron Wallace:

You have the famous scene of Max returning to his room and there's this camera shot looking through the gaps in the closet door at the unsuspecting Max that I still find so unsettling to this day. It's straight out of John Carpenter's playbook. There's a very similar shot in *Halloween* where Michael Myers is stalking Laurie Strode [played by Jamie Lee Curtis] and she's hiding in the closet. There are these moments in *Hocus Pocus* that take us right to the edge of horror.

William Cuthbert (@SpookyWil; Cohost, *The Black Flame Society* Podcast):

In an earlier script, instead of Sarah using song [to lure kids], the Sandersons make candy crows for the kids to eat. This story line is much darker than what we [see in the movie], but it does appear in the Todd Strasser novel that was released alongside the film. It's now out of print, but if you want to see how much darker *Hocus Pocus* could have been, read the novel.

Tobias Jelinek:

The origins of *Hocus Pocus* are that you had these rather incredible horror writers and producers like Mick Garris and David Kirschner. Some of those adult undertones managed to slip by. There is no formula for a film that really resonates with more than one generation, but there's enough in this film that speaks to both an adult audience and a younger audience.

Doug Jones:

Hocus Pocus is a kid's tale where kids are empowered to go after these evil entities and win. I think any kid is inspired by that and wants to relive that moment again and again and again even as they grow up. As adults we remember that with the right collaboration and the right ideas and faith we can get through the monsters that are before us.

William Sandell:

Kenny really walked the line terrifically where a grown-up can watch that movie and the kids can watch it, too. There's nothing too scary or lascivious that happens, but there is innuendo. You know, there's the bus driver, but a little kid doesn't know what all that stuff is.

Don Yesso:

About four or five days before the bus driver scene was set to take place, Andrew Dice Clay, who was supposed to play the bus driver, dropped out. I heard that his agent might have talked him out of it. He did a movie called *The Adventures of Ford Fairlane*, I don't know how many people remember that picture, but I guess he thought he was the lead and didn't want to take a part in this movie. My friend Chris [L. Spellman] was a set decorator on *Hocus Pocus*, and he gave Kenny my name. They called my agent and I went directly to the set and auditioned and I got the job. Dice Clay, at that time, was known for those nasty nursery rhymes, you know, "Little Miss Muffet sat on her tuffet." If Dice was going to do this, I had to figure out why they wanted him. I told Kenny I had a couple of ideas and he said, "Do whatever you want, let's see what you got." The whole thing with the spitting the gum out, that's all me, and after that I was on my own. Now, I don't know if Bette remembers this and, of course, I don't want to cause any bad blood, but I think she was upset because I wasn't saying the exact lines in the script. As a professional actor, I can understand why she was upset with that, but I thought this stuff was funny.

Neil Cuthbert:
Yabbos? That wasn't me. I didn't even know that word at that time.

Mara Wilson:
Kids don't need to know the details of things. Kids like to know that there is something that's right over their head that they don't understand right now, but they're going to understand in a couple of years. You could call it the "*Grease* Effect." There are a lot of things you don't understand when you see *Grease* when you're nine that you do when you see *Grease* again when you're fourteen.

Vinessa Shaw:
I watched all the Bugs Bunny cartoons and did not recognize all the innuendo in there. I loved *Peanuts* and there's innuendo in there, too, but also intelligent, thoughtful topics. I feel like we shouldn't treat children with kid gloves. I think *Hocus Pocus* toes that line pretty well. It talks about believing in yourself, using your own powers to overcome things that may seem insurmountable in your life. The youth have the power and the ingenuity to problem solve. I mean, where are Allison's parents in this movie? Max and Dani's parents are literally under a spell. Parents are there to guide you, but you have to become your own person.

Nell Minow:

In most kids' movies, you have children having an adventure where the adults are superfluous. That's what kids like to see and a lot of times it's upsetting to parents. The child can't have an adventure if the parent is there. The parent will be saying, "Wear a sweater! Do your homework! Don't go on that yellow-brick road!"

Alex Steed (Cohost, *You Are Good* Podcast):

I do remember seeing it on television and being really taken by how much the plot revolved around needing a virgin. I think I found the movie at that time when I had an awareness of sex, so I thought, *This is a very, very strange thing to be in a children's movie.* But I did think, *This is actually interestingly about the anxiety of someone very much being a young person.* I think that spoke to me, I'm not going to say more than it should have, but I think it spoke to me more than I was aware of at that time.

David Kirschner:

One note I remember, and I lost this battle, was that they wanted the person who lit the Black Flame Candle to be a virgin. I just remember talking to Jeffrey Katzenberg about it and he said, "It works." Basically that's it, he shut me down. I always cringed over the whole virgin thing, but sometimes you have to let studio executives pee on the fire hydrant so to speak.

Gail Lyon:

I don't remember that specific conversation [about the word "virgin"], to be honest with you, but I do remember us really honestly kind of feeling our way through. . . . It was the crux of rebuilding that brand for live action.

Jeffrey Katzenberg:

One of our goals at Disney was to expand the audience for a Disney film while still being suitable for the whole family. This was the case with animation as well as live action. The issue you raise [about the use of "virgin" in the film] was one of countless judgment calls we made as we tried to keep Disney contemporary while true to its roots.

Mark I. Pinsky:

I don't want to be pejorative, but *Hocus Pocus* doesn't have the saccharine Disney feel to it. It's a movie where if you didn't know that it was produced by Disney, you might not suspect that.

Mara Wilson:

I remember when they kept saying the word "virgin," everybody was giggling. We asked, "What does that mean?" and one of the cooler girls in the class said, "A virgin is somebody who hasn't done *it* yet." They said it just like that. They emphasized "it." We were giggling about that, but I remember also thinking, *Well, why is that such a big deal?* We were all virgins and I figured you pretty much stay a virgin until you're ready to have children. That was my understanding of sex.

Thora Birch:

When I read the script, I asked [my parents] about it. I was like, "What is 'virginity'?" That was the big talk. Well, actually, I didn't get a *talk*. I got a book. "Spend some time in your room, read this. You're good."

Omri Katz:

A lot of people have told me that they learned what the word "virgin" meant because of *Hocus Pocus*. I mean, showing the movie to your kid for the first time and then it's like, "What's a virgin, Mom?" that would probably catch some people by surprise.

Larry Bagby:

An actress on a set I was working on, I think it was a Chili's commercial, realized I was in *Hocus Pocus* and told me she had mixed emotions about the film. Her parents taught her about the birds and the bees when she asked about the Black Flame Candle. That must have been so horrifying.

Vinessa Shaw:

People have to give teenagers more credit. I mean, in high school they're having all these talks anyway; they know what's going on. My first role I played a pregnant fourteen-year-old girl from the Dust Bowl era, so I had already gone beyond that, you know? I felt it was very tactful the way that it was done in the movie. It's done in a tongue-in-cheek way.

Tobias Jelinek:

The way virginity and adolescence is tied into this story is pretty brilliant. You don't have to address it as a parent because it's not a coming-of-age story per se. It's part of the mythology and magic.

Mara Wilson:

If you look at any kind of mythology, the virgin is usually the most powerful. Vestal Virgins were believed to be able to carry water in a sieve. They could commute sentences. They were dedicated to Artemis. They were considered pure and powerful. Virginity is actually a very common strength in a lot of mythology and a lot of religion. So I think that if you wanted to get a little bit pretentious, you could say, "Well, maybe it's not a bad thing to be a virgin. You get to have the power."

Chapter 12

"FOR WHATEVER REASON, IT JUST DID NOT STRIKE A CHORD"

*W*hen Hocus Pocus *was released on July 16, 1993, it wasn't the box office hit that those who worked on the film hoped it would be. It made $8.1 million its first weekend on a $28 million budget, landing in fourth place right above* Free Willy. *The reviews for the film ranged from bad (the* New York Times *called it an "unholy mess") to absolutely awful (*Associated Press *said, "the only real curses in this film will be yours as you walk up the aisle to leave"). At the time those who made the movie were disappointed by the lackluster release, but after three decades, everyone seems to have their own theory as to why* Hocus Pocus *wasn't a hit straight out of the gate.*

David Kirschner:

Disney didn't do a premiere, but they did a screening at the gorgeous El Capitan Theatre on Hollywood Boulevard. Coming out of the movie, Jeffrey [Katzenberg] said, "Well, we did it, buddy!" and he hugged me. Jeffrey's not a hugging kind of guy. I just remember feeling like life could not be better than this moment. I just thought, *We've got a hit here!* I didn't see what was coming and that knocked me over like a tsunami.

Liz Kirschner:

Jeffrey came up to Dave after the screening, and I don't remember his exact words, but he was beyond thrilled. He was thanking Dave because, that's the thing, the audience loved it. Nothing is guaranteed, but we were not expecting the response from critics.

Kenny Ortega:

Not only was it great fun making the film—certainly, working with Bette Midler, Kathy Najimy, Sarah Jessica Parker, Doug Jones, and all of the kids—but I was entertained by it [when I saw it] and so were others, including the cast. So it kind of really threw me that my sense of humor and my appreciation for this kind of moviemaking was being pooed on [by critics].

Alexis Kirschner:
To finally be sitting in a movie theater, watching it on a big screen, thinking back to my dad telling me this story was a really cool experience. I don't want to say it was an out-of-body experience, but to have watched the evolution of this story and know there were a bunch of people experiencing my story, too, was a really cool experience.

Omri Katz:
I don't even recall if there were paparazzi at the El Capitan screening, but I do remember feeling nervous. My name came up in the credits and I was like, "Oh god, I don't want to see it." At the time, I was already kind of an adult, I was seventeen, so it felt like it was oriented toward children and had that kind of Disney, I guess you could say, cheese factor to it. It wasn't like watching *The Godfather* or *Easy Rider* or *Scarface*, but it was cool. By the end, I was proud of it.

Vinessa Shaw:
I was completely entranced from the first shot of the movie when the witches are flying over. I thought, *Oh my God, this is going to be so good!*

Peggy Holmes:
I do remember really wanting to see the flying in its full glory. I remember feeling pretty happy about that and the musical number because Kenny shot a lot of stuff. A lot of close-ups, shots of feet, shots of hands. It was fun to see that musical number come together.

Doug Jones:
I went to the cast and crew screening and took [my wife] Laurie and a couple of close friends. I was nervous as could be. This was the biggest role and the biggest film I'd ever been in. Every time I was on-screen, I think I held my breath. As soon as I was off camera, I could let the air out.

Amanda Shepherd:

I went to the screening and I think that's when I signed my first two autographs. I'll admit I was excited about it. Everybody thought it was going to be this big huge thing, so my mom was almost preparing me, saying, "This is a big movie, Amanda. You may become known for this" so I was kind of expecting that. That wasn't my goal, but when you have somebody telling you that it's going to be this big hit, you're like, "I'm ready for this!" Like, "All right, bring it on!" When that didn't happen, it was just kind of like *womp-womp*.

Tony Gardner:

When I read *Hocus Pocus,* it was a very dark story and I really liked Mick Garris's darker script. I remember when I went to the cast and crew screening, it was a very different film. I knew the script had been changing, but I didn't realize how tonally it had shifted, so when it was over, I remember turning to my wife and going, "That's so different from what I was expecting. I don't know if I'm disappointed or if I just need to process it."

Chet Zar:

If people love the movie, I think that's great, but when I saw it, I didn't really like it that much. Personally, I was kind of disappointed. It was a little too family friendly for me. It definitely wasn't a bad movie, it was obviously well-made and everything, but I do remember not liking it that much.

Colin Brady:

When we saw the very first rough cut of *Hocus Pocus*, the music wasn't in there yet and it was very long. To be honest, I remember being really disappointed, but it's all about the editing; editing can save almost anything. Jeffrey Katzenberg came in and, to his credit, basically said, "This is a chase movie. Take out everything that's not related to them being chased by these witches." And it worked. When it came out I was like, *Oh, it's better than I thought!*

Doug Jones:

The screening was kind of low-key, but we had a little after-party. They had a dance floor and I got to see Kenny Ortega dance, which was wonderful. It was a very celebratory night. I had people coming up to me and just fawning all over me. Whatever I couldn't see in Billy, they did.

Vinessa Shaw:

I danced my head off at the party. I was obviously a teenager and I probably went with my mom, but I felt like it was equal to any bar mitzvah that I went to that had good tunes and good food. I have photos of that party; I'm just sweating and dancing. I remember seeing members of the crew just pointing across the room—"I love this jam, too!"

Amanda Shepherd:

I'll never forget, I was wearing a red-and-white polka-dot dress, and Kenny Ortega picked me up and whirled me around and said, "You are going to be a big star!" He was so happy and so excited, it was just really magical.

Doug Jones:

You know the scene in *Once Upon A Time... In Hollywood* where Margot Robbie as Sharon Tate goes by herself to a matinee in the middle of the day? She buys a ticket, sits among other people watching the movie, and she's just kind of having the experience that an audience member would have. Well, I did that with *Hocus Pocus*, more than once. I was living in the San Fernando Valley and I went to a matinee by myself just to kind of take it in one more time. There was never anybody there, but it was quite fulfilling for me. The first time I watch something all I see is what I should have done. The second viewing, I'm a bit more lenient and kind to myself. I was able to give myself more credit. "Okay, maybe I didn't suck as much as I thought."

Tobias Jelinek:

I had a similar experience when I was in Santa Barbara and went to a mall theater. I remember I had just met up with a skater kid who was a friend of a friend and we're cruising down State Street. I look up at the marquee and it reads "*Hocus Pocus*." I hadn't seen it yet so I said, "Hey, why don't we go watch this Halloween movie?" I remember he said, "Are you kidding me? It's a Disney film." I convinced him, I said, "I heard there's some interesting characters in it." It was a matinee and there were other people in the theater. It was far from full. We sat way in the back and I remember when I popped up in the cemetery scene, he turned his head and looked at me. His mouth was just open. I did not know him well, but he starts laughing and the people who were there start turning around thinking we're just snickering, you know, "Why are you even in this theater?" None of those people knew I was in it.

Larry Bagby:

I went on a mission for my church not long after *Hocus Pocus*. My manager was like, "This is ridiculous. You're leaving at your high point. I've got a lot of momentum with you. Are you sure you want to go?" What was funny was I ended up in Argentina on my mission. I was in this really small desert town with dirt roads, and there was a little movie theater and *Abracadabra* was playing there. Turns out, it was *Hocus Pocus*, so I ended up walking in to check it out. There were maybe two people in there, and I think they got up and left at some point, but someone had dubbed my part in Spanish. I thought, *Man, if they just waited another year, I could have done it myself!*

Vinessa Shaw:

When it came out and it didn't do that well, it was kind of heartbreaking for us all. I felt like we all thought it was going to be a sure hit and it wasn't. We just felt like that magic was there and it wasn't actually conveyed to the audience. It was crushing.

Tobias Jelinek:

There wasn't that celebration, that excitement of even having been in a film. I remember I was taking acting classes at the local city college, and one of the first exercises was you share your biography with a scene partner. It was right after *Hocus Pocus* and I remember sharing it and thinking they'll be so impressed that I've been in a film with Bette Midler, which had just been in the theaters. Nobody knew about it. It was really this feeling of, *Did it happen?*

Larry Bagby:

There was very little notoriety about it at all. The movie just kind of came and went. Of course, we opened a few weeks after *Jurassic Park*. It was the biggest movie I'd done to date so I was so excited about that. We got some cool auditions because of it, but it just kind of fizzled out.

Jason Marsden:

Most of my work was on TV, I didn't do a lot of features, so I definitely paid attention to how it was being marketed. I knew something was off when you saw the posters for it and it's a July release. "Are you kidding? It's a Halloween movie!"

Ralph Winter:

I mean, what's the right way to talk about Halloween in the heat of summer?

David Hoberman:
It was a weird choice and I can't for the life of me remember why we released it in July. It should have been a fall movie.

Gail Lyon:
What you have to remember is, especially back in those days, it was a radically different world. Collectively between Touchstone and Disney, we probably released twenty-four to thirty movies a year. The release date conversation was very nuanced and one that got decided really quite early. I didn't even actually remember that *Hocus Pocus* came out in July, to be honest with you, but in retrospect, that doesn't sound like the sweet spot. But again, I can't even begin to mention what a different era it was in terms of massive feature films from someplace like the Walt Disney Company. They just weren't as skilled as they are now in sort of placing these things. I mean, it was just such a totally different reality for the feature film box office.

Jeffrey Katzenberg:
The two best times for family films are summer and the Christmas holidays, since kids are out of school, whereas Halloween is one day and not even a [school] holiday. So, it seemed just a logical choice to swing for the fences and give this film a shot at the best possible release window, i.e. summer.

Aaron Wallace:
I'm a '90s kid, so I can remember the lead-up to the movie's release. I don't know that there was a lot of promotional fanfare in the summer of 1993 for this Halloween film, but I do remember being very aware of it. I was always into witches and all things Disney. I wanted to see it and I did end up seeing it in theaters. I was probably among the precious few who did. I think so many of us who knew this film and loved it didn't realize that anyone else did for decades.

Michele Atwood (CEO, *The Main Street Mouse*; Co-Founder, House of Mouse Expo):

I would say I'm a *Hocus Pocus* superfan. I was actually one of the people that did see it in theaters and I've just been a fan ever since. The cast was teasing me. They're like, "Oh, you're the one who saw it in the theater!" But this movie grew by word of mouth: "Oh, you haven't seen *Hocus Pocus*? You have to see it!" I still do that. If somebody tells me they haven't seen *Hocus Pocus* yet, I sort of gasp, but then I have a project. I tell them, "I need you to go and watch it and tell me what you think, because you're going to love it!"

Kimmy Blankenburg:

I was fortunate enough to see *Hocus Pocus* on opening day. I had just turned ten; my family and I were on vacation. We had rented a cottage on the lake and the weather was horrible, so we decided to go to a local mall that had a theater. Oh my goodness, I was captivated from the moment the opening scene started! My parents were amazing and let me see it two more times back-to-back that day. I couldn't get enough. Since then, I have been a fanatic, lover, and collector of all things *Hocus Pocus*. I lost my dad when he was only forty-nine, and this memory is one of my most favorite with him.

David Kirschner, 2018:

Everybody likes to say [the movie got] mixed reviews, but I'm so sensitive so I say "terrible" because I thought they would love it. The audiences loved it, it tested huge, but it also came out the same summer as *Jurassic Park*. No one was thinking about witches in July.

Kenny Ortega:

I remember one review, I don't remember the details, but the review said, "It's as if Kenny couldn't decide whether he was making a family movie or making a movie for adults." I was making a movie for everybody—and that's what it turned out to be. The movie is loved by a broad spectrum of people, from kids to grown-up folks, [and] that was what I had set out to do.

Chris Bailey:

It got fine reviews, but I think there was a sense of disappointment with a lot of people associated with it. I think if the cat got a mention, it was, "Was it necessary or could you just put peanut butter on its mouth?" I think that's what Rex Reed said. But then I remember there were also some really nice notes about the CG cat. I remember a couple of people sort of pontificated about what it said about the future. The work was received well within the industry.

Mary Vogt:

The reviews were terrible. It was not the kind of movie that reviewers especially liked back then.

Desson Thomson (Film Critic, *The Washington Post*, 1987–2008):

I think the thing to understand is, when you're a movie critic, you are like McDonald's, serving 297,000 burgers a year. In any given week you could get *The Last Temptation of Christ* and you could get a movie about three witches. You might get *Jackass 3D* and then you might get a European movie with subtitles. What I'm saying is, it's like being a quarterback, you're going to throw some interceptions. I don't remember saying anything [in my review of *Hocus Pocus*] that I would take back. My recollection of [the movie] was that it was incredibly uninspiring. I panned it, I guess, because it just seemed so innocuous.

Susan Wloszczyna (Film Critic, *USA Today*, 1989–2001):

I'm known for two things: I didn't like *Hocus Pocus,* and giving the only sort of good review to *Showgirls.* Those are my two notorious things. *USA Today* keeps reprinting [my *Hocus Pocus* review] and saying, "Our critic didn't like it." I guess I'm a villain, but no one ever got angry [about my review at the time]. There wasn't email, so people couldn't reach you. Sometimes you remember when you're sitting in a movie if it's really bad, and I can't remember seeing this movie. I haven't given it much thought except for what I wrote about it at the time. I guess it was a pan, but I loved writing it. It was brief and to the point, but I love those three actresses.

Thora Birch:

I mean, it is all good now, more than all good now, but largely everybody at the time thought that there was a problem with when they chose to release it. Like, "That's stupid. Why would they put it out in July?" So that was bad and then the print and advertising and publicity that was around for so many films of that era wasn't supplied for us. Some members of the cast chose not to promote it and that was surprising and disappointing. Then on top of it, the critics, and there was no audience. It was like watching a slow death and nobody wants to watch that when they're so emotionally invested in the experience. Especially when they're eleven years old. It was a real downer.

Aaron Wallace:

Some of those reviews were so harsh, it's funny to read them now. Stephen Hunter from the *Baltimore Sun* wrote a Shakespearean poem just totally ripping apart the film. It's a blast to go back and read that.

Neil Cuthbert:

It's too painful to read all the reviews unless you know they're going to be really positive, and I remember they weren't mostly. I think it was Janet Maslin [at the *New York Times*] who was negative.

Janet Maslin (Film Critic, *The New York Times*, 1977–1999):

If you look back at the 1993 reviews, I was more or less on the same page as Roger Ebert, who didn't see it as a cult classic either. Has it become one? I guess so, or you wouldn't be writing about it. But often the sources of staying power aren't obvious. They take shape over time, as with the once-terrible action movies that now look so predictive of 2020s tastes. One thing I can say about the new popularity of *Hocus Pocus* is that its Disneyness must be a significant factor. It was part of the '90s Disney revival in which undervalued actors were instrumental in the studio's relaunch, and Midler was Exhibit A. As for any '90s nostalgia that may be helping it or the increasing commercial importance of Halloween, I can't speak to either. I'm always glad to see something catch fire over time. I wouldn't have bet on this one. But every now and then I catch wind of one of these revisionist waves. My review of *Meet Joe Black* kept recirculating, and I thought that was because it's a funny review. It is, but now people like the film better, so maybe they're laughing at me. It happens. I have regrets, but these aren't among them.

Jason Marsden:

Everything I heard was kind of positive. Truthfully, I think because it didn't make a lot of money it became known as a critical failure as well. It's not show talent, it's show business. No matter how shitty a movie is, if it's made three times its cost at the box office, it's a hit, a success. I had been in the business about eight years at that point and I still had enough experience to know, "Oh, that's it. Just move on to the next thing." It hurts every time, every time. You have to allow yourself to feel the feelings, to feel the sadness, the frustration, the bitterness, the jealousy, and then you have to move on. I didn't feel anything that heavy. I was just kind of sad. I thought, *Oh man, this is a really good movie. I wish more people would see it. Maybe on video.*

Joseph Malone:

I was paying attention to the box office. I was invested because of Kenny. Who doesn't want to see that man do well? When I saw the movie, I thought it was just really unfairly judged. This is a nice movie, a good movie. It hits all the marks, so I didn't understand what they were all fussy about. It's not supposed to be *Titanic*. I was unhappy that it didn't do better because I thought he had done a really good job.

Doug Jones:

I paid attention to how long it stayed in the theater. It didn't stay in as long as I'd hoped. You see the box office numbers come out in the *Hollywood Reporter* or *Variety* and you see that we weren't number one after all. We didn't stay in the Top 10 for weeks and weeks and weeks, so I thought, *Well, that ship sailed, onto the next thing, I guess.*

Omri Katz:

It pretty much flopped. Part of it was the marketing; part of it was that they released it against *Jurassic Park* in the summertime because they obviously didn't want to compete with *A Nightmare Before Christmas,* which came out that October. I saw that it flopped and just moved on. I did my job.

Mary Vogt:

Before *Hocus Pocus* came out I was invited to a screening at Disney. It was me, my costume supervisor, I think Kenny was there, and then mostly Disney executives and their kids. The kids were young, like three and five years old; really too young for this film. They're playing the movie and it's all going well and then the cat gets run over by a car. All of a sudden, all the kids start crying. They're crying hysterically. I'm like, "Uh-oh, this isn't good." The executives are going, "This is not a Disney movie. This makes kids cry!" I was thinking, *Did you see* Bambi?

David Kirschner:

I don't think I was sophisticated enough to understand that there was very little marketing. In retrospect, I look back and say, "Oh my God, there was no marketing on this film!" There was a movie trailer, maybe some TV spots, but there weren't any billboards. There wasn't this Disney machine that got it out there in this huge way. There was really nothing.

Steven Haft:

Disney had a famously successful marketing team back in those days, but the marketing department is only as aggressive as the market research would give them permission to be. I don't know that our test numbers were so huge that there was an urgency to throw a lot of money against it.

Mick Garris:

I always feel like an audience is going to find and embrace a movie in spite of, not because of, the advertising. It was complete folly to release it in July, but I understand releasing a family film in the middle of summer when the kids are out of school and they can go see it any day of the week. It's easy to second-guess the marketing campaign, but I think, if it had the appeal to the audience that it was intended to have, they'd have found it. For whatever reason, it just did not strike a chord.

David Kirschner:

How do you put a Halloween movie out in July? I wanted to say, "Jeffrey, you were the guy that responded to Halloween as a billion-dollar business!" But I think he probably did remember that and put Tim Burton's *Nightmare Before Christmas* out there in the fall. That's the truth.

Rosemary Brandenburg:

Tim Burton's *Nightmare Before Christmas* won the race as far as getting the funding for marketing. They didn't want to have two movies competing with each other at the box office. So *Hocus Pocus* kind of became the stepchild. It was kind of dismissed to some extent at the time.

Mary Hidalgo:

I was involved in *Nightmare Before Christmas,* too, but I was not aware of that bias. . . . *Nightmare Before Christmas* took forever. It was all stop-motion and back in those days that took years. They had this movie from Tim Burton and they had no merchandise for it when it was released, which I thought was strange.

David Kirschner:

I think honestly, they had *Nightmare Before Christmas*, and they felt that that was the film. I think we were just kind of viewed as silly and Tim's movie is a brilliant movie. I mean it is a classic and it was a classic from the very beginning. We weren't a classic. We were a film that failed.

David Hoberman:

I don't remember anyone saying, "Let's push [*Hocus Pocus*]," but if we pushed it to summer that would indicate we felt pretty good about it. We knew that summer and the holidays were the best times to release big movies. We probably could have put both of them back-to-back and not have to compete with each other. I mean, that's what I would do today. Put *Hocus Pocus* out and then follow up with *Nightmare Before Christmas*, which also wasn't a hit to begin with.

Hocus Pocus *did have a few famous fans, however, that were not shy about their love for the film.*

Vinessa Shaw:

Michael Jackson called my agent a few months before *Hocus Pocus* was released and said, "Would Vinessa like to go to the *Home Alone 2* wrap party? [Macaulay Culkin and I] saw the movie *Hocus Pocus* and we love it." My agent calls me and says, "Michael would love to talk to you. You can call him at this time." My mom and I were in the car and we were just driving around LA, so we pull over and my mom had a car phone,

one of those brick phones. I put it on speakerphone so my mom could hear and a person goes, "Hello?" I knew that wasn't Michael and I said, "Um, is Michael there?" like, *I can't believe I'm asking is Michael Jackson there!* Then they said, "No, hold on," and the next person gets on and says, "Hello? Is this Vinessa? I'm sorry, I'm really nervous because I just really enjoyed your performance." I said to Michael, "You're nervous!" and I said it just that way. He said, "Would you like to go to the *Home Alone 2* wrap party? And if it's okay, Macaulay Culkin would like to call you." Of course, I knew *Home Alone*, and I loved him in *My Girl*, but I was thinking, *This kid is eleven or twelve and I'm sixteen.* I get this call later at my house from Macaulay and he says, "I'd really like it if you come to the wrap party." I said, "I would love to. Is anyone else going?" I didn't get an answer, but we started chatting and he's like, "We're finishing this movie. It's going to be good. Just like the first one." He's just like a sweet kid. I could tell he was trying to be cool. I was just like, "Well, I'm so honored you invited me, I'll definitely be there." Then cut to the day it was supposed to happen, the day the Rodney King riots happened in Los Angeles, which, of course, changed the history of the US. So I'm glad I had the opportunity to connect with both of them, but I never saw them.

The inauspicious release of Hocus Pocus *affected the cast and crew in different ways.*

Omri Katz:

After *Hocus Pocus*, I pretty much left the industry. I did a few parts here and there, but because of the relationship I had built with Vince [Welnick, the keyboardist for the Grateful Dead] I went on the Dead tour. I started following the Dead all over the country. I always had tickets at every show waiting for me with backstage passes. I guess there are some perks to showbiz. I should go and kiss Kenny's feet and thank him again for allowing me to have that experience, but I just kind of left Hollywood all behind to go see what else the world had to offer me. I never really had a desire to come back to acting. Actually, I did have a desire to come back, but for all the wrong reasons. It was for money and not because I was truly passionate or driven to act, and that didn't work out too well. This was kind of a blessing because I really got to learn more about life and myself and dig deep and have different experiences other than just being caught up in that Hollywood loophole. This business can chew you up and spit you out. A lot of child actors struggle to move on and find their identity. I went through that as well, but I think I got out early enough to discover that there's more to life than what Hollywood has to offer.

Vinessa Shaw:

After *Hocus Pocus,* I didn't want to be a bright light that faded too quickly. It was a challenge because a lot of my peers were growing up too fast or becoming lost in drugs and alcohol, losing their lives. It was a lot for me. I just kind of had to make my own path and that was hard because a lot of people didn't understand me. They were thinking, "Well, why wouldn't you want to just be famous and be in this top movie?" All these years later, I'm proud of my integrity, but you know, there are times when I'm like, "Why didn't I just take that movie so that I could have done a little bit more," you know? I really chose from early on to be a person of integrity and do roles that I really felt were expressing humanity, and that's just hard as a teenager, especially in the early 2000s. I mean, it was an *American Pie* world. *Eyes Wide Shut* [in 1999] was what kind of put me on the path of where I really wanted to go. I feel really happy that I took the time to grow as a person and, this is a Gen X mentality, but not sell out. I needed to do that for myself.

Chris Bailey:

It's funny because after *Hocus Pocus,* for a while, I had a nice career as a CGI 9-1-1 guy in movies. After these early movies, everybody thought it was easy. Everybody thought computers animated it. I was brought on as the animation consultant mid-production on *Deep Rising*, which was Stephen Sommers's movie before *The Mummy*. I then went on to do *Mighty Joe Young*, which wasn't quite jelling together. I think there was a great deal of enthusiasm for CGI back then, but people's eyes got a little bigger than their stomach.

Colin Brady:

Three or four years after *Hocus Pocus*, I found out that the next *Star Wars* movie [*Star Wars: Episode I – The Phantom Menace*] was in the works. They were looking for an animation director for what was going to be a fully animated talking character mixed with live action. They were very impressed that I did all this work on Binx the Cat, so they offered me the job. When *Phantom Menace* came out [in 1999], I was shocked that the character's name was Jar Jar Binks. I thought that was the strangest coincidence in the world. I've had a wonderful career; after *Hocus Pocus*, I went to Pixar to be one of the first animators on *Toy Story* and now I'm running my own animation studio, doing some cutting-edge AI. Someone once joked that I'm the "Forrest Gump of computer animation" because I've had so many different reincarnations in this industry. I've always tried to find movies that were the first to do something and it goes back to *Hocus Pocus*. It really opened up a lot of doors for me.

Neil Cuthbert:

I actually did another project or two for Disney. They were happy with me and I liked working for them, but *Hocus Pocus* didn't help my career per se. I was doing indie scripts, and then [the 1999 superhero comedy] *Mystery Men* came along. So *Hocus Pocus* didn't help me, but it didn't kill me either.

Amanda Shepherd:

In grade school, everybody knew I was in it. I already had fake friends, but the thing was, it didn't bother me. I knew the movie was the only reason they were hanging around me. Now I feel different about someone wanting to be fake friends with me, but when you're young, you don't think about that stuff. You're just, "Oh, they really like the movie and they really like me and that's cool."

Don Yesso:

I became really good friends with Sarah Jessica Parker after this movie. We did a film in Vancouver together for three months; it was me, Brendan Fraser, and Sarah. Talk about a flop. You've probably never even heard of that movie, you'll probably have to google it, but it was called *Dudley Do-Right*. I don't think it made ten thousand dollars. We all spent Thanksgiving dinner together. SJ, we called her SJ on set, came to my wife's birthday party. She was a big Yankees fan and they were in the World Series [in 1998, when we were filming *Dudley Do-Right*] so we would all get a table at the bar and it would be twenty guys and Sarah, plopped in the middle. But it's interesting, we never once mentioned the movie *Hocus Pocus*. I guess neither of us wanted to bring it up; it was too painful. It really was such a bomb. All we would say was "Oh yeah, we worked together."

Mary Vogt:

It's funny, because the movie wasn't successful; the costumes were rented out for years. They don't do it anymore, but twenty years ago, all the big costume houses, including Disney's wardrobe department, would open up on Halloween to make extra money and they would rent out costumes from their movies: *Tron*, *Hocus Pocus*, all the big films. After they were worn, they went to the dry cleaners. I'm amazed those dresses have any color left in them at all; when you hand-dye stuff it doesn't really hold up. Now the studios are very sort of precious about everything, but then, if you had seventy dollars you could rent Bette Midler's costume for a couple of days.

Ralph Winter:

It's funny, when we came for *Hocus Pocus 2*, our costume designer [Salvador Pérez Jr.] went back to the studio to look at the outfits and some of them were in tatters. It was just sort of sad that no one saw the future of that or protected that. A lot of those things, props, et cetera, were gone.

Kevin Haney:

Unfortunately, Winifred's teeth and those molds from *Hocus Pocus* were lost. When it came time to do *Hocus Pocus 2*, we started with a new cast and for whatever reason we couldn't get them to stay in Bette's mouth. I had consulted with an actual dental technician and he said Bette has a difficult mouth so the new ones just took a long time to get right. Every time I made them look like the original, she was like, "They're too long. I can't close my mouth. I can't talk." I think we did like ten sets of teeth. Bette's face has changed, obviously, and just trying to get the right shape for her face now was difficult. I actually took the teeth that were too large for Bette and used them for Ginger Minj. But I haven't heard anybody say, "Why are her teeth different?" I mean, there are a bunch of people out there that freeze-frame movies to try to find errors and mistakes and, you know, we hate them. I take this to mean, fans accept these teeth as the total look, but they are different from the original.

Liz Kirschner:

When it first came out, it didn't do well. It was painful and sad. But I said to David, "It doesn't matter because look where it is now. It's one of the most beloved Halloween films." I mean, it was a Halloween film released in July against *Jurassic Park*. How is that going to work? You always have to look at the glass half-full and, boy, the glass is really full, because here we are.

Allison Dubrosky:

I just think it's so funny that they gave such harsh reviews. I mean it had horrible reviews. One reviewer, I believe it was the weekend it came out, basically said, "Years from now, you will expect to find this in the five-dollar bin at Blockbuster." Here we are thirty years later; people are paying massive dollars for anything that they can collect with the *Hocus Pocus* brand. That delayed success, I think, really plays a role in why people love it so much. If it would've been an instant classic, I don't know if we'd be in the same spot we are here today.

Don Yesso:

Kathy and I almost did another movie together with Kenny Ortega where we were going to play husband and wife. It was something where we had a girl who was a hip-hop dancer in the Bronx or Brooklyn. We did a table reading, but *Hocus Pocus* was such a flop, we didn't get to make it. It's funny, I realize if the movie would have been a huge hit, life would have taken a different direction for me. I don't know where I'd be. But if it was a hit, it might not be a classic now.

Desson Thomson:

Movies are immortal. They're almost Buddhist. They can have a new life that's nothing like the life they had before. That's thanks to the variety of human beings that the planet is blessed with. A movie can always have an afterlife.

William Sandell:

I knew in my heart that *Hocus Pocus* was going to be a perennial Halloween movie. I knew we were going to be *the* Halloween movie, and you know what? We got our revenge.

Chapter 13

SAVED FROM THE BARGAIN BIN

*I*n *the early 2000s, thanks to its DVD release,* Hocus Pocus *began a word-of-mouth resurgence. But it was cable television that turned it into the hit it is now. In 2002, the Disney-owned basic cable network ABC Family (now known as Freeform) began airing the movie as part of its "13 Nights of Halloween" marathon. In 2016, Freeform estimated that a whopping 23.4 million viewers watched the movie on the channel. Two years later, the network launched the expanded "31 Nights of Halloween" and played* Hocus Pocus *even more times in the lead-up to the holiday. The resurgence was a surprise to the cast and crew, but looking back, there were clues all along that* Hocus Pocus *was not the disappointment it originally appeared to be.*

Neil Cuthbert:

I remember going to the Disney Store a year or two after the movie came out, there was literally no merchandise from *Hocus Pocus,* but then this thing started happening. I remember mothers coming up to me and saying, half-jokingly, that they would like to kill me. "You're one of the writers of *Hocus Pocus?* Well, I have a five-year-old daughter and she has played that VHS over and over and over again." That was really the beginning of the surge. Little girls were the first ones to discover [the film] and now they're all thirty-five or forty years old and it's still one of their favorite movies.

Doug Jones:

I did that thing where you go into a Blockbuster or your local video store and you go see if it's on the shelf. When it wasn't, I thought, *Maybe it does have an afterlife because people are renting it.*

Blake Harris (Screenwriter, *Hocus Pocus 2*):

It wasn't a big theatrical success, but yet every single friend of mine, when naming some [of their] favorite movies, *Hocus Pocus* would come up and it was almost always met with extreme passion, like, "Oh my god, me too!" That was kind of a telltale sign, like, "Wait a minute, there's a reason why that VHS was always checked out."

Mara Wilson:

Matilda was never a big box office success, but I hear from people every week who loved it growing up. I think there was this ritual of going to Blockbuster or going to your local video store in the '90s, renting a video, and staying up to watch it with your friends. *Hocus Pocus* had this life that shows that maybe in some ways box office is less important than we think. A lot of times it's really more about staying power, what does and doesn't appeal to kids.

Ginger Minj ("Drag Queen Winifred," *Hocus Pocus 2*; *RuPaul's Drag Race*):

When I was younger, we never had the money to go see first-run movies, we always had to wait for them to hit the 99-cent theater near the house. Usually the wait was excruciating, but somehow we got *Hocus Pocus* during the Halloween season; it made the experience even better. I've always loved the magic, the spells, the music, the whole aura of that film. Those three women taught me so much about being a queen before I ever even discovered drag.

Amanda Shepherd:

I went to a Catholic high school and every Halloween, *Hocus Pocus* was the movie they played. Every. Single. Halloween. This was before it was a hit. They took everybody to the cafeteria and put on *Hocus Pocus*. Of course everyone was like, "Please say the line! Come on, come on!" Throughout my entire life, it's always been great for me. It was always there and there was always a little bit of buzz around it. Just a little bit.

David Kirschner, 2018:

The first moment I really realized it caught on was when my daughter told me her friend could recite the film. She brought her to the office at the house and said, "Okay, do it!" and she started reciting complete passages from the film. She had watched it over and over and over and over again. I was blown away by that and didn't realize how many others could do the same thing.

Michele Atwood:

There are a lot of people that can recite the movie by heart. I'm one of them.

Jessie Wolfson:

The kids at school would want to be the Sandersons for Halloween, but it was an odd phenomenon. When you're younger, you feel like your world is small. My parents were not Hollywood people; my dad still to this day will probably not go down a red carpet, so when I would see people knowing *Hocus Pocus*, it was, *How do you know that?*

Alex Steed:

There is a generation of kids for whom this was one of twenty movies they owned and could watch the entire year so they watched it maybe twenty times a year. There are probably many kids who can recite to you the commercials that played in between because that was part of their viewing experience.

William Cuthbert:

In 1994, the film was apparently shown on Pay-Per-View or the Disney Channel, it's unclear which, with deleted scenes. Someone shared screenshots online from the alleged VHS recording. Not to sound braggy, but I have an original script from 1991 so I know the ins and outs of these deleted scenes; the pool scene, where Sarah and Mary push Winifred into the pool at the high school, and the supermarket scene, which is seen briefly in an early trailer. When I asked the person who posted those images about these scenes, he described them so accurately it made me believe that this VHS must exist somewhere, maybe in someone's attic or under someone's bed.

Allison Dubrosky:

We tell our listeners and our followers to check their VHS copies. You might have been recording it that one time they allegedly aired that special version. You could have a golden ticket!

Kenny Ortega:

Well, I cannot for certain confirm that there was a high school pool scene. There may well have been, but I don't remember. However, there was definitely a grocery market scene. In fact, my sister, Debra Lee Ortega, was in it. I don't recall it ever being cut into a version of *Hocus Pocus* that aired, but it was in our first cuts and it, along with other fun bits, found its way out of the movie in order for us to get the film to time. There wasn't anything that I can really think of that I felt [bad cutting] except for maybe the grocery scene because my beloved sister was in it. I thought the scene, which featured Kathy Najimy, my sister, and a baby, was very clever and gave Kathy another great comic moment. Maybe someday Disney would be open to letting me put that back in for a special screening. That would be fun.

Mara Wilson:

I saw *Hocus Pocus* at my friends' house, the twins, Dana and Rebecca. There are always those twins who are the cool girls in every school for some reason. Most, if not all, of the girls in my first-grade class were there, and we all watched *Hocus Pocus*. I found it terrifying, but also enthralling. The rest of the girls all completely loved it. We were quoting it and making jokes about it the whole rest of the night.

Nell Minow:

There are two times in a child's life when they particularly want to watch the same movie a thousand times in a row, and it's not coincidental that they're both the times of the greatest transformation in a child's life: the late toddler period, going from being a baby to being a child, and early adolescence. Everything around them is suddenly different, so it's tremendously comforting to have something that's always the same. The thing about a movie is, it's always the same. Your reaction to it may shift over time, but it's always the same. People will sometimes write me and say, "My twelve-year-old is having a slumber party. What is a good movie for them?" I say, "No, no, no, no. When they're twelve, you ask them what they want to see." And don't say, "Well, you've seen it two hundred times already." The sameness and the reliability and the predictability of it is an enormous comfort during turbulent times in their development. *Hocus Pocus* is directed at that age group and it hits that sweet spot. There are certain movies that imprint on us the way the mother goose imprints on the gosling. It's the first time that you experience certain responses to a film and it just becomes a part of your life completely disconnected from whether it's a good movie or a bad movie.

Belissa Escobedo:

I think growing up, for me, [*Hocus Pocus*] just meant Halloween entirely. We'd always watch it right before going trick-or-treating. I love the Sanderson sisters. I just think they're hilarious. I never thought there would be a sequel, just because it's so iconic and a lot of time had passed. When I got the audition I was like, "Oh my God, this is crazy!" I was just excited either way to have part two. Now being in it, I feel like the first one is much more sentimental. I feel very much connected to that world now. It's almost like when I watch the first one, it feels like I know the place. It just feels more familiar now.

While some saw Hocus Pocus *for the first time on VHS, others caught it on the Disney Channel, where it aired every October between 1996 and 2006. But it wasn't until 2007 when ABC Family, now Freeform, added* Hocus Pocus *to its "13 Nights of Halloween" slate that it officially became a spooky holiday staple.*

Debra OConnell (President, News Group and Networks, Disney Entertainment):

When you look back on the history of "13 Nights of Halloween," the stunt reflects the network's brand, rooted in a curated mix of broad, family-friendly content that celebrates the Halloween spirit, leaning into "spooky not scary." *Hocus Pocus* exemplifies this lens perfectly, so what started as a thematically aligned scheduling strategy expanded over the years as audiences discovered this unique title and fell in love with the Sanderson sisters. It's certainly no fluke that the movie found its way to cable. Before streaming put movies at audiences' fingertips, cable was and continues to be a great place to discover or relive curated content in a lean-back experience.

Tony Gardner:

It was always fun to watch it on TV instead of on your VHS, because it looked better. Then there was a year where it was like, "Oh, they're playing it twice." Then all of a sudden, probably about ten years ago, it was playing once a day and the fan response was massive.

William Sandell:

I remember realizing that ABC Family was playing it every Halloween and then all of a sudden it was like thirty days of it.

Debra OConnell:

In 2012, we started programming *Hocus Pocus* with even more fre-quency. In collaboration with our social team, we really started focusing on *Hocus Pocus* in "13 Nights of Halloween" and the audience responded, making it the number one movie on cable in October. Execs knew they were onto something and increased the usage in 2015, airing [the movie] ten times throughout the month. Ratings really grew in 2016 and 2017 when we were running the movie almost every night of the stunt. Fans couldn't get enough and wanted more, helping it retain its number one ranking, and cementing its status as the crown jewel of the Halloween stunt.

Bette Midler, 2022:

We went from, like, nothing to suddenly we're getting these sort of checks and wondering, *What the heck's going on?* They were presenting it as a thing during October, first a week, and then two weeks. And then suddenly it was a month.

Kate Fox:

I don't know if it was because Freeform started showing it, you know, thirty-one days in October or what the contributing factor was to the *Hocus Pocus* phenomenon, but we have two websites, Salem.org and HauntedHappenings.org. We have the *Hocus Pocus* filming locations listed on both of them and they are consistently one of the top four pages visited on our websites year round. It's not just October, whenever they're coming, they want to see the *Hocus Pocus* sites.

Doug Jones:

You can't flip channels without coming across *Hocus Pocus* during the month of October. It's like, "Oh, well, there it is again. Oh, there it is again."

Debra OConnell:

Absolutely *Hocus Pocus* was a key piece in expanding "13 Nights" to "31 Nights of Halloween" on Freeform. We had seen ratings and fandom increase the past few years, and in 2018 we had a great curated set list of

Halloween titles, none more important than *Hocus Pocus*, so we knew we had the goods to deliver a full "31 Nights." Our marketing team rebranded the stunt, and we really focused on making it feel like a giant celebration of all things Halloween with *Hocus Pocus* being the anchor. Freeform aired *Hocus Pocus* twenty-seven times that year across "31 Nights of Halloween" and ratings just kept growing, reaching more than twenty-four million people.

Kimmy Blankenburg:

My husband, Pete—who thankfully accepts my addiction—and I did a rough estimate of how many times I watch it in one year. It roughly comes out to twenty-five times, and I can confidently say I've seen this film well over a thousand times [in my life], give or take a few. We have a rule in our house, if *Hocus Pocus* is on, we watch it, no matter what. So when they're playing it thirteen times in a Halloween season, that's thirteen times I watch it in one month.

Neil Cuthbert:

It plays well on television, which, by the way, is where I saw all the comedians that I loved as a kid. I was watching them on a little black-and-white TV. This kind of comedy plays really well on TV.

Allison Dubrosky:

I was one when it came out in theaters, but I do remember seeing it when they started playing it on ABC Family. I remember just immediately falling in love with Winifred Sanderson. I wanted her to be like my fun aunt. I would have been like, "Suck the life out of me, sure, go for it!"

Mark I. Pinsky:

It is a feel-good movie; you will leave wherever you're watching it feeling good.

Matt Piwowarczyk (Cohost, *All Things Cozy* Podcast):

I would look forward to every Halloween getting to watch it and especially at the time, they would do all these intercuts of behind-the scenes footage. There's this clip I loved of Bette Midler scratching Thora Birch's face accidentally with her nails when she's swooping down to grab her. I can picture myself in front of the TV watching that scene.

Thora Birch:

I barely remember it, but it wasn't even [Bette Midler's] fault. I'm somebody that always has been very nasty to her stunt double because I don't want them to have their job. I want to do it. That was always my fight: "I can do it. She doesn't even look like me!" At this moment, they were like, "Okay, well, we'll try it" and I think the edge of the broom kind of scraped the top of my head or something. It wasn't anything. The rig that she was on went faster than they had anticipated. She was super apologetic, but it was one of those things where the adults panic a little bit more than the kids do.

David Kirschner, 2018:

When Disney started running it on ABC Family was when I started hearing about sororities having huge *Hocus Pocus* parties where there would be drinking games every time the word "book" was said.

Don Yesso:

I've only seen the movie two times. First was at the cast and crew screening, and the second time was when my son was probably around seven or eight. We watched it all the way through and he went, "Okay, I want to watch wrestling now." I realized, "Oh, that didn't impress him." What's funny is that when he was in college, he and his friends used to use me as an icebreaker with all the girls. "You know who his dad is? He's the bus driver from *Hocus Pocus*." It became a pickup line and it sure worked a lot.

Dr. Carmen Phillips:

I know I watched it all the time on VHS as a kid, but it almost feels like it just magically showed up. There is something very childhood about that, like, it was there one day, you know? But I got really into the movie again in my twenties. I remember I got it on Netflix, back when Netflix would mail DVDs to your house. I remember the first year I thought, *Oh, I should watch* Hocus Pocus. *It's Halloween*, and all the copies were already taken. I remember saying, "I'm going to place my Netflix order in September and just hold on to it!" The nostalgia of it really stuck with me. I watched *Hocus Pocus* when I was a kid and I enjoyed it and then when I was older, it made me feel like a kid again. There are so few movies that can perfectly take you back. Not in a weird longing way. Not in a weird distant, *Oh, remember when* kind of way. For me, there's something so pure and joyful about *Hocus Pocus*. It feels like Snickers bars, those teeny tiny Snickers bars.

Jessie Wolfson:

It's almost like *I Love Lucy*, you could see the same episode fifty thousand times, but it's just so good. I could watch *Hocus Pocus* three times today and not be tired of it. It's like opening a new world every time I see that movie.

Doug Jones:

The movie came out back in the day when you had a theater run and then VHS, and maybe a network TV airing here and there. The life of a film was only so long then. This movie did the opposite of what movies normally do. The afterlife of the movie has been unexpected. It was received moderately and then grew over time instead of fading away. The *Hocus Pocus* home collection has been an ongoing thing through all of its iterations, going from VHS to DVD to Blu-ray to 4K. Now of course, it streams on Disney+ at the push of a button.

Allison Dubrosky:

In probably the late 2000s, I was in high school, and that's when I started my [*Hocus Pocus*] VHS and DVD collection. I have over sixty versions now between a few laser disc copies, VHS, DVDs, Blu-rays. I have a Japanese version, a German version, a French version, an Australian version, a UK version, and a Mexican version. They all have different subtitle options, some of them have different voiceovers and different languages. I think it's a bit crazy, my husband does too, but I just feel like it shows how worldwide *Hocus Pocus* actually is.

William Cuthbert:

As a kid [growing up in the UK], *Hocus Pocus* was kind of like a glimpse at American Halloween. Allison's house was piled high with food, there were pumpkins and trick-or-treaters everywhere. It was exciting, it was like, *Look how good it is in America!*

Daniel Henares (Filmmaker):

I didn't realize how popular *Hocus Pocus* was in Brazil [where I live] until I made a documentary about *Hocus Pocus* and saw all the comments on YouTube. We don't have trick-or-treating here, but I think the movie is about more than Halloween. It's this beautiful story about love, family, and magic. It's got heart and here in Brazil, our heart, beats the same as yours. *Hocus Pocus* is this magical thing that we can all share.

Peggy Holmes:

Kenny has a pulse on a very special kind of movie and it shows. Look what we're talking about thirty years later! That is one of his superpowers: knowing what's going to attract an audience. He's very, very good at that.

William Sandell:

Many women and men, but it's mostly women, have built *Hocus Pocus* into this Halloween juggernaut. They love sitting there with their daughters to see it for the first time. They've got one eye on the screen and one eye on the kid to see if she likes it. The kids always love Binx, that's their favorite part.

Neil Cuthbert:

Kenny as a director is more into this theatricality and flamboyance and kind of over-the-top-ness . . . [*Hocus Pocus*] goes big and he has to get credit for that. He probably has to take the blame for what happened in the beginning, but he also gets the credit for the success it's had since then.

That success includes a yearly run at the Walt Disney—owned El Capitan Theatre, a fully restored 1920s movie palace located on Hollywood Boulevard.

James M. Wood (Vice President/General Manager, El Capitan Theatre):

We are always looking for classic titles from the Disney vault to bring back on the big screen. Back in 2015, we had a summer intern who suggested that we show *Hocus Pocus* as it was one of her favorite films and many of her friends that were the same age felt similarly. So, we decided to try it out, and as we were planning the screenings we reached out to Kenny Ortega, who was a great supporter of the El Capitan over the years, and he agreed to participate and bring along cast members and the composer John Debney. The first year was so popular that we have continued to bring it back year after year. And I'm happy to say each year Kenny and John have come and welcomed the fans and collaborated with us to make each year unique and special. I think that this is one of those magical films that takes viewers on a ride—there is laughter, sadness, anger, and joy. People still want to see movies on the big screen in a communal experience, and El Capitan provides that like no other. Whether it is seeing the Sanderson sisters perform live or John Debney bringing an orchestra to do part of the score before the film, you know that you are going to have a special experience that can't be replicated at home.

John Debney:
Every year they've played [the movie] at El Capitan, they'd ask me to come. Some years it was just me. I sort of felt like I was a torchbearer. I remember David Kirschner and I would talk about it a lot back then—"We really think there's a big fan base here!" And we were right, but Disney didn't want to know anything about it for a long time. For years, I was trying to organize live concerts with an orchestra playing to the film. They would just sort of laugh. Then they did a bunch of concerts [in 2022]. The Disney people are wonderful; I love that they finally came to the party.

Aaron Wallace:
There was a time when just no one really talked to Bette about [*Hocus Pocus*]. I mean, it never came up in interviews with her. I recall that she had a sitcom [in 2000] in which she played a sort of exaggerated version of herself. There was an episode all about Halloween and Bette Midler's Halloween legacy, and *Hocus Pocus* was not even included anywhere in the episode. It's unthinkable that that would be the case if that sitcom premiered today. You also have to imagine she would not have included the song ["I Put a Spell on You"] in her set list throughout the '90s and even the 2000s, but then there was this cultural turning point. The millennials had grown up and now suddenly there was this audience where Bette could step into the role that she loves the most and perform it for a sold-out crowd. On [her 2015] tour, she had a backdrop of the Sanderson sisters' cottage, she had the wig and the gown and the whole getup. One clearly gets the sense that Bette Midler has always been personally proud of the film.

Bette Midler, 2016:

I have to say, I'm flawless in that movie. I do, I have to say that. First of all, it's the only time I've ever actually disappeared behind a real mask. It was so liberating. It was so much fun, you know, to find this way of moving and this way of holding your hands and this voice. It was just great.

Nell Minow:

It's kind of the *lingua franca* of that [millennial] generation, it's a shortcut. You can make a reference to the Sanderson sisters. Everybody knows what it is. It may not be as primal for the next generations, but I think it will remain popular because the things that make it appealing are still very appealing.

Doug Jones:

When I was a kid, I watched *The Wizard of Oz* every year. It came on broadcast television once a year, and if you missed it, you missed it, so you did not miss it. I saw *The Wizard of Oz* and became a huge fan of that movie. It changed my childhood. Having never seen it in the theater, the original box office of that movie was unimportant to me. What was important was that I got to watch it now. *Hocus Pocus* kind of has become *The Wizard of Oz* of our day. The original theater box office numbers do not even matter. It's here now. We're going to enjoy it now.

Jason Marsden:

About five years ago, I was invited to a friend's Halloween party and it was a *Hocus Pocus*–themed party. I was like, "Oh, that's cool. I'll wear a black suit and get some cat contact lenses and I'll get some cat ears. I'll go as Binx and I'll be in character and I'll annoy everybody!" I didn't realize how serious it was. They had *Hocus Pocus* playing on the TV. The hosts were dressed as the Sanderson sisters; they looked fantastic. I just played with it and pretended to hate them the entire time. Someone took a photo of me and put it on the internet and then *BuzzFeed* took it and ran with it. And I'm like, "Oh, this is for real." People really care about this in a big way. I had no idea.

Thora Birch:

Coming off of *American Beauty* and *Ghost World*, I was flying at a certain level and I often heard, "Aren't you the girl from *Hocus Pocus*?" I'm like, "What the fuck? What are you talking about, man?" It was where I was hearing that, too. It wasn't in LA or New York or Toronto or London. It was when you stopped off in an airport somewhere in Ohio or Florida.

Rosemary Brandenburg:

The number of young crew people that I have [worked with] that say, "Oh my God, you did *Hocus Pocus*? It's my favorite movie." I can't claim tremendous credit for it, but when you're three or four or five years old, those kinds of movies go straight into your DNA. They can't believe they're meeting someone who worked on it. How lovely to give them that experience.

Russell Bobbitt:

When I'm on set, I'll read the room and I'll know when or when not to mention *Hocus Pocus* based on people's ages. I can pick out a *Hocus Pocus* fan no problem. I always use it as a freak-out factor, like, "I worked on *Iron Man* one, two, and three, but I also worked on *Hocus Pocus*," and they're like, "Oh my God!"

Mary Hidalgo:

I was checking out at Trader Joe's and this guy came over to bag my groceries and he said to the cashier, "Are you excited for *Hocus Pocus*?" I looked at them and I said, "I worked on *Hocus Pocus*." They went, "Oh my God!" They thought I was the queen. It was so funny.

Michael McGrady:

I didn't really follow the box office. I just went on to the next project. I told a few people I was in it, but little did I know that this little movie would take on a life all its own. Even to this day, I get recognized from it. People are like, "Oh yeah, you're in *Hocus Pocus!*" I've done over two hundred things since then and you're still calling me out for *Hocus Pocus?* A little dinky role with a few lines in it? I've done big, big projects that do not get any traction at all and you never hear from 'em again. You never know what the audience is gonna claw on to. I'm proud of the fact that the movie has done so well. It actually vindicated me because I do remember when it was not doing well and my agents at the time were like, "See, we told you." I kept saying, "That's not the reason I did the movie, guys. I didn't do it for the money. I did it for the role. I did it because I wanted to do something my kids can see me in."

Bonnie Bruckheimer:

I went to Israel with a group of people. I was going to go alone and someone told me to call this Broadway producer who takes people to Israel every year. I went, but I had to get there a day later so I wasn't properly introduced to anybody on the tour. The first night I went to bed, and when I came downstairs in the morning, one of the guys, a young guy who was on the tour, came over to me and he said, "You're Bonnie Bruckheimer?" I said, "Yes." He was like, "Oh my God, you did *Hocus Pocus!*" He was walking around shouting to everybody that I did *Hocus Pocus.* He was obsessed with *Hocus Pocus.*

Vinessa Shaw:

For the longest time, I was not known for *Hocus Pocus.* I was mostly known amongst Hollywood people, especially cinephiles, for being in *Eyes Wide Shut*, Stanley Kubrick's last movie. I saw the change when people started talking more to me about *Hocus Pocus* than *Eyes Wide Shut*, which I had done only four years later. I think *Hocus Pocus* resonates with their inner child, but it doesn't really resonate with people who are older than me or Omri. People don't understand the obsession with it unless you're a grandma or an auntie of people that were my age or younger. Even the other actors who are my age are like, "What is this movie?"

Blake Harris:

There is certainly a genesis point where people are like, "This wasn't a big hit in theaters. I don't really understand where this came from." Whereas others are like, "Oh, it's just always been a hit."

Aaron Wallace:

I think film criticism has a lot in common with archeology. It's digging to find something that's been there all along. Often it's very deep and can be more complex than you expected. The critics of the time were dismissive of this film. We can get into all the reasons why that might have been: I think certainly it was a straight-male-dominated body of criticism. There was a lot of skepticism toward musicals at the time. This was just at the beginning of the Disney Renaissance so there was skepticism towards Disney films and toward films being led by women who are funny. But I think there's this very neat generational opportunity in this particular moment for millennials, my generation, but even some in Gen X and Gen Z, who had a chance to grow up with this movie, to stand up and say to the milieu of cultural criticism, "Hey, wait a minute, this thing that you neglected, this thing that you dismissed, there's something to it that you missed." If there are tens of millions of us who were powerfully affected by this movie and are still holding on to it thirty years later, then clearly there's something that critics at large perhaps overlooked in 1993.

David Kirschner:

Something that doesn't make me proud about the first film is a complete lack of diversity. In the first film, it's all white people. There's clearly strong women in there, but they're mostly white women. There really aren't any people of color in the movie and that makes me cringe. I think any one of us would've pushed for it now, understanding something that we really weren't very understanding or sensitive to then. On *Hocus Pocus* I made a huge mistake; it was not that it was conscious, but it was from the point of being a white man and not thinking beyond that. The truth is I'm guilty and I should have been a voice that spoke up, and it didn't even cross my mind. I'm embarrassed by that.

Amanda Shepherd:

I'll never forget when I realized people were aware of this movie. It was around ten years ago, I was selling real estate and I was in my office and I got a call from *Cosmopolitan*. I think they just googled me and they asked, "We were wondering if we could do an interview with you and talk about *Hocus Pocus*?" The funny thing is, everybody assumes, "Oh, you've always been famous!" No, I haven't. I'm just becoming famous now.

For many years IMDb listed former YouTuber Jodie-Amy Rivera, known then as VenetianPrincess, as the actress who played Emily Binx, not Amanda Shepherd. It wasn't until 2015, when Cosmopolitan.com *published a story about the mix-up that many fans learned the truth.*

Jodie-Amy Rivera (Internet Personality), 2015:

I used to do a lot of radio shows and [during one interview] they asked me if I had been in any films. When I was a kid, my mom had me doing commercials and extra work, so I said I was in *Hocus Pocus* and the DJ then went on to something else, so I didn't get to say I had a very small part. After that I remember people saying, "Oh, you're Emily Binx," and I'd be like, "No, I'm not!" It was funny, but not really, because I was on Facebook and I'd see these articles from like *BuzzFeed* and I'd see my face and it says, "Where are they now?" but they'd got it all wrong. If you google the trailer, you can see me perfectly clear. The whole concept the director had was that we're half in our pajamas, half in our Halloween costumes [because we'd come back home to sleep after trick-or-treating], so I was in pajamas and then I had a bridal veil on. I got ahold of Amanda and talked to her on the phone, because every Halloween, this becomes a thing again. I explained to her what happened, and she was so understanding and very kind. She said, "Don't worry about it, it was so long ago, I really don't care."

Amanda Shepherd:
Jodie-Amy Rivera called me at work one day in 2015, tracked me down. I think she knew that there was going to be some press coming, but it was very sweet of her to call me and to say, "Hey, I just want to say I'm really sorry for the mix-up." The mix-up bothered everybody else, but it never bothered me. You want me to be honest? I was getting the check. When people would tell me, even family would say, "Somebody's stealing your identity!" I would go, "I'm the one getting the check. I'm fine." Now I have to admit, it's become such a big deal that it does kind of bother me. Sometimes I will post things and they'll go, "Oh, but it's not really you, is it?" I'm like, "No, it is me! Go look on IMDb!" That's a little frustrating. That's why my social media is "the real Emily Binx," even though that sounds pretentious, I have to do it.

Don Yesso:
When I started selling pictures on the internet, someone wrote in the comments, "Man, don't you know this is a scam? How do you really know it's him?" I finally sent off a thing: "Who the hell would want my goddamn life? Why would someone want to impersonate me?" I never had a problem after that.

Basic cable helped get the movie in front of more people, but Halloween's growing popularity in the years since Hocus Pocus *hit theaters clearly helped the film's popularity as well. Halloween spending in the US reached an all-time* *high of $12.2 billion in 2023, according to the National Retail Federation. Yet some fans argue that* Hocus Pocus *is really a film for all seasons.*

Allison Dubrosky:

There were people who were like, "Oh yeah, I know that movie. I watch it around Halloween." And I say, "No, it's August. Are you watching it?" "It's February, why aren't you watching it?" I think what made it such a success is that whenever you turn it on, it feels like it's Halloween. It's pure nostalgia magic. [My podcast cohost] Wil said it feels like they bottled Halloween. It's just the perfect Halloween film.

Daniel Henares:

Hocus Pocus is nostalgia in the best form of the word for me. It takes me back to one of the happiest moments of my life: my childhood, watching the movie a million times, re-creating the scenes with my friends and my family on my father's camera. Now I work in video, which is how I met David [Kirschner]. It's not hard to imagine that the premise of a magical movie came from his beautiful soul. He is one of the most generous people I've ever met in my life. [After watching my documentary,] David invited me to a screening [of *Hocus Pocus*] in Los Angeles. He thanked me for my documentary in front of everyone at the screening; who does that? This made me believe in magic because what has happened to me is truly magical.

Aaron Wallace:

Certainly there is our nostalgia for *Hocus Pocus* as an audience, but also within the story, the characters are driven by their own deep nostalgia. It's really a world of characters who are all pining for their respective pasts. You have Max pining for his past in LA. You have Dani longing for the past where her brother spent quality time with her. You have a whole town of people in Salem who are defined by this obsession with this legend from their own past. Allison is trying to escape that version of the past for a different past. Where does she go when she leaves the party? She goes to the museum that her mother ran when she was a child. Throughout the movie, Winifred, Mary, and Sarah are obsessively mourning the loss of their mother and looking back to their own childhood. There's this recurring theme for them, Halloween isn't what it used to be, and they're sort of lamenting that and are driven by that forlornness. I think that we as an adult audience of this film now feel that way about our own Halloweens. So much of the love of Halloween as an adult is a longing for an attempt to get back to the magic and the mystery of what Halloween was for us when we were young. I think the movie validates that feeling within us by mourning Halloween's past along with us.

Gillian Walters:

I honestly have no idea how it entered my life, but it has stayed in my life. It is a tradition every single year. Now I watch it with my partner and it's just something that we continually look forward to. I don't think I could ever watch it not in October. That is something I wouldn't do; that would feel sacrilegious to watch it outside of October.

Thora Birch:

The thing I hear most [from fans] is, "We watch it all the time." That's the number one thing, "We don't even watch it during Halloween. We watch it all the time."

Matt Piwowarczyk:

It is a film that can sustain the abuse of constant rewatching. I love the movie and think it's so well made. I could see why people could enjoy it all year round. Every time I watch it, there is a new detail that reveals itself.

Michele Atwood:

When it comes to Disney, I always tell people either you get it or you don't. You have your super Disney fans and you have your super *Hocus Pocus* fans. Those of us that really enjoy that fandom, we don't think it's silly to celebrate it all year. Maybe an outsider looking in might not fully understand, but if you get it, you get it.

A. W. Jantha:

I love this fanbase! I used a pen name for [*Hocus Pocus and the All-New Sequel*], so it's especially fun to run into fans "in the wild" and get unfiltered opinions. It allows me to learn what they love about the movies and share what I love as well. At the end of the day, I feel a little bit like I wrote some highly publicized fan fiction.

Neil Cuthbert:

The connection to Halloween means every year it has a seasonal surge. That's a plus. And yet, early in my career, I wrote a version of *Miracle on 34th Street* for Fox. It came out really well. They were really happy with it. Scott Rudin, who was the vice president of Fox at the time, was riding around in the Macy's Thanksgiving Day Parade and they were scouting locations. Then I got a call from my producer and she said, "Guess what? They're not making the movie." They walked it down the hall to the marketing department and the marketing department said, "Oh, you can't do this. It's just a seasonal picture and we don't know if it will work in Europe." Now you have *Hocus Pocus* that succeeds because it is a seasonal movie.

Aaron Wallace:

The story of *Hocus Pocus* is really the story of a Christmas movie. Max Dennison is an Ebenezer Scrooge, he's a Grinch. This is a character who has grown bitter with the sort of trajectory of his life to date and who is very skeptical toward the holiday at hand, in contrast to all of the more loving family members around him. It is only through an unwanted encounter with the supernatural that he overcomes that and reconciles himself to the holiday, and as a result, reconciles himself to his family and his sense of home. That is exactly the story of Scrooge. It's exactly the story of the Grinch and of so many other Christmas films. I think what is very clever about *Hocus Pocus*, which at the time of its release was one of the few features linked to Halloween, was that it was able to travel that well-worn path and sort of plug into the emotional power of *Miracle on 34th Street* or *It's a Wonderful Life*, borrowing that story structure and translating it authentically to a different holiday setting.

Ralph Winter:
There was really nothing else that was a Halloween movie for families in 1993. When you think about Halloween, you think about horror movies. I think the ongoing success of *Hocus Pocus* took up all the available oxygen for that genre.

Rosemary Brandenburg:
Honestly, *Hocus Pocus* kind of gave Halloween a shot in the arm all over the country and maybe all over the world. Halloween wasn't anything in Europe before that. I give us credit for reviving Halloween.

William Cuthbert:
Halloween and the film are tied together. As Halloween's grown, the film's grown as well. I feel like without the other, neither would have the success it has today. Halloween continues to grow, especially in the UK [where I live]. I give it five years and I think we'll be at the same level as America for Halloween; it's that popular here now. As Halloween gets more popular, the film's just going to keep growing.

Michele Atwood:

Sometimes you watch an older movie and you're like, "Oh, wow, that's a really old movie." Not with *Hocus Pocus*. It's timeless, it really is. It's one of those things that year after year you can enjoy and you don't feel like time is getting away from you. You don't feel like, "My gosh, I was a teenager when I watched this movie." You still feel like you're visiting old friends every Halloween.

Vinessa Shaw:

Halloween is now synonymous with trick-or-treating, wearing a costume, and watching *Hocus Pocus*. Halloween has become more and more of an event and going beyond what anyone could imagine Halloween could do, which is why I think *Hocus Pocus* is going beyond what was expected as well.

William Cuthbert:

You can see how big the film's gotten by the amount of merchandise that the Sanderson sisters are on now. If someone had said to me ten years ago, you're going to go into a shop and there's going to be sponges with the Sanderson sisters on them, I wouldn't have believed it. If you looked hard enough you could probably have your entire home decorated in all *Hocus Pocus* merchandise. I think this is the result of a shared appreciation of something that for the longest time was very niche. Up until around the twentieth anniversary, when it started to really explode, loving *Hocus Pocus* was kind of like being part of an exclusive club.

Members of the cast and crew point to the twentieth anniversary in 2013 as a watershed moment for the film. For the special milestone, the cast and crew reunited for a screening held by D23, the official Disney Fan Club, at the Walt Disney Studios in Burbank, California. It's when they first realized how popular the film had become.

Omri Katz:

Vinessa and Thora convinced me to do the twentieth-anniversary *Hocus Pocus* thing that we did on the Disney lot. I was hesitant, but a lot of people attended. So many were dressed like the witch characters and I saw the influence it had on this new fan base. I thought, *Wow, I guess, this movie is having a revitalization.*

Vinessa Shaw:

Omri, Thora, and I were just kind of hanging around outside catching up afterward and all of a sudden we had all these fans coming up and asking, "Can I take a picture with you?" Don't get me wrong, it wasn't like an insane amount where we were mobbed, but all of a sudden I realized, *Oh, this movie means something to people.*

Debra OConnell:

From a Freeform perspective, the biggest difference in 2013 was how popular ABC Family had become on social media. Despite only having the film for two airings that year, the marketing team ran very clever campaigns for "13 Nights of Halloween" and *Hocus Pocus* celebrating the iconic characters. From there it really took off, with fans responding with their own posts, tagging both the stunt and the movie. Ratings among young women, [ages] eighteen to thirty-four, jumped +25 percent year over year.

Tobias Jelinek:

It was funny, "Ha, *Hocus Pocus* is popping up again," but you're expecting it to go away. Then it did all kind of come to a head with the twenty-fifth anniversary. The fact that they pulled that together was surprising.

The star-studded Hocus Pocus 25th Anniversary Halloween Bash *aired on Freeform in 2018. It became the network's most watched special ever, attracting 1.67 million viewers on first airing, according to Nielsen.*

Debra OConnell:

We knew the film's twenty-fifth anniversary was an opportunity to celebrate the film and potentially get the cast and crew to participate to mark the milestone. It was a true Hollywood story wrangling agents and managers, but once Kenny Ortega committed, the spell was cast and the special took on a life of its own, which culminated in our *Hocus Pocus 25th Anniversary Halloween Bash* special, which premiered on Saturday, October 20, 2018. Shot on location in Hollywood Forever Cemetery and hosted by superfans Vanessa Hudgens and Jordan Fisher, with appearances by all the main cast members and Kenny Ortega himself, it was a love letter to *Hocus Pocus* as well as to the fans who were growing the franchise year over year. The *Hocus Pocus 25th Anniversary Halloween Bash* reached almost eleven million total viewers in 2018.

Larry Bagby:

Vanessa Hudgens had a crush on Tobias. I remember [at the *Hocus Pocus 25th Anniversary Halloween Bash*] she was like, "You were my childhood crush."

Tobias Jelinek:

I remember Kenny Ortega letting me know, "Someone here has a crush on you." I was surprised. I then started a friendship on Instagram with Vanessa Hudgens and her fans would start messaging me about how to get in touch with Vanessa. I just thought, *Oh my goodness. Oh no.* It let me know just how many young people were fans of this film growing up.

Thora Birch:

It was just like one of those moments where you realize how lucky you are to have been a part of something that made such an impact for so many people. That's a cheesy thing to say, but it's true. I think that was the most heartwarming part of it all.

Amanda Shepherd:

I didn't keep in touch with the people from the cast for a long time. It wasn't until the twenty-fifth anniversary that I connected with everybody again. It was like reconnecting with family. We all found each other again. I've always felt kind of like an outcast my whole life, but it just feels like this is where I belong. I call them my soul family.

Larry Bagby:

That's where we all really reconnected and started exchanging numbers and keeping in touch again. Over the last five years we've definitely grown even closer.

Omri Katz:

We actually have a text thread. All of us, even Kenny, are on the thread. We just send all kinds of funny memes and you can just feel that there's just this love and camaraderie between all of us. I'm very grateful to be back in touch with a lot of these people.

Jason Marsden:

Some of us don't text; we'll just emote as responses. But Larry, he's funny and he'll record songs and share stuff from movies he's working on. Then Doug will send an outfit that he's wearing on some project. I'm like a Doug Jones fanboy so I show this to my girlfriend and we're like, "Is this cool or what? We get this behind-the-scenes look at what he's working on. Doug Jones sent that just for us! This is so cool!"

Tobias Jelinek:

In many respects, that twenty-fifth anniversary felt like the *Hocus Pocus 2* for the original cast. Of course it was a reunion, but the reason it felt like such a celebration was having thousands of fans who were able to meet the cast and come in full regalia from not just around the country, it was an international gathering. It was really singular. It's the only time we had Kenny and the producers all together again. It really was that celebration and a chance to connect.

Jennica McCleary:

I was at the *Hocus Pocus 25th Anniversary Halloween Bash*. I had just finished my third round of chemotherapy for breast cancer. I was very thin, very gray, and very bald. I just kept my wig on all day and said nothing to anyone. I didn't say that I was the OG Winifred [from the *Hocus Pocus Villain Spelltacular*], nothing. I wasn't ready to own it in that way publicly yet, but that night, Kenny Ortega came up to me and just wrapped his arms around me and said, "My dear, you are quite the showman." It was so crazy.

Kenny Ortega, 2018:

That was the first time that I saw the tattoos. I was so drunk with love that I just went walking through the crowd. They were hugging and high-fiving and they were rolling up their sleeves and their pant legs and they had Billy and Winifred and Binx, and they tattooed their bodies with the characters.

David Kirschner:

At the twenty-fifth anniversary, [*Hocus Pocus* composer] John Debney and I sat right next to each other with his wife, Lola, on his right side and [my wife] Lizzie on my left side. At the end of the movie, which always makes me cry, when Thackery Binx has died and Thora Birch is giving just this amazing performance, John and I held hands and just watched that scene as two guys that were twenty-five years older than we were when we started this journey. It was incredibly emotional and something I will remember for the rest of my life.

John Debney:
I'll never forget that. It was the most magical, sweet, beautiful moment—a culmination of our friendship and our belief in the magic of the film. But I have to confess something: Whenever I watch the ending of this movie, I cry.

Blake Harris:
David is someone that believes in that magic of storytelling, believes in bringing people together. He is generally as excited to chat with you [about *Hocus Pocus*] as you probably are to chat with him. That in itself is also just incredibly special and incredibly rare. His heart is, I think, the core of *Hocus Pocus*.

Tobias Jelinek:
Larry and I became an iconic bully duo and one of the things that we were inspired to do when we reconnected at the twenty-fifth anniversary was to visit some high schools and talk about bullying. We got in touch with the theater teacher who was actually responsible for me getting the *Hocus Pocus* audition. He was the one who directed that community theater production in Santa Barbara. He was still teaching theater and we drove up to Santa Barbara and we spent the day with his class. It was very inspiring for us to be able to bring the bully conversation into the present context.

Larry Bagby:
We did some acting stuff and we had fun with the kids, and then the teacher asked if anybody would like to stay after class and just talk about their experiences with bullying a little more. There were about ten or

twelve kids who shared things that even the teacher knew nothing about. In the future, we'd like to team up with some anti-bullying campaigns.

Fan conventions have become a way for the cast to connect face-to-face with those who love the movie. For Doug Jones, it was where he first realized just how popular Hocus Pocus *had gotten.*

Doug Jones:

I had seen the growth of the *Hocus Pocus* fandom when I started doing conventions back in 2006 and 2007. People would come up to the table and be looking at all the images of different characters I've played over the years. They would look at Billy and say, "Oh wait, now what's that from again?" Then they would get a different picture. That has grown into them waiting in line dressed as Billy and can't wait to meet me. That evolution has happened slowly over the years. Now it is the number one thing people ask about at my table.

Tobias Jelinek:

Doug Jones has really taught us a lot about how to make the most of these conventions and their potential for connection. Doug is famous for his hugs. He hugs every single person that comes to see him. People will take every opportunity to come back and to wait in line for hours in some cases for the Doug hug.

Don Yesso:

Doug's a sweetheart. The first time I met him was at a convention, I walked in the room and put my hand out and he pulled me toward him. He goes, "Everyone's always asking me, 'If you could have played another character in *Hocus Pocus . . .*' and I always say, 'The bus driver.'" That meant so much to me. I said, "Doug, you're saying that on camera." He said, "Oh, I'd love to!" He put it on camera and I put it on Instagram. He's so sweet, oh my god.

Jason Marsden:

My joke is, "I've traveled to all these places. I've seen the inside of so many convention centers!" You're sometimes there from ten a.m. to seven p.m. It's wonderful, but it's exhausting because, for me anyway, I love to meet people. I stand in front of my table and I greet everybody. Like I said, I love the adoration. I get to meet people that I'm a fan of, too. Vinessa, Omri, and I all got a picture taken with [*House of the Dragon* star] Matt Smith. We snuck onto his line to get our picture taken with him and we get the picture and we leave. Moments after, Vinessa says, "Guys, come back!" Omri and I are like, "What's going on? Did we do something wrong?" Matt had called us back in because he recognized us and he was totally fanboying because he was a big *Hocus Pocus* fan. He says, "I was just talking to my mates the other day about how *Hocus Pocus* is one of the classic Halloween movies." It was fantastic.

Michael McGrady:

There was a time when conventions were considered the boneyard for actors, where you go after your career died and you still want to make your mortgage payment. I never did the cons in the '80s and the '90s and the early aughts. But Vinessa called me and said, "Hey, we do these conventions all the time for *Hocus Pocus* reunions and you never come. Why? People are always asking us, 'Where's Eddie the cop?'" I said, "One, I don't do conventions. Two, I don't even know where to start with that. I don't have an agent." Vinessa says, "You do have an agent, actually, my agent. I'd love to get you in touch with him and let's see if we can get you on board." She said, "Michael, it's changed, believe me, with social media now, the days where actors can just go live their private life and be left alone. That's long gone. You have to interact with your audience." When Instagram first came out, I actually thought it was just gonna be some crazy fad that would go away. Little did I know, casting directors and producers and studios would look at your following before even casting you. They want to see how many eyeballs are watching you. I did my first one, the House of Mouse Expo in Florida. I thought nobody was going to come to my booth. I was gonna be standing with egg on my face, completely humiliated, but just the opposite happened. I had people showing up with their posters saying, "When we found out you were going to be here, we were so happy because you're the one signature we don't have." Suddenly I became a commodity. My signature was needed by so many people to complete their collection. That was an eye opener for me.

Michele Atwood:

When my husband, Scott, and I decided we were going to do the House of Mouse Expo in Orlando, I said, "You know what I'd really love? A *Hocus Pocus* reunion." Four of the actors came to our first expo in 2022—Jason Marsden, Doug Jones, Larry Bagby, and Tobias Jelinek—and it was the most talked about panel of the weekend. I think when it was done, I cried because it was just a dream come true. We all had such a great time so we decided to do the thirtieth-anniversary reunion panel in 2023. We had nine actors from the original film, they had never had a reunion so big. I learned that a lot of them hadn't seen each other since filming and some of them had never met. It was almost like a big family reunion. To see them interact with each other after all of these years, it kind of did my heart really good. Looking out into that audience to see how excited and energized and happy they were to be there with that cast. If you watch that movie every year like I do, they become almost part of your family. It was just really exciting to be able to pull that together for the fans.

SaraRose Orlandini:

I think every person who doesn't understand the conventions will be like, "Oh, it's kind of sad," but there are people who will pay forty dollars a pop to have Nick Castle, who played Michael Myers, sign something or take a picture. We had him here [at the SugarMynt Gallery] and there were about seven hundred people who bought tickets, maybe a little more, and they waited in line for up to six hours. We were there till three a.m.

Larry Bagby:

Going to these conventions is almost like being in a band. You have a bunch of hits and then everybody goes their own way, but the people are demanding, they want to hear the music so you get the band back together and you go on tour and these places are packed. They're getting bigger than they were during the first go-round when you did it because people have had time to appreciate it. The fandom is growing and I'm so grateful to have been part of this.

Blake Harris:

Seeing what the marketing team did with the sequel really highlighted how big *Hocus Pocus* is with fans. They were teaming up with candle companies. They had a "Black Flame Latte" at [the LA-based coffee chain] Alfred Coffee.

Becky Coulter (Marketing Director, Alfred Coffee):

We're kind of known for our buzzy partnerships. We've worked with Disney on a few different occasions and every time we work with them it's always a success. This really started as the [coffee cup] sleeve partnership. They had four different designs—one for each Sanderson sister and then a fourth one that had all three of them—and those were distributed at all of our locations for the month of September [before *Hocus Pocus 2* premiered].

Jordan G. Hardin (Director of Food & Beverage, Alfred Coffee):

The Disney team had suggested [a drink] around the Black Flame Candle. We took that and ran with it. It's a layered drink with a little bit of all-natural black food dye, which was actually a concentrate of grape juice and spirulina, with apple cider and espresso over milk and caramel apple puree. I will say some people weren't necessarily a fan of the kind of slight acidic tang. It wasn't necessarily one of our best-selling specials ever, but people were very excited to take a picture, like, "I got the *Hocus Pocus* latte!"

Becky Coulter:

We did have a lot of *Hocus Pocus* superfans outside of LA reaching out asking if we could send them the sleeves to save for their personal collections. Obviously, we couldn't do it for everyone, but we definitely sent some out. I know that for a fact. I will say, I don't think we've ever gotten random people from Wisconsin wanting us to send them our sleeves. If that passion says anything, then I think *Hocus Pocus* is here to stay.

Jennica McCleary:

I would hear from friends that work at city hall [in Orlando], and still hear from friends that people will come and complain that they want me back [in the *Hocus Pocus Villain Spelltacular*].

Amanda Shepherd:

When I started doing these conventions, I was shocked by the emotional connection that they have with the characters. I had no idea that there was this level of fandom. I feel like I've been living under a rock! It's a trip to see adults, who are into the movie, with their children who are now also into the movie. What's also kind of shocking is there will be a line for me and I either get these big burly men or I get these little children that are super young.

Jason Marsden:

For the longest time, just to be funny, I would sign photos of Binx with "No virgins. Stay away" or "Don't go anywhere near that Black Flame Candle!" People love the Binx line "I shall always be with you," so I've evolved to that.

Thora Birch:

The worst for me is meeting a young child who loves the movie and they've been told that they're going to meet Dani and then they see me and I'm, like, this old lady. That's tough. Getting to hold on to the ten-year-old me through other people's eyes is a unique experience that I'm grateful for, but I also don't know how to analyze it. Not a lot of other people are constantly reminded of when they were ten years old.

Omri Katz:

After I left the industry, I kind of developed stage fright. When I started to do these conventions, I was extremely nervous about engaging with fans and having all this kind of attention brought to me. But as we've been doing more of these, I've been finding my footing again. I don't feel nervous now at all. I feel like if I was given a role to play in something right now, I think I would actually do a pretty good job. I'm kind of overcoming these fears that I've had for the last few decades. So who knows, maybe Omri Katz will be back on the silver screen one day.

Larry Bagby:

I had some heart failure and I was sick for many years. I just kind of lost my love for everything for a while. I had a little bit of depression and then I lost my dad, but I'm back up on my feet now. The *Hocus Pocus* stuff has helped me kind of gain confidence in what I've done and how people feel about my work. For us to be able to hang out and build each other up, all of us, is a beautiful thing. We just love each other, you know?

For the film's thirtieth anniversary, a few cast members put on their own event in Salem with help from the local community development group Creative Collective, the Horror Squad Podcast, and Salem's Black Hat Society, founded by Brian Sims. The two-day inaugural celebration held in October 2023 allowed fans to connect with the film's stars in the city where it all started.

Jason Marsden:

Omri, Vinessa, Thora, and myself decided to put this event together on our own. Omri had gone to Salem [in 2022] to do a private signing through the *Horror Squad Podcast* and he told us, "Dude, people came out in droves!" He said he had never been recognized in public before, but everywhere he went people were like, "Hey, Hollywood!" Our intention was to not just show up in Salem, but to employ and invite as many local people and businesses as possible to be part of it. We set up a tent in Salem Common and signed autographs for eight and a half hours. It poured rain nonstop, and I think we must have met six to eight hundred people.

Brian Sims:

It rained so hard, but there was no showbiz, no arrogance, no rushing from the cast. They took their time to meet everyone and hear the stories of how *Hocus Pocus* changed their lives. They really had no idea how much Salem has embraced *Hocus Pocus*, and how much the fans have embraced Salem because of *Hocus Pocus*.

Jason Marsden:

It was surreal being in Salem. We went on a tour of the *Hocus Pocus* locations—nobody knew we were there, by the way—and we could hear another tour within earshot saying, "Here is where you heard Allison talk about yabbos." Thora and Vinessa were cracking up. We are determined to make this an annual event: a celebration of Halloween, Salem, and this movie that people love so much and we just happen to be a part of.

Chapter 14

A NEW CLASSIC

A fter initially being deemed a disappointment, Hocus Pocus *has reached a level of popularity that most films can only dream of. The film has inspired countless Halloween costumes, a LEGO set, scented candles, a tarot card deck, an unofficial cookbook, drinks on Starbucks's secret menu, a cat scratcher toy, and numerous drag shows across the United States. Its dedicated fan base is certainly the secret to its unlikely resurgence, but is it a cult classic? For years, there has been a growing debate over whether the Disney film that certainly has inspired obsession in its fans should be considered a cult film or something else entirely.*

Neil Cuthbert:

When you've been on a project and it's not going well, one of the things they say when it's done is, "Well, it's just gonna find a cult following." It never does, but this one did.

Bonnie Bruckheimer:

Well, it happened to me with *Beaches,* another movie I produced with Bette Midler. *Beaches* became a cult movie because, for years, mothers would tell their daughters about it. With *Hocus Pocus,* people showed it to their children and it took on a life of its own. I was hoping it would be a big hit, but nobody ever imagined that it would become what it is.

Nell Minow:

You can never predict a film's cultural impact when it comes out, and you can't predict it in terms of the box office or the critical response at the time. *Blade Runner* was not in a single Top 10 list the year that it came out. Now it's considered a classic.

Dr. Catherine Lester (Lecturer, Film and Television):

Defining "cult" can be tricky. If you take any two cult films they could be so wildly different, but I do think there are certain elements that come up most, if not all, of the time. The idea of something having been initially perceived as a failure is something that's usually present and the nostalgic appeal. I think another important part of *Hocus Pocus* being a cult film is that it was replayed every Halloween multiple times over and over. There's this whole generation of millennials who have grown up watching it, especially queer and female viewers. A really important element with cult films is also this idea of transgression. Cult films can transgress all kinds of boundaries. That could be boundaries of taste or of cultural norms the way that something like *The Rocky Horror Picture Show* is transgressing all kinds of boundaries of sexuality and gender.

Xavier Mendik (Professor of Cult Cinema Studies, Birmingham City University; Director, Cine-Excess International Film Festival):
It's not a dramatic leap from *The Rocky Horror Picture Show* to *Hocus Pocus*. Both have very self-referential dance routines that draw in the audience. Both have very powerful performances that exceed the boundaries of the role. One of the features of the cult film performance is what's often known as "histrionic performance." The idea that the actor is so impassioned or crazy that the role is just a thinly veiled exercise for them to be themselves. It could be argued every Nicolas Cage film is a cult film because of Nicolas Cage. This is Bette Midler's movie, right? That iconic performance by a middle-aged woman, not a traditional icon, is one of the elements that [makes] *Hocus Pocus* a cult film. Some of the acting is consciously over-the-top. She's hamming it up, almost like Vincent Price in a 1950s horror film.

Russell Bobbitt:
I had a great moment with Tim Curry once. I'm professional on set, but I went up to him and said, "I hope this doesn't freak you out or whatever. But I got to tell you, I grew up with you every weekend at *The Rocky Horror Picture Show*, throwing rocks and all that." He's sixty years old at the time and his reaction was, "Why would that freak me out? How many people do you know that have had a box office hit for thirty years running?"

Dr. Catherine Lester:

It's the witches themselves who I think are really the focus of a lot of the cult appeal. They are the villains of the movie, but they're also so much fun to watch. They really are these figures of camp appeal, but I would also say feminist pleasure as well. They're very much drawing from the tradition of the witch as almost like a symbol of feminist resistance. They are transgressing all kinds of patriarchal roles that women are supposed to fit into. They don't have any maternal instincts. Instead, they want to kill children and suck out their souls to make themselves young and beautiful.

Ernest Mathijs (Professor of Film Studies, University of British Columbia):

There is something called "safe transgression." A film that is transgressive in a way that allows the audience to entertain that transgression knowing very well that in the end all will be okay. It's a step into the unknown knowing that someone will pull you back safely at the end. I think that's what *Hocus Pocus* does. It doesn't push you off the cliff, it holds you by the hand and says there is something there, but you're okay.

Peaches Christ:

When it came out, people just didn't know who *Hocus Pocus* was for. Adults didn't know how to respond to it. I think it was one of those movies, like a lot of cult movies, that just had to find its audience. The way it found its audience was through cable television and home video, and kids growing up with it, especially young queer kids.

Xavier Mendik:

There aren't any outwardly queer characters in this film, but you could say that heterosexuality is not explicitly celebrated in this film. The witches have to be released by a virgin who isn't a woman, which might be the stereotype, but a guy. The film interestingly, doesn't end on an image of heterosexual union, Max and his new girlfriend, Allison. It ends with the image of Dani, whose name, short for "Danielle," is quite ambiguous. In terms of the LGBTQ+ focus, Bette Midler is an LGBTQ+ icon and there are real elements of camp in the costume and music that draw in a disparate set of audiences.

Alex Steed:
Hocus Pocus was one of my early relationships with camp. I feel like it's a gift that Kenny Ortega gives to children on repeat for decades.

Gail Lyon:
The campy nature of it, which Kenny Ortega obviously intended, just had legs way, way beyond 1993.

Jeffrey Katzenberg:
Maybe it is the magic of Kenny Ortega! He achieved the same long-term success with *Newsies*. If I learned one thing, it's that moviemaking is more art than science, and the movie gods always surprise us!

Mark I. Pinsky:
[Legendary screenwriter] William Goldman said, "The first rule of Hollywood is nobody knows anything." Some directors just do one hit after another. There's no guarantee that the next one they do will be the same. It's only in retrospect it becomes clear they had the formula, they knew what the public taste was. For a time it was Orson Welles and then it was the Farrelly Brothers, you know, go figure.

Tobias Jelinek:
In a way, *Hocus Pocus* feels like the end of an era. The Disney films being made for family and children really started to change after this. It's the early '90s, so some of these adult themes made it through and I think that's part of why it's a cult classic and a part of the popular culture's

memory. People would love to figure out that formula, but we don't know what's really going to make it into our popular psyche until it does.

Xavier Mendik:

Let me just say, cult movies can't be created. They're incredibly happy accidents. If you go out and create it, you'll fail.

Chet Zar:

I remember so many of the movies we worked on at Alterian were cool movies and we'd get so hopeful about them and they'd come out and they wouldn't do that well. It was almost like a running joke, like, "We're cursed!" *Hocus Pocus* wasn't a hit when it first came out and everyone was all disappointed, but it's funny, maybe ten years ago, I started noticing that people about ten years younger than me started telling me, "I grew up on that movie!" That's how things get cult status, you have to see them at the right age and at the right time.

Bette Midler, 2020:

It was a picture that started off a little bit sleepy, but somehow it found its niche, and it became kind of a cult classic and now it's everywhere. I wish I had a nickel for every person who turned out in a Winifred Sanderson costume.

Tony Gardner:

When something grows organically like this, it has real value to people. It wasn't a marketing experiment. It was achieved because people liked it and then they loved it. The fans really created the response to it and the fans created a sequel. I don't think you could get any more genuine than that. I think that's pretty unique and that's what makes this really special.

Alexis Kirschner:

I'm used to my dad doing movies. I just didn't expect the amount of fan culture that became attached to [*Hocus Pocus*]. People were obsessed with it. Even to this day, it's amazing that it's that serious to people. I think it's a beautiful thing, but I didn't expect it at all.

Neil Cuthbert:

I think *Hocus Pocus* was a cult classic until they made the second one. I think you lose your cult-classic status when you make another one.

Dr. Catherine Lester:

In a way, I think that almost cements its cult status because it's Disney acknowledging how much the fans love this film. They gave this follow-up in recognition of that fandom. I had my reservations about the sequel, you know, can you make a cult film a second time, but this time do it on purpose? So while I think the original *Hocus Pocus* is still a cult film, I'm not sure if I would say that *Hocus Pocus 2* is a cult film.

Peaches Christ:

There are these ideas that cult has to be gritty or cheap or underground or trashy and while I think that a lot of amazing cult movies are those things, my definition of cult is, "Does it have a cult? Is there a group of people who have made this movie their religion?" As someone who has been on the front lines of *Hocus Pocus* with [my drag show] *Hocum Pokem* and dealt with the fandom, yes it does and it has. This explosion that has taken place to me, it's the ultimate example of a cult because only cult movies can come out and decades later are being celebrated in this way.

Xavier Mendik:

Wizard of Oz is the classic example here, which is referenced endlessly for *Hocus Pocus*. Those films have a darker air to them and have an element of the horrific or are difficult texts. So it doesn't preclude a children's film from becoming a cult classic. I think it's the way these films reach out to different genres of different audiences that give them the cult flavor.

Dr. Catherine Lester:

I think people forget that just because something's a children's film doesn't mean it can't be other things, which is also the case with horror. Sometimes people are like, "What do you mean children's horror? That's not a thing." I think that cult and children's cinema overlap quite a lot precisely because one of the big defining elements of a cult film is that it was a failure to begin with, right? But the people who would've been writing those reviews are adults. Children can have very different perceptions about quality and taste. They might also become reappraised over time as the years go on and those children grow up into adults who are passionately defending the things they grew up with.

Ernest Mathijs:

There is something about cult films like *Hocus Pocus* that sort of allows you to hook into them and take them with you on a sort of journey. A lot of films, they come out, they get released, you consume them, and that's it. They're disposable in that sense; cult films are not disposable. They have a longevity that is unique thanks to the people who watch and re-watch them.

Alex Steed:

I kind of feel like the term "cult classic" is as antiquated as the term "selling out." It meant something at a time when there were limited channels for distribution, limited channels for ownership and who got to make things. Something would kind of fail by specific expectations or rubrics and then find a new life, but in order to find a new life, you need to really seek it out. You needed to give it new life. I have a hard time understanding what that means in a time where pretty much anything can be found somewhere and keep living a life.

Nneka McGuire:

I think [*Hocus Pocus* is] cult movie *lite*. It does have a fan following, it is beloved by many, but I think that there's still something more commercial about it than what I typically think of as a cult movie, like *The Room*. *Hocus Pocus* feels like it sort of has a foot in that world of being a cult movie because it wasn't a massive success [on its initial release]. It got horrible reviews, but there are still people who really identify with it and relate to it and enjoy it. But it doesn't feel to me like it's going to live on in the pantheon of cult movies that people talk about when they teach classes about cult movies, you know? It seems like an addendum: *This was something that a lot of people liked.*

Dr. Catherine Lester:

It probably sounds a bit weird to lump *Hocus Pocus* in the same category as the films of John Waters, but there is a link in the sense that John Waters's films are cult films partly because they're all about trying to shock you and push the boundaries of taste. The Sanderson sisters are also there to mess things up and challenge dominant structures. There is the extravagance of the Sanderson sisters and the way that they are just so willing, especially Winnie, to shout about the fact that they're pissed off. They don't fit in with polite society and, in a way, cult films are often like that as well.

Xavier Mendik:

A cult classic is a dialogue of obsession, something that people return to and debate endlessly. I think you have to have that longevity to move from a conversation to a dialogue of obsession. In my opinion, *Hocus Pocus* is definitely a cult classic. This was a movie that was reclaimed by fans, and it's the sustained interest in those fans that have made it a cult classic and arguably led to a sequel.

Peaches Christ:

Hocus Pocus, I think, is one of the most interesting examples of cult. The fans basically got to create the magic of bringing the Sanderson sisters back to life just like in the movie.

Mick Garris:

I think *Hocus Pocus* has become way too mainstream to be called a "cult classic," you know? When you have a movie that appeals to people of all ages and all generations, and it lasts thirty years, and looks like it will last more, that's just a classic. *Hocus Pocus* is embraced not just by a cult, but by everyone.

Dr. Catherine Lester:

If a cult film becomes too mainstream or too popular, does it stop being cult? Well, for something to be a classic, you know, presumably it would have to be known by the majority of people so it almost feels like those two terms may be in conflict with each other. But I don't feel like people question the cult status of popular things like Star Wars and Star Trek quite as much. Whereas when it comes to maybe more feminine franchises geared toward girls, Twilight being another one, people tend to raise those questions a bit more. There are academics who have done work on the gendered aspects of cult and I do have to wonder, *Why are you questioning the legitimacy of this film as cult, the one that's about women and for girls, but not the legitimacy of Star Trek's status as cult?*

David Kirschner:

It has really grown into being a cult classic and then gone beyond that . . . I mean, I'm seeing people say it's the number one Halloween movie of all time. I don't know how to articulate what *Hocus Pocus* is. I just know the feeling that those tears from that painful first weekend have been replaced by tears of joy and pride.

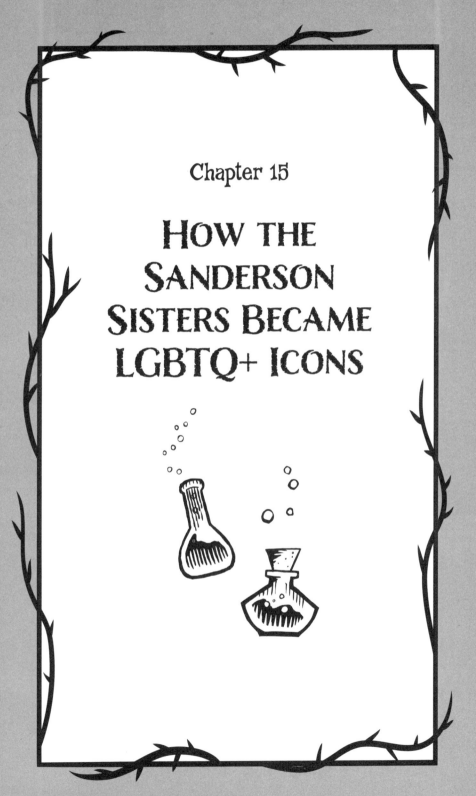

Chapter 15

How the Sanderson Sisters Became LGBTQ+ Icons

Hocus Pocus *has zero openly LGBTQ+ characters, but Kenny Ortega, who is gay, has admitted that drag culture was an important influence on the film. While that may not have been clear to everyone back in 1993, there were many in the LGBTQ+ community who embraced* Hocus Pocus's *broad humor and campy nature from the very beginning. The film has become an important piece of LGBTQ+ iconography thanks to its stars, Bette Midler, Sarah Jessica Parker, and Kathy Najimy, who are longtime supporters of the community.* Hocus Pocus *has inspired countless drag performers, including Peaches Christ and Tina Burner, to create their own shows in salute to the film. (Nicole Halliwell's* It's Just a Bunch of Hocus Pocus: A Drag Tribute, *which debuted in 2012, is billed as "the original and longest-running* Hocus Pocus *tribute show.") There are many reasons why the film has connected with members of the LGBTQ+ community, but the most important one may be that it has made many of them feel seen.*

Kenny Ortega:

It has been extraordinary to see how the LGBTQ+ community and drag artists have embraced these characters. I'd worked with drag artists for many years before and many years after [*Hocus Pocus*], and I just felt that the spirit of drag was there [in this film] in the humor, the artistry, and that heightened theatricality. Obviously, our ladies are not drag queens, but I felt that they sort of embraced the spirit of drag in their portrayals, so it's not a surprise to me that drag artists embraced the performances, took them into their world, and incorporated them into their repertoires.

Vicente Saintignon (Actor/"Clair Voyance," Drag Queen):

We've all seen a queen do a *Hocus Pocus* number as Bette Midler with the buckteeth. Clearly, this is a classic movie within the community.

Kahmora Hall:

In college when I started doing drag and just being more involved in the LGBTQ+ community I realized, "Oh, drag queens love *Hocus Pocus*, like, these are gay icons." They're over-the-top, they're dramatic, they love boys and just want to be young forever, I mean, that is relatable content right there.

David Kirschner:

I love that it has spoken so strongly to the LGBTQ+ community. There's such a strong following there and that makes me proud. There was a drag show that Peaches Christ did in San Francisco that even went to London.

Peaches Christ:

When we did *Hocum Pokem,* I had never seen anyone do a drag tribute show before. I came up with some ridiculous parody story; drag queens returning from the dead to suck the life out of young queens. I mean, it's not *Hamlet*, it's not Mamet, you know?

Tina Burner:

Witch Perfect is a parody based on these really drag-personified versions of the Sanderson sisters. I was always drawn to movies with that strong female energy as a member of the homosexual society. I think gay men love fierce women.

Nicole Halliwell:

When the movie came out in the nineties, I'm sure there were lots of classic drag queens that were playing the character, but when I was launching my show [*It's Just a Bunch of Hocus Pocus: A Drag Tribute*] in 2012, nobody was really doing it the way that I had imagined it. I wanted to actually re-create the film. I wanted to have uncanny lookalikes that when they walked onstage, you thought, *Oh my God, that's Bette Midler!* So I went to this bar where I'd been working for years and said, "Hey, I've got this idea for Halloween, let's do this *Hocus Pocus* show." . . . We're backstage getting ready on the first night, and the bar owner comes back and goes, "Hey, why don't you look out the curtain and see the audience." The bar holds three hundred people; they had almost six hundred in there. I thought, *Oh, we've got something here!*

Drew Gaver ("Bev," Drag Performer):

I wanted to combine the movie with an actual standard drag show where each character gets their own solo. Mary's big solo is right after the calming circle; she does Enya while her sisters do an interpretive dance. . . . The show is definitely geared toward adults.

Kenny Ortega, 2020:

There's just kind of a spirit and a fun that is representative of my own spirit and fun that lives under some of my work. That makes it, I think, queer-friendly—if that's a good way to put it. And I think that there has been so much progress that you can actually say that now, and people won't freak out.

Alex Steed:

Hocus Pocus is one of those movies that is layered in representation. In any family of five there is someone who sees themselves in this movie in a much different way than the rest of the family does. Most will connect with the movie's spooky Halloween vibes, but then there's one kid who is like, "This is me." I would have been that kid.

Gillian Walters:

I didn't have any inkling that I was queer until past high school, so looking back, as a child, I think there's this undercurrent that I knew that something was different and I had to assimilate in some way. I was very introverted. I still am, but more so then. I was always in my head, always creating these alternative worlds and realities and narratives, and I was in constant conversations with myself all the time. Those imaginary folks I had in my mind were outsized personalities. They were creative and strange and weird, so the Sanderson sisters were the perfect accompaniment to that. It was like watching my imagination and it felt validating in that sense. I think a lot of queer kids do that, create these worlds, not necessarily to "escape," because that word often has a negative connotation, but to see yourself reflected. This movie gave me the opportunity to live out loud in a way. I think that is why *Hocus Pocus* has a very special place in my heart as a queer person.

Megan Townsend:

Any movie that you can find a relationship to can be powerful and meaningful, but in terms of where storytelling was in the '90s, so much of it was based in queer coding and subtext. You had to read into it. . . . They were not going to commit to doing it explicitly. Similarly, a lot of films, if they were explicitly queer, were very much object lessons. *Philadelphia* is a great example; it builds understanding and empathy, but it's not a fun movie that you want to watch with your friends or that is necessarily aimed at you as a queer person. A lot of those were aimed at our straight friends and family to kind of let them know more about us.

Dr. Carmen Phillips:

I remember, as a child, thinking Bette Midler was like the funniest human being. There's something about the campiness of her humor that I latched onto as a kid. I loved the high drama of it. I loved how much she felt like a diva. Lots of kids can love that and not grow up to be gay, but I think for me, those things are very tied. As a young person, that really tapped into something for me. Bette's ties to the gay community go back longer than I've been alive, but it felt like I got tapped into something before I even knew that, which has always felt really special to me.

Drew Gaver:

I remember riding on my scooter and being like, "Pull over, let me see your driver's permit!" I just thought that line was hilarious. I didn't know what a driver's permit was; I was eleven years old, but I immediately knew that Bette's delivery of that line was funny.

Ginger Minj:

I have to admit I was so intimidated by the thought of working alongside Bette Midler [in *Hocus Pocus 2*]. She's this barely five-foot-tall, iconic force of nature! Of course, I had rehearsed how I would greet her in my head for days, but she didn't give me a chance to be nervous. The second I stepped foot on set, she stopped everything, threw her arms up, and screamed, "Ginger Minj, you were *robbed*!" Now, I have no idea if she's ever seen an episode of *Drag Race*, but she immediately made me laugh and put me at ease. She really took me under her wing, showed me how to make sure my close-up looked as good as possible, and kept us queens riveted with stories from filming the first movie.

Peaches Christ:

Bette Midler is maybe one of the greatest living queer icons. You've got her camping it up in drag playing a witch. Witches are also queer iconography. Margaret Hamilton as the Wicked Witch in *Wizard of Oz* is something so important for us. . . . Queers have always identified with victims and villains and the reason is we've been seen as monsters. Witches in general have a very special place in our heart. These are people that were burned at the stake for being who they were or who they were suspected to be.

Matt Piwowarczyk:

Gay kids love villains. If you are queer and bent to drama and being extravagant and over-the-top, I guess you could say camp. That was definitely part of this movie's appeal.

Mara Wilson:

For a very long time, queer people were told, "You can't be what you are. You are too much. You're too this, you're too that. You need to hide yourself and you need to change yourself." When you see people that are out there being themselves and being over-the-top and taking up space that they feel is owed to them, that can feel liberating. You want to live sort of vicariously through these people who are being very performative and being very demonstrative because we're not allowed to be like that. A lot of villains were very queer coded, but I don't think you necessarily see that in this movie. Although they are all women who ostensibly didn't marry and [who] live with their sisters, which was probably seen as suspicious. Speaking as a queer woman who lives with her sister, that can be seen as kind of witchy in certain circles.

Megan Townsend:

What a lot of different research has shown over and over is that horror is one of the top, if not the top genre for queer audiences. A lot of that, I would assume, is because that's the kind of storytelling that we had to find ourselves in and find allusions to when we were growing up. These people who are monsters or are living on the outskirts of society, and have something about them that they are being kind of persecuted for or something that just sets them apart. As queer people, especially back thirty years ago, there was a lot to relate to in seeing yourself in somebody who is kind of on the edge of society. With the three sisters, there's also an element of chosen or nontraditional family. These three sisters are going to spend eternity together if they can get the lives out of all of these children. They aren't interested in having a romance or fitting into the kind of mold that society had for them like going to school, graduating, and having a family of two point five kids.

Gillian Walters:

For me, it's just a film of misfits. Max is struggling to find his place. Dani is feeling left out. The Sanderson sisters each have their own element of not fitting in even within their trio. That misfit-dom is what I think also draws us to it.

Mara Wilson:

Binx's whole thing is that he is out of his own time and he's lived this very lonely existence, which can be what it's like when you're the only gay teenager.

Matt Piwowarczyk:

As a kid, I'd go to a friend's birthday party; I'd end up hanging out with the moms. I feel like there's some element of that with *Hocus Pocus*. I love when the Sanderson sisters are on-screen because I get to hang out with the moms.

Vicente Saintignon:

Even though we know that the Sanderson sisters are evil, and they want to suck the souls out of these children, we're kind of like, "Let's give the girls a chance!"

Alex Steed:

There are so many pieces of its fabric that just speak to people. I have a friend who is an actress and who is trans and Doug Jones was kind of the first thing that they wanted to be. I think that there's something about what Doug Jones is; there's a shapeshifting element that speaks to the queer community, too.

Both the sequel novel, 2018's Hocus Pocus and the All-New Sequel, *and the sequel film, 2022's* Hocus Pocus 2, *acknowledge the role the LGBTQ+ community played in the film's comeback. While A. W. Jantha's book features a same-sex relationship, the movie features former* RuPaul's Drag Race *contestants Ginger Minj, Kahmora Hall, and Kornbread "the Snack" Jeté, as drag queen versions of the Sanderson sisters.*

Matt Piwowarczyk:

It was a great acknowledgment of the impact and/or the embrace of *Hocus Pocus* by the drag community to include them in that scene. Drag queens really helped carry the banner of this movie forward and kept it present. For a long time, the only people I would see dressed up [as the Sanderson sisters] out and about were drag queens, so it was inclusion that I appreciated.

Tina Burner:

If they hadn't even touched on it, it would've been a huge cultural thing. I love that they did this, but if you're going to ask me as a drag queen, "Do I want more representation?" Yeah, I want more, I want The Night of a Thousand Winifreds.

Kahmora Hall:

Ginger, Kornbread, and I talked a lot about this; we're literally a part of history now. I think we're the first drag queens to be in a Disney movie and we're also a diverse group; Kornbread is a Black trans woman, Ginger is nonbinary, and I'm an Asian American drag queen. Everyone really cared about us as people and as artists. We never felt like we were a prop in the movie. We never felt like we were part of a political agenda or anything like that. They truly just wanted us there. We felt respected. We were truly treated like queens. Just to be at the premiere doing press shows that we're a part of this film just like everyone else, we weren't just a five-second gag. I think it just shows that our society is changing, our views are changing and that queer visibility is so important. I'm very grateful to Disney for taking a chance on this.

Ginger Minj:

So many times people shoehorn drag into TV or movies just to be part of the trend, but they rarely treat us like "real" actors. I actually got into drag through acting, I know more about stage and screen than I do about wigs and makeup. It was so nice to be a part of a project where we were treated as equals, by the stars, the crew, by everybody.

Megan Townsend:

Even though it was a kind of short moment in the film. I think for queer audiences, it was kind of a way of showing support or solidarity and, sort of saying, "I see you and thank you." I won't say we've single-handedly done it, but we've been up there in the groups of people who have kept the movie in the zeitgeist for the past thirty years. I think it was kind of a small little way to say, "Thank you for loving this and being involved in this," but I think that that kind of costume scene overall is a way of saying, "These characters can be for anybody."

Jennica McCleary:

So many of us looked to *Hocus Pocus* as one of those films that got us. I really love that I'm able to use *Hocus Pocus* as an outlet to entertain you but also remind you that we stand against adversity. We have nonbinary and transgender members in my show, *Winnie's Rock Cauldron Cabaret*. We're very much aware that we may be protested for it, but we are all part of the *Hocus Pocus* legacy.

Alex Steed:

I'm grateful for Kenny Ortega. I think that a lot of the ways he touched popular culture were significant to people beyond words. Meaning it wasn't just entertainment; it was giving a form of recognition in very visible places at times when those forms of recognition could not always be very visible. . . . Art sometimes speaks when the culture can't. I know that there might be people who say, "Well, is this movie art?" Yes, he's an artist and his art is appreciated.

Vicente Saintignon:

Maybe [*Hocus Pocus*] wasn't originally representative of us, but we've identified ourselves there and now it is representative of us. I think that's an important distinction: *We* have identified ourselves with these characters.

Chapter 16

MORE THAN JUST A BIT OF HOCUS POCUS

*T*wenty-nine years after the release of Hocus Pocus, a much-anticipated yet still surprising sequel featuring the film's original stars Bette Midler, Sarah Jessica Parker, Kathy Najimy, and Doug Jones premiered on Disney+. The film, directed by Anne Fletcher and written by Jen D'Angelo, marked the return of the Sanderson sisters, who were back to get revenge on a new cast of young people who grew up watching the original. Much like its source material, the sequel, based on a story by D'Angelo, Blake Harris, and David Kirschner, took nearly ten years and half as many writers to get made. Shot in Rhode Island, now the stand-in for Salem, during the fall of 2021 amid the COVID-19 pandemic, Hocus Pocus 2 is a sweet and silly tale for a new generation of kids. While the sequel is packed with Easter eggs for lovers of the first film, this is a kinder, gentler Hocus Pocus. Gone are the talking cats, risqué humor, and virgin references that defined the original. (Though there is one funny, rather meta reference: A little boy asks, "What is a virgin?" only to have an adult nervously respond, "A person who has never lit a candle.") Instead, the new film, which also features Veep co-stars Tony Hale and Sam Richardson, as well as Ted Lasso's Hannah Waddingham, leans into the fish-out-of-water humor and focuses on the power of friendship and finding your own coven.

When Hocus Pocus 2 finally did arrive on Disney+ in September 2022, it broke records in the U.S., becoming the most watched movie premiere to date on the Walt Disney–owned streaming service. Audiences appeared to love the ways in which it expanded the universe. By flashing back to the young Sanderson sisters, led by Taylor Paige Henderson's Young Winifred and introducing Waddingham's Witch Mother, Hocus Pocus 2 opened up a world of possibility for where the series can go next—with or without the original cast.

Kenny Ortega once said that Hocus Pocus didn't find its audience, "the audience found us." Thirty years and one sequel later, audiences have found this movie and have no plans to give it up. The love and admiration the film has received, especially in the last decade, has been validating for the cast and crew, and even the film's biggest fans, who always thought they had a hit on their hands. Now it's more than a hit, it's a phenomenon—and a rare one at *that, which has got those with connections to* Hocus Pocus *thinking about the film's legacy and their place in it.*

David Kirschner:

I'd love to say, "Yes, I always knew people would discover it," but I didn't. I spoke at colleges and high schools about Halloween and what all this means, and just doing everything I could to, in my tiny little way, keep the movie alive, never dreaming that it would become what it would become. I was proud of it and wasn't ashamed of the fact that it failed. It was my childhood and it was our daughters' childhoods and maybe I didn't want to let go of it for those prideful reasons. I'd like to think it was more than that, but I'll leave that to other people to decipher.

Omri Katz:

It's amazing how it's grown into something that most of us didn't anticipate. I think we all just kind of saw it die, swept it under the rug, and thought, *Oh, that was fun.* Now it's the gift that keeps on giving.

Vinessa Shaw:

It's proving to be the classic I thought it should have been from the start, but now, for the first time, I feel like it's going beyond what I thought it could be.

Bette Midler, 2018:

It was like an ugly duckling. A little creature that nobody thought could do anything and now it's a swan. It's found its wings and it's just flown away. I think it's fantastic.

Neil Cuthbert:

Being a screenwriter is dealing with mostly disappointments. So many things you write, especially back in the '80s and '90s when they were buying a lot of scripts, just didn't get made. They'd shelve them and it would be like they're just dead. For me, it's been thrilling to realize, "Wow, there's all these people that love this movie." There's all these little girls who love this movie. There's all these LGBTQ+ people who love it. That thrills me because that wasn't expected.

Ron Underwood:

Even though I didn't make [*Hocus Pocus*], it holds a very dear place in my heart. I was hired by a studio to make a movie that I really thought had great potential—and it did have great potential! Even though I didn't get to make it, it was very satisfying to be part of it, however short-lived. It's a fun movie about Halloween, the first of its kind. I think it will always have an important spot in film history.

Liz Kirschner:

Our grandkids were at Disneyland with friends. It was around Halloween, and it was so cute. They called from the park and they went, "Listen, they're playing the music from *Hocus Pocus!*" They're showing us on FaceTime all the people that are wearing *Hocus Pocus* T-shirts. It couldn't be better, you know? There are just so many factors that are beyond someone's control as to why a film will or will not succeed. So to be here now makes you feel so proud and happy that it is so loved. I don't take it for granted. I pinch myself every day.

Jessie Wolfson:

It just feels good every time you turn it on and I'm not saying that because it's my dad's movie. I'm always very honest with him. I definitely could not turn on a Chucky movie every day. *Hocus Pocus* is like *Chicken Soup for the Soul.*

Kahmora Hall:

Every Halloween, everyone's going to watch *Hocus Pocus* and *Hocus Pocus 2*. It's going to be watched by millions every year. Just stepping back and just thinking about it. That's amazing. I better see everyone dressing up as Drag Queen Sarah and saying my one line. I better see it. Of course this means I have to dress up as Sarah every holiday. I have to, it's required.

William Sandell:

I just love that there are *Hocus Pocus* tours. I get such a kick out of that. It's like following the Inca Trail or the Yellow Brick Road. They go to Salem and they say, "All my life I wanted to stand in front of the Max Dennison house." You could walk around Salem thirty years ago, it wasn't that crowded. I really think, not to sound too egotistical, *Hocus Pocus* helped put Salem back in the tourist trade.

Omri Katz:

Seriously, Salem should just be called *Hocus Pocus* Land. That place was just a small, quaint little town, and this movie has made it this mega tourist attraction, especially in October. It's great for the economy, but I'm sure it's annoying. I mean it's all mom-and-pop storefronts. There are no Walmarts, Targets, or Starbucks. It's just these quaint little beautiful shops; I have sympathy for the residents.

Kate Fox:

In 2022, we had over a million people come to Salem in October alone. Salem's a city of forty thousand. It's a small city, so a million visitors in a month is substantial. One of the things that we wrestle with is over tourism and too much visitation for a small historic city. I don't think Disney understands the impact they've had on Salem as a destination. Most of it is fun and we love it, but when tourism of any type in any destination clashes with the residents' needs and quality of life, it can be tricky.

Rachel Christ-Doane:

It was really one of my favorite Halloween movies and not so much anymore. It's just when you're faced with it all the time, it gets a little like, "I really can't watch that movie anymore." I know that's the case for a lot of people in Salem.

Rosemary Brandenburg:
Film tourism is a funny phenomenon, isn't it? I mean all the little shops [in Salem] with the little *Hocus Pocus* tchotchkes. It's weird to go to a historical place like that and see all the stuff for sale.

Kate Fox:
The Salem Witch Museum has a section in their gift shop for *Hocus Pocus* merchandise. It's a children's movie and people are turning that into Salem's identity. There are a lot of people here who want Salem's identity to be more closely aligned with the maritime story, with the true history, with the significant stories, and the remarkable people who have come from Salem. Not the Sanderson sisters, who are a work of fiction.

Brian Sims:
Hocus Pocus actually feels real to me. This might sound weird, but I don't think of it as the Ropes Mansion anymore, it's Allison's home. People have embraced the movie so much that it kind of supersedes the real history in some ways.

Heather Greene:
The legacy of this movie is those three witches. They're not as iconic as, say, the Wicked Witch of the West; nothing can be that iconic. But those three have become popular and iconic figures for the modern witchcraft community and the broader culture. It's given the modern witch a fun way to celebrate who they are. Will the Sanderson sisters last? I hope so.

David Hoberman:
I think it's the trio that made it what it is today. I really do. I think people just loved those characters and loved the dynamic between them.

Don Yesso:

No matter what I do I'm going to forever be known as "Mortal Bus Boy." People say, "You're in *Guarding Tess*?" I go, "I'm in thirty scenes!" I'm only in one scene in *Hocus Pocus*, but I'm a key chain. I'm on coffee mugs. Someone told me they were thinking about making a Funko? I don't even know what a Funko is, but I'm going to continue riding this wave. I'll be Mortal Bus Boy–ing my ass off for the rest of my life.

Larry Bagby:

By the way, if you can put in a plug, Tobias and I would like to have a Funko Ice and Jay. I just want an action figure and I'm good to go.

Brock Walsh:

I've been at this a long time, since 1975 when I moved out here to LA, and I wrote a lot of shitty songs. Honestly, I hear some of them, and they make me cringe, so when I hear something that I did a long time ago that stands up and still has currency, emotional currency in the world, that makes me feel good. We do this to express ourselves and to have other people hear things and feel those things expressed and feel better for having heard the expression of them.

Mary Hidalgo:

I don't know what makes something successful at all. I have no idea what it is that all these kids are connected to, but it's those kids, who are now adults, who have made it what it is now. We have nothing to do with it, but this is part of my legacy now. I can appreciate that I've had this influence on so many children.

Michael McGrady:

As an actor, you think you're just making a commodity that just kind of comes and goes and that's it. But certain movies are turning points in people's lives. It really helped me understand that what I do is important. I'm not a brain surgeon, but I entertain brain surgeons, and that's important.

Rick Lazzarini:
I have worked on some very cool projects, *Spaceballs* among them. What a dream job that was, working with John Candy, intimately, for weeks on end, having Mel Brooks as my director. Working on *Hook*, with Steven Spielberg's direction and compliments. You want to pinch yourself because you feel so lucky to be there! What stood out with *Hocus Pocus* was the freedom I was given to do the best possible work that I could. And that the film was just destined to be a well-received, well-loved work. You could feel that from the beginning. There's just an innocence and playful aspect, and even a loving "hokiness" about it that makes it stand apart from a lot of other films I've worked on.

Jennica McCleary:
I always say that my obituary in the *Orlando Sentinel* will probably say, "The woman who played Winifred Sanderson." But everybody wants to be Winifred; she's legendary and iconic in so many ways. For Bette to have created an original character that will stand the test of time, and that the fans begged for more of, is incredible. For me to have had a tiny piece of that legacy, to have people call me "Disney's go-to Winifred Sanderson," that's all I need. I'm good.

Taylor Paige Henderson:
I felt a lot of responsibility to do the character [of Winifred] justice and I think we did. It's just such an iconic movie and people love it. It's crazy that I'm forever going to be a part of it. I'm always going to be young Winifred Sanderson. It's really cool and I'm really, really honored.

Ginger Minj:

To be a part of a legacy that has captured the hearts of so many people over the last three decades is not something I will ever take for granted. In the world of *Hocus Pocus*, there are three Winifreds: Bette Midler, Taylor Paige Henderson, and me!

Tobias Jelinek:

The authenticity of its fan base really is what's responsible for this, it's not Disney. It's the fan base that has kept it alive—and Doug Jones. That's no joke! The amount of character work he's done, he has fans coming from so many different films and franchises.

Allison Dubrosky:

Every time we've spoken to anyone from the cast or crew, they do credit the fans. They say, we're the ones who kind of carried it along, brought that love back. We always try to credit them right back. If not for your story, if not for your acting, if not for bringing that character to life, it wouldn't exist. Whether it be meeting a best friend or getting through a breakup or getting through a family death, this silly little movie about Halloween has really changed people's lives.

A. W. Jantha:

I think this movie is here to stay, and my own story of becoming a fan testifies to that. Before I watched it, I'd considered it a classic kids' film, but it's so much more. There are elements about belonging and standing up for yourself that resonate across age brackets, and the campiness gives it adult appeal and fantastic rewatchability. I hope the original movie continues to inspire audiences to leave a little room for magic in their lives.

Nicole Halliwell:

The movie really has changed my life in so many ways. As a kid, it was something that I loved and connected to. It's given me a chance to express myself. It's helped me feel validated and complete as a person.

Mara Wilson:

I think the things that affected you when you were a child will affect you for the rest of your life. I've seen that personally because I've been in children's movies, but also Beverly Cleary, Judy Blume, Bruce Coville, K. A. Applegate, all of the authors that I grew up loving, I still hold them in such high regard. Maybe there was a point in my life where I was like, "Oh, maybe I'm too old for Beverly Cleary now," but as an adult, I'm like, "Are you ever really too old for Beverly Cleary?" Because now you appreciate it. Now you look at it and you marvel at the work. You marvel at the lessons that they taught you. The thing about this movie is that my relationship with it has changed so many times from fear to fascination to appreciation, especially as I learned about what it was like behind the scenes and I got to meet some of the actors who were in it. Now I'm putting it on for children I know. That's the great thing, I think, about good children's media, well-thought-out, well-developed children's media, you get to enjoy it over and over again on several different levels.

Debra OConnell:

A film like *Hocus Pocus* works on many levels that different audience segments relate to because, at the core, it is really a story about family. Thackery and Emily, the Sanderson sisters, and Max and Dani each have their dysfunction, but in the end, they are in it together. I think that's why audiences are so drawn to it—it's relatable and no matter how many times you watch, the story and performances are so spectacular, the quotes so hilarious, that you are moved each and every time. It's like an old song that you love. It comes on and you just feel happy and nostalgic. I think that is what makes the movie such a perennial favorite. If you are familiar with the movie, audiences can drop in at any point and are immediately under *Hocus Pocus's* spell.

Michele Atwood:

Describe what this movie means to me? Oh my goodness, that's a loaded question. Do you want me to cry? I think because not everybody saw it at first, but I did, I felt like kind of an advocate. Then when I had kids, I wanted to introduce it to them because it meant so much to me. I'm not even sure what it was about the movie that really struck me. It kind of gets you in the heart in some weird way. To see the fandom grow and to be able to share that with other people, there are no words to describe it, my heart is so full.

Blake Harris:

Fans made [*Hocus Pocus 2*] the biggest streaming premiere movie ever. That tells you everything you need to know about the fandom. People want this as a part of their lives—give the people what they want.

Vinessa Shaw:

I have nothing but fond memories of that time and I just love the joy that everyone has when they come up to me and tell me how they watch it every year. One couple came up to me and said that they watch it every night before they go to sleep because it's so comforting. It's funny, people watch it regularly, not even on Halloween.

Omri Katz:

We get asked by fans a lot, "Where would Max and Allison be now?" I think Allison's running the witch museum. But if the movie was reality, we would be traumatized after going through something like that. Max would probably run away from Salem as fast as he could, like, "I'm never coming back to this witch town!"

Thora Birch:

There were multiple definitive storylines and possibilities for bringing me back [for *Hocus Pocus 2*] and I was completely on board for pretty much all of them—except the last one, which didn't work out anyway. Personally, I'd like to know what happens with Dani.

Don Yesso:

To me, that [*Hocus Pocus 3*] would be a huge summer tentpole movie. They could make the bus driver an Uber driver. Allison and Max could be putting their kids in a carpool or something.

Sarah Jessica Parker, 2022:

Kathy had a good idea that the third one should be animated. That would be cool and a smart idea. It's fun, funny, and could be interesting and innovative, like old-fashioned or new [animation].

Belissa Escobedo:

I would love to see something where somehow the Sanderson sisters are brought back but it's the children's versions. The baby witches are amazing. A prequel about the little Sanderson sisters would be hilarious as well.

Taylor Paige Henderson:

I love young Winifred and I think she is so complex. I think it would be great to be able to step back into her shoes again. I think people would love more of the backstory.

Ginger Minj:

I think there's a lot of potential there for me, Kahmora, and Kornbread's characters. We didn't win the costume contest, so there's some unfinished business there. Maybe the judges didn't think our costumes were historically accurate enough and we three queens break into the witches' old house and try to find some of their actual outfits to make our looks a little more authentic. Of course, we can't see in the dark, so we light the nearest candle and, voilà, here we are again!

Blake Harris:

I heard from so many people that nothing could ever top the original [for them], but their kids actually preferred the second one.

Vinessa Shaw:

When I showed [my son] *Hocus Pocus*, he loved it and he just ran around the room talking about it. His favorite was Sarah. "She's so pretty and she sings!" Then I asked, "Well, what do you think of Allison?" And he said, "Who's Allison?" Then he wanted to watch *Hocus Pocus 2* and then he wanted to watch more *Hocus Pocus 2*. I'm like, "What about *Hocus Pocus* one?" He's a *Hocus Pocus 2* fan because he loves all the singing in it. He loves that song "The Witches Are Back."

Michele Atwood:

From a true fan perspective, it was disappointing that not all the original cast was back [for the sequel]. It's kind of like the Star Wars fandom. *Hocus Pocus* fans want to see the familiarity of what they've loved for thirty years.

Amanda Shepherd:

I think [*Hocus Pocus 2*] was a good movie, especially for younger kids. The witches kind of get to become good at the end. It's definitely catered to children, whereas *Hocus Pocus* felt like it was for adults and children. But, oh my God, it felt like Bette Midler was almost going back into her skin when she did that role. Like it's part of who she is. Her performance was on point.

Bette Midler, 2022:

I've always been envious of people who get to do their favorite character more than once. The fact that we got to do [a *Hocus Pocus* sequel] finally, after thirty years of promoting the idea, I'm glad we got to do it. I'd love to have a franchise—especially a character I love playing.

A. W. Jantha:

I would love to see more *Hocus Pocus* books and movies. They will never touch the original, and I think that's okay so long as they are handled with the same madcap joy as the original. When I watch *Hocus Pocus*, I get a distinct sense of, *We have no idea whether this is going to work, but we're going for it.*

Thora Birch:

The world that David Kirschner created was something special and unique. I think the creative mind of Kenny, the burgeoning CGI, and just the willingness of Disney to try something that was a little bit experimental for the time creates a mystique around the film. But at the end of the day, I think it's really the fans of the film that have carried us through, because there was a time when we didn't think we had any. And because we keep talking about it, the memories stay alive. It probably was the happiest time in my life, apart from now.

Kenny Ortega:

My favorite memory [from making *Hocus Pocus*]? The laughter and good times. There were times when we were all on the floor and we couldn't get up because we were laughing so hard.

William Sandell:

I take great pride and pleasure in the whole thing. Many people reach out to me and say, "How's it feel to be the guy that worked on *Hocus Pocus*?" And I say, "It feels great." I never get tired of talking about *Hocus Pocus*.

Mick Garris:

I can't imagine *Hocus Pocus* lasting another thirty years, but however long it lasts, we've seen something incredible. It's appreciated by people in a way that is incredibly meaningful. I've learned to appreciate everything about *Hocus Pocus*.

Kimmy Blankenburg:

If I have anything to do with it, we most definitely will be talking about *Hocus Pocus* thirty years from now! One thing I do each year is gift the movie to anyone I hear hasn't seen it. One year, I gifted the movie to eleven people that hadn't seen *Hocus Pocus* yet. It's so gratifying to be able to spread the magic of *Hocus Pocus* to so many people. *Hocus Pocus* is a comfort to so many. It's a movie that sticks with you forever.

Doug Jones:

Hocus Pocus has such a tender place in people's hearts. I think anything that we saw as a kid that moved us, entertained us, made us laugh, cry, think, hope or dream about the future sticks with us. If I ever met Ray Bolger at a convention, I would cry in front of him and be like, "I'm meeting the person who I idolized as a kid." I'm getting that reaction from so many grown-ups now who grew up watching *Hocus Pocus*. A lot of life has happened for these people and I've been a part of it all. I've been in tears several times as fans tell me their personal stories.

Larry Bagby:

My dad passed away on October 20, 2020, due to COVID complications. He was a wonderful father, married to my mom for over fifty years, and just a fine example of a Christ-like man. We decided to do the memorial service on Halloween and we all went and watched *Hocus Pocus* after. My dad was so proud to be able to sit with the whole family and watch a movie with me in it. His name was Larry Bagby, too, I'm a third, and he was there on set filming a lot of the behind-the-scenes when

I wasn't. That movie kind of healed me in a new way that night. I think that's what people feel when they watch it—and I get it, it's a movie that connects people and can help get you through the hardest times.

Kenny Ortega:

I'm extremely grateful that people found the movie, and that over time our audience grew and grew, decade after decade.

Blake Harris:

I think *Hocus Pocus* is such a great testament to [the idea that] a great story can truly come from anywhere. This was a story that David was telling people that he loved, and seeing what it evolved into is extremely special. For David and for all of us [who love *Hocus Pocus*], it's really become much more than just a bunch of *Hocus Pocus*. It really is magic.

David Kirschner:

The idea of something that has been brewing in me since I was big enough to go trick-or-treating, to see that made into a movie and then die, just the anguish and the tears of that, and then all of a sudden, things started to change and then grow into what it's become. It's so overwhelming. I'm very proud of the career that I've had and what I've created, but nothing will ever touch *Hocus Pocus*. Maybe I should be cooler about this, but I'm not a very cool person. It moves me.

Acknowledgments

I have never written a book before and because there are no guarantees in this life, I may never write another, so there are many people I want to thank for helping me get here. First, I want to thank every single one of the ninety-five people who spoke to me about *Hocus Pocus* across 2022 and 2023, often on long Zoom calls or phone calls due to the pandemic making it difficult to meet in person. Everyone was so kind, making time for multiple follow-up calls and emails to share their memories, photos, documents, and contacts with a complete stranger. Thank you for trusting me with your stories, I hope I did them justice.

I want to send a special thank-you to those who spoke to me in 2018 for a twenty-fifth-anniversary piece I wrote about the "I Put a Spell on You" scene for *Bustle*, never imagining those conversations would lead to this book: David Kirschner, Thora Birch, Doug Jones, Stephanie Faracy, Mary Vogt, Joseph Malone, and Marc Shaiman. Many of their quotes from those original interviews had never been published before this book, and I am extremely grateful that they agreed to speak with me all those years ago.

I'd like to shout out a few people who went above and beyond to help me in this process. Thank you, Vinessa Shaw, Omri Katz, Tobias Jelinek, Larry Bagby, Jason Marsden, Amanda Shepherd, Doug Jones, and Thora Birch for being so candid about your time working on the film and all the years after. Bill Sandell is the keeper of the *Hocus Pocus* records and he was kind enough to pass along so many of his original budget sheets and other documents to me. If he ever decides to write a book about his time in Hollywood, I will be first in line to buy it. Aaron Wallace, the author of *Hocus Pocus in Focus: The Thinking Fan's Guide to Disney's Halloween Classic*, and Allison Dubrosky and William Cuthbert, the hosts of *The Black Flame Society* podcast, are truly *Hocus Pocus* scholars, who were kind enough to share their knowledge with me. I want to thank Tony Gardner and Chris Bailey for breaking down the complicated art of making a cat talk in terms that a novice like me could understand. A big thank-you to Kenny Ortega for making the time to be a part of this. It really does mean the world. I will never be able to thank David Kirschner enough for all the time not only he, but his whole family—Liz, Jessie, Alexis—gave me to talk about a movie that means so much to so many. *Hocus Pocus* couldn't have been made without you, and the same could be said of this book.

It's also safe to say, I would have never written this book if literary agent Rick Richter didn't email me in 2022 asking if I wanted to write a book on *Hocus Pocus*. You are so good at what you do and I am honored to have you on my side fighting for me every step of the way. My name on this book is all thanks to the hard work of you and your incredible colleagues.

As a first-time author, my editor, Jennifer Levesque, was an indispensable resource and an incredible sounding board throughout this entire process. She's also one of the best people to talk about movies with. Our meetings always started with a debrief about what we'd just seen that made me feel at ease no matter how stressed I might have been at the time. This book wouldn't have gotten over the finish line without your guidance and perseverance. Thank you, Elias Kotsis, for catching the things I didn't see and dealing with all of my emails. I would like to thank Guy Cunningham and his amazing team of copy editors who looked over the book at every stage of its development, cleaning up all my mistakes along the way. And thank you, Stephanie Sumulong for designing such a wonderful cover and Yunika Kadarusman for making me look like a real professional in my author photo.

My first job in journalism was at *Beyond Race*, a small arts-and-culture magazine founded by David Terra, who put his faith in me to run the quarterly magazine's music section when I was right out of college. I can't thank Dave enough for believing in me so early in my career. Thank you, Bob Boilen, Robin Hilton, and everyone who worked at NPR's *All Songs Considered* when I interned there in the summer of 2011 for teaching me about good music and good music writing.

Getting a master's degree in journalism from the Craig Newmark Graduate School of Journalism at CUNY in 2011 is one of my proudest accomplishments. I had so many great professors during my time there, all of whom helped me become a more proficient writer and reporter, but no one was better than Jan Simpson. She taught me how to get the best out of any interview, which was an invaluable skill when working on this book. She was kind enough to officiate my wedding in 2019, and people still come up to me and say she was their favorite part of the day. Maybe I should feel slighted by that, but honestly, I get it! She is the best of the best at what she does.

There are so many people who have taken my pitches or given me opportunities throughout my career, but I want to specifically thank Courtney E. Smith, Brian Ives, Heather Stas, Jillian Mapes, Kelsea Stahler, Samantha Rollins, Kadeen Griffiths, Mallory Cara, Olivia Truffaut-Wong, Genevieve Koski, Nneka McGuire, Lena Felton, Mahita Gajanan, Elisabeth Garber-Paul, and Amber Sutherland-Namako for working their magic on my copy. Most of all, thank you, Rachel Simon for saying yes to my *Hocus Pocus* oral-history pitch back in 2018.

Dragica Dabo has been my best friend since fifth grade and has seen me at my best, worst, and most anxiety-ridden. We also shared a byline on my first-ever published piece for the Connetquot High School newspaper. I can honestly say, I wouldn't be me without her. Pia Mannino is one of the most caring people you will ever meet and an impossibly talented artist, though she is way too humble to admit it. Kayley Hoffman was the first person to tell me I should write a book, which I considered a ridiculous proposition at the time, but we all need friends who dream big when we're thinking too small. Chris Hernandez and Leesa Haspel are the best publishing/lawyer duo anyone could ask for and I will never be able to repay them for all the free advice they gave me in the early days of this project. Thank you, Adam Neuman and Kelly Conniff, for always being down to see a movie. Stefanie Ferraro has been kind enough to read my work for a very long time. I don't think I deserve such loyal readership, but it means the world to me nonetheless. And thank you, Dottie, for being by my side—or, more accurately, sitting on my computer keyboard—as I worked. (And thank you, Joan Wong, for trusting us to care for her.)

My sister, Melissa Carlin, was the first person who had to deal with my movie takes and is the only person who understands the importance of the Mary-Kate and Ashley Cinematic Universe. You deserve the very best of everything this life has to offer and I hope you know that. My dad, Billy Carlin, showed me how to be a hard worker and coached every sports team I ever played on. He also drove me to a local Long Island B. J.'s on the release day of the Backstreet Boys' *Millennium*, to buy a second copy of the album when the first one didn't arrive in the mail. That is love. My mom, Jeanne Lamb Carlin, is my original movie-watching buddy, who introduced me to so many of the films I still adore today. Her decision to buy a subscription to *Entertainment Weekly* was life-changing for me. She, a writer herself, is the reason I wanted to become a writer. I will never be able to thank my mom and dad for everything they've done for me, but that won't stop me from trying. I love you both so much.

Finally, my husband, Kyle McGovern, I love you and I like you more than anything in this crazy world. You are my favorite person to talk about movies (and everything else) with. I wouldn't have been able to do this without you. This book is as much yours as it is mine. You are the most talented writer and editor I know and I am in awe of everything you do. I am so lucky to get to spend my life with you.

Selected Sources

Aguilera, Leanne. "*Hocus Pocus* Turns 25–Watch Young Sarah Jessica Parker Spill On Set Secrets From 1993!" *Entertainment Tonight.* July 16, 2018. https://www.etonline.com/hocus-pocus-turns-25-watch-young-sarah-jessica-parker-spill-on-set-secrets-from-1993-exclusive

Allaire, Christian. "Kathy Najimy Knows She's a Gay Icon." *Vogue.* October 6, 2022. https://www.vogue.com/article/kathy-najimy-hocus-pocus-2-interview

"Bette Midler Has Her Fake Teeth Ready for the *Hocus Pocus* Reunion." *Late Night With Seth Meyers.* October 28, 2020. https://www.youtube.com/watch?v=Zc4DfQmcHko

"Bette Midler Loves Her *Hocus Pocus* Performance: 'I'm Flawless in That Movie.' " *Today Show.* December 2, 2016. https://www.today.com/video/bette-midler-loves-her-hocus-pocus-performance-i-m-flawless-in-that-movie-823091267860

"Bette Midler Talks *Hocus Pocus.*" *Today Show.* July 1993.

Birch, Thora; archival author interview with (2018).

Carlin, Shannon. "An Oral History Of The Most Famous Scene In *Hocus Pocus*, As Told By The Movie's Cast & Crew." *Bustle.* July 16, 2018. https://www.bustle.com/p/a-hocus-pocus-oral-history-of-the-movies-most-famous-scene-as-told-by-cast-crew-9724620

Cipriani, Casey. "What It Was Really Like Playing Thackery Binx in *Hocus Pocus.*" *Bustle.* October 16, 2018. https://www.bustle.com/p/wheres-thackery-binx-from-hocus-pocus-in-2018-sean-murrays-kids-arent-all-that-impressed-that-hes-in-the-halloween-classic-12270623

Fanning, Jim. "Tricks and Insider Treats From *Hocus Pocus.*" *D23.com.* October 24, 2013. https://d23.com/tricks-and-insider-treats-from-disneys-hocus-pocus/

Faracy, Stephanie; archival author interview with (2018).

Hocus Pocus Press Release. Walt Disney Company. 1993.

Jones, Doug; archival author interview with (2018).

"Kathy Najimy Talks *Hocus Pocus.*" *Today Show.* July 1993. https://www
.today.com/video/kathy-najimy-talks-hocus-pocus-in-1993-today-
interview-150305861742

Kirschner, David; archival author interview with (2018).

La Jeunesse, Marilyn. "Kathy Najimy: Mother, Activist, and Actor. In That
Order." *Glamour.* October 10, 2022. https://www.glamour.com/story
/kathy-najimy-interview.

Lenker, Maureen Lee. "See the *Hocus Pocus* Stars All Grown Up—And
Celebrating the 25th Anniversary." *Entertainment Weekly.* October 4,
2018. https://ew.com/tv/hocus-pocus-stars-are-all-grown-up-and-
celebrating-the-25th-anniversary/

McCluskey, Megan. "The Story of Leonardo DiCaprio's *Hocus Pocus*
Audition Is Everything You Want It To Be." *Time.* October 19, 2017.
https://time.com/4989996/leonardo-dicaprio-hocus-pocus-audition

Nolfi, Joey. "Bette Midler, Sarah Jessica Parker, Kathy Najimy Reveal If
They'd Do *Hocus Pocus 3* After New Sequel." *Entertainment Weekly.*
September 27, 2022. https://ew.com/movies/hocus-pocus-2-
stars-discuss-potential-sequel-hocus-pocus-3/

Novak, Analisa. "Bette Midler, Sarah Jessica Parker and Kathy Najimy on
the Magic Behind *Hocus Pocus* and Potential Third Film." *CBS Mornings.*
September 30, 2022. https://www.cbsnews.com/news
/bette-midler-sarah-jessica-parker-kathy-najimy-hocus-pocus/

Ortiz, Andi. "How *Hocus Pocus* Went From Box Office Bomb to Disney's
Halloween Darling." *The Wrap.* September 21, 2022. https://www
.thewrap.com/hocus-pocus-oral-history-box-office-bomb/

Rees, Alex. "You Really Won't Believe What Emily Binx, the Little Girl
From *Hocus Pocus* Looks Like Now." *Cosmopolitan.* October 22, 2015.
https://www.cosmopolitan.com/entertainment/movies/news/a47653
/emily-binx-hocus-pocus-jodie-rivera-amanda-shepherd/

Reinstein, Mara. "Sarah Jessica Parker, Bette Midler and Kathy Najimy
Reveal the Secret to the Success of *Hocus Pocus* and Why They Agreed to
Make a Sequel." *Parade.* September 30, 2022. https://parade.com/movies
/hocus-pocus-sequel-bette-midler-sarah-jessica-parker

Riley, Jenelle. "Leonardo DiCaprio Unleashes a Fearless 'Wolf'
Performance." *Variety.* February 11, 2014. https://variety.com/2014
/film/news/

leonardo-dicaprio-tackles-roles-that-push-the-envelope-1201096254/

"Sarah Jessica Parker Enjoyed Being Airborne in *Hocus Pocus.*" *The Late Show With Stephen Colbert.* October 30, 2018. https://www.cbs.com /shows/video/ano7k_2c5cYKl28GkIGmzkfDHy__fGGA/

Shaiman, Marc; archival author interview with (2018).

Setoodeh, Ramin. "Director Kenny Ortega on the Queer Aesthetic of His Movies From *Hocus Pocus* to *High School Musical.*" *Variety.* June 30, 2020. https://variety.com/2020/film/news/director-kenny-ortega-pride-high-school-musical

Stern, Sophie T. "Bette Midler on *Hocus Pocus*'s Enduring Appeal: It Was an 'Ugly Duckling' and 'Now It's a Swan.'" *People.* October 31, 2018. https:// people.com/movies/better-midler-on-hocus-pocus-enduring-appeal/

"Watch *Hocus Pocus* With Director Kenny Ortega." Oh My Disney. October 9, 2018. https://video.disney.com/watch/watch-hocus-pocus-with-director-kenny-ortega-oh-my-disney-577be14d8f26b33004c7d0b6